MYTHS AND LIES OF 'THE IRISH REVOLUTION'

MYTHS AND LIES OF 'THE IRISH REVOLUTION'

COLUM KENNY

EASTWOOD BOOKS

First published by Wordwell Books, 2025
Dublin, Ireland
www.eastwoodbooks.com

Eastwood Books is an imprint of the Wordwell Group

Eastwood Books
The Wordwell Group
Suite 5, Hub 17, Corrig Road, Sandyford,
Dublin, Ireland

The Wordwell Group is a member of Publishing Ireland,
the Irish Book Publishers' Association

ISBN: 978-1-916742-96-3 (paperback)
ISBN: 978-1-916742-97-0 (epub)

British Library Cataloguing in Publication Data.
A catalogue record for this book is available from the British Library.

Copyediting: Emer Condit
Internal layout and cover design: Wordwell
Printed in Ireland by SprintPrint, Dublin

Front cover illustration: 'Sackville Street in flames—A photograph taken by a *Daily Sketch* photographer under fire', Dublin, May 1916 (postcard; courtesy of the National Library of Ireland, EPH A652). It is unclear whether the image, of what is now named O'Connell Street, has been manipulated to enhance the effect.

For our grandchildren
Aoife, Sophie and Olivia

'To Ireland in the Coming Times'

'What then is, generally speaking, the truth of history?
A fable agreed upon.'

—*Napoleon Bonaparte*
(Saint Helena, 1816)

'Thousands of children are hungry and naked, huddled together like swine in their so-called houses. In all parts of the country we hear cries of desperation, cries of: "What is going to be done for us?"'

—*Thomas Johnson*
(Dáil Éireann, 10 January 1922)

CONTENTS

PREFACE

Kathleen Clarke was republican royalty. The widow of rebel leader Tom Clarke, executed by the British in 1916 for his leading role in the rising of that year, she was 'driven by a fierce commitment'. Kathleen believed that Harry Boland blocked her from standing for Sinn Féin in 1918, in favour of a male candidate, but at the next election she made it into Dáil Éireann (the Irish parliament). On 17 December 1921 she told her fellow deputies that she had been present weeks earlier when Éamon de Valera informed Arthur Griffith 'we must have scapegoats' (or made a remark 'such as this'), even as Griffith left for the treaty talks in London. De Valera stated he could not recall what particular idea had been in his mind when he said it.

The unreliability of memory is just one of the reasons why the history of a nation may become what Napoleon called 'a fable agreed upon'. Pride and vanity and self-interest also play their parts. So it is that the decade in Ireland from 1913 to 1923–from what some regard as an heroic failure of organised labour to achieve its objectives in the great Dublin lock-out, through the suppressed 1916 rebellion that saw Ireland's leading socialist intellectual and activist James Connolly also executed, to a bitter civil war that poisoned Irish politics–has come to be defined not just as a 'revolutionary' decade or as a period of 'Irish revolution' but as the very epoch of '*the* Irish revolution'. There was certainly then a national independence struggle that was partly successful. Hundreds of combatants died in it. Many more Irish joined the British Army and died in World War I. Risk in itself is not revolution. Partial liberation from imperialism and injustice is not necessarily economic or social transformation. There was little in the plaintive address that trade unionist and Labour Party leader Tom Johnson made in Dáil Éireann on 10 January 1922, between its approval of the Anglo-Irish Treaty and the commencement of civil war, that suggests he was confident of an imminent improvement in the living conditions of workers and the poor. Not until 1961 was the new state able to reverse the overall continuing decline in its population since the Great Famine. It was ultimately to the benefit of both sides in the Irish civil war, after its losers in the 1920s themselves became winners in the 1930s, to commemorate the decade of troubles from 1913 to 1923 in ways that bolstered the reputations of survivors who had become part of a new state establishment.

This book highlights misrepresentations regarding the struggle for Irish independence. The greatest fruit of 'the Irish revolution' was the independent Irish state founded on an agreement for a treaty between British and Irish negotiators in December 1921. Yet ideas that people now hold about what occurred in Ireland in the early twentieth century are still too often informed by the propaganda of two sides that fought a civil war rather than by hard facts.

Whether one believes that the treaty agreement signed in London was the best deal possible for Irish nationalists in the circumstances of that time or one regards it as an unnecessary and unprincipled surrender of territory and of republican principles, one should try to be fair about what happened and to respect the motives of those who acted honourably on each 'side'—and, indeed, of those who acted honourably on neither 'side'.

The revolutionary struggle forced Britain to the negotiating table in late 1921. Arthur Griffith and Michael Collins led the team of five negotiators in London, and they alone of the Irish had a full grasp of what had transpired there. After both men died tragically in August 1922 their efforts and achievements came to be represented in ways that were misleading, but that ultimately suited the objectives of some people on both sides who survived the Civil War of 1922–3, not least Éamon de Valera who had demanded talks but refused to participate in them. If the Irish Revolution was somehow incomplete, then claiming that the negotiators had been duped or even duplicitous might serve to persuade the public that this was the reason. Had their negotiations been represented instead as a triumphant if imperfect outcome of the War of Independence, in the face of a mighty British Empire, how much more positive would have been the foundational myth of the independent Irish state, how less likely a civil war and how more difficult it might have been to thwart political and social objectives of the most advanced or radical nationalists.

This book challenges in general the myth of some kind of definitive Irish 'revolution' between 1910 and 1922, a 'revolution' proclaimed by the titles of many recently published histories, and examines incidental misconceptions along the way. The author posits an alternative quest, for a clear appreciation of what was actually achieved during those years, including the treaty on which the state was founded. Griffith and Collins represented the terms of that treaty as stepping-stones to greater independence, as 'the freedom to achieve freedom'. It is one of the ironies of Irish history that whilst pro-treaty governments of the 1920s dragged their feet when it came to taking further steps towards greater sovereignty, de Valera eventually dropped his anti-Treaty civil war antics and formed governments in the 1930s that used the state's powers and status under the Treaty of 1922 and under the UK Statute of Westminster of 1931 to strip away its chief remaining trappings of inferiority. De Valera fulfilled rather than undid the Treaty.

This is the final volume in a suite of five related books written by the author in the past decade, two of which are fresh studies of key figures—Arthur Griffith and Éamon de Valera—and two of which are succinct accounts of key events: the treaty negotiations of late 1921 aimed at ending the War of Independence and the bitter Civil War of 1922–3. My publisher, Ronan Colgan, believes that the present explicit exploration of certain questions that challenged me along the way will interest general readers and historians alike. I am grateful to Eastwood Books for its support and encouragement.

'The Irish revolution' of the early twentieth century came into focus for me when I was invited to write about Arthur Griffith's journalism for a collection of essays published in 2014.[1] Griffith founded Sinn Féin, was a leading propagandist for independence, acted as president of Dáil Éireann in 1919–22 for longer than Éamon de Valera had done, and by the time of his death on 12 August 1922, aged 51, had spent more time in jail than most other active nationalists, including de Valera. He was a pragmatic man who lived among the poor of central Dublin and was particularly conscious of the economic and social impact of violence on the lives of the working class.

My consideration of Griffith's writings and life led me to ask why his standing today is not as high as it might be, and to interrogate more generally the idea that events in the early years of the twentieth century may be defined properly as 'the Irish revolution'. That idea is rejected below as complacent and inaccurate.

Various beliefs, justifications, delusions and fictions are explored here. Especially important to our understanding of the period and of its legacy when considering the Irish state today is the 'damnable lie', as Griffith called allegations that in 1921 he somehow gave Prime Minister Lloyd George in advance both binding and 'secret assent' in respect of aspects of the proposed Anglo-Irish treaty. Frank Pakenham, later Lord Longford, sanctified those allegations in his book entitled *Peace by Ordeal* that he wrote with Éamon de Valera's assistance in the 1930s. Personally and professionally, Pakenham was well connected to leading Tories when he began his research. A few years after his book appeared he returned to Dublin at the behest of the Ministry of Information in London to approach de Valera, whose trust he had won by it. I have previously identified some of the defects of Pakenham's book but undertake here a far more detailed and fully referenced analysis of its influential shortcomings The section in which I do so is, of necessity, by far the longest below. I also provide relevant details of its author's background.

If this volume achieves nothing else, it should serve to warn against assuming that Pakenham's *Peace by Ordeal* is somehow a definitive or unquestionably reliable account of the treaty negotiations of late 1921 upon which the Irish state is founded. His book has been given authoritative status for too long, with Nicholas Mansergh, for example, describing it in 1991 as a 'classic study'.[2] Its influence historically cannot be overstated, for it represented de Valera as the victim of a secret sell-out and thus slyly justified his behaviour in 1921–3 and has been slavishly followed by too many writers.

As they prepared to begin treaty negotiations with the Irish in late 1921, as we shall see, Prime Minister Lloyd George told his fellow British ministers that 'Men will die for the Throne and Empire. I do not know who will die for Tyrone and Fermanagh.' He believed all along that he could safely insist on Ireland remaining in the British Commonwealth and accepting the king as head of state, secure in the knowledge that British people and those of the main dominions of Australia and Canada wanted for reasons of identity and self-interest a strong empire united under the Crown. If the Irish government walked away from a deal only on those grounds, given the concession of political independence for most of Ireland, it would get little international sympathy and very limited support at home. He was even prepared to make concessions on the border, not least because there were nationalist majorities in Tyrone and Fermanagh, and he feared international opinion in that regard.

But what might have been was to be overtaken by events, and the Irish revolutionary momentum was thwarted. Shortly after the talks ended in the early hours of 6 December 1921 Griffith wrote to tell de Valera 'I was determined not to let them break on the Crown.'[3] Yet he himself was prevented from breaking on Northern Ireland, because the British suddenly threatened immediate and terrible war if the Irish did not sign the agreement that very night. Lloyd George had failed to deliver on a promised response from Ulster unionists to a proposed revision of the Irish border but the Irish felt obliged to sign anyway, albeit conditional on the Dáil approving the proposed treaty.

In my opinion, it would have been better had all Ireland become an independent republic in 1922, but violently pursuing that objective after 1921 was both counterproductive and contrary to the wishes of most Irish people at that time. In the Irish general election of June 1922 voters did not make decisions in a void but knew that the British Empire threatened to unleash further and terrible violence if the War of Independence was resumed. I trust that readers will find that what I write here is even-handed and will accept that my research was undertaken in a spirit of exploration and understanding rather than one of partisan judgement.

In a neat essay on objectivity, a contemporary philosopher has stated the obvious by observing that 'consequent judgments are objective or subjective to varying degrees'.[4] Nowhere is that truer than in the field of history. Principled historians aspire to the truth, but the potential for discrepancies between one's perceptual impressions and the 'real' qualities of perceived objects is vast. Subjectively, writers may be influenced by their existing view of related events and by unconscious prejudices, as well as by subconscious attitudes arising from personal or ethnic or social circumstances. Objectively, limitations in the range and quality of sources constrict one's ability to understand clearly what may have once happened. And this is not yet to consider some writers who consciously bend the truth to further a cause or to reinforce egotistically their own opinions.

Few, if any, people are entirely free of bias, but there are—as noted above—'varying degrees' of subjectivity. The appropriate moral response to subjectivity is not to forsake in despair the pursuit of truth or 'objectivity'. If there is no absolute or complete objectivity, we can still strive for clarity and fairness.

While historians ought not to interpret the past in a way that imposes their wishes for the future on it, we may at least learn something about human behaviour and societal trends from what has already happened. In attempting to do so, historians must seek to distinguish between reliable information on the one hand and myths and fables on the other. The *Oxford English Dictionary* defines myth in part as

> 'A traditional story … which embodies and provides an explanation, aetiology, or justification for something such as the early history of a society … A widespread but untrue or erroneous story or belief; a widely held misconception; a misrepresentation of the

> truth … A person or thing held in awe or generally referred to with near reverential admiration on the basis of popularly repeated stories (whether real or fictitious) … A popular conception of a person or thing which exaggerates or idealizes the truth.'

In respect of any or all of these senses the matters considered in this volume will be interrogated. The *OED* also gives 'fable' as a synonym for 'myth'.

Sources on which statements in this book are directly based are identified in endnotes, and many other relevant works are mentioned in the text when 'the Irish revolution' as a concept is considered below.

My family's background is that of the Catholic nationalist middle class that emerged from the nineteenth century. One of my great-grandfathers was a printer and a member of the Dublin Fenians who mounted a brief revolt in 1867. One of his sons, my grandfather, knew and sometimes worked on publications with Patrick Pearse, Arthur Griffith and Seán MacDiarmada (MacDermott) and managed the production of early editions of the *Sinn Féin Year Book*.[5] My Kerry grandmother was descended from the Gaelic chieftain Domhnall O'Sullivan Beare and was directly related to a renowned parish priest of Kenmare who worked to alleviate suffering and to change British policy during the Great Famine. My mother admired de Valera, while my father was inclined towards Fine Gael. I try to see the good and bad on all sides.

From an early age the story of Ireland, as presented in history, politics and current affairs and as expressed in everyday life, has intrigued me. For much of my life I have interrogated and communicated it through journalism and academic research and was greatly encouraged in the latter respect by the late W.N. ('Nial') Osborough, professor of legal history at University College Dublin and Trinity College Dublin. As the supervisor of my doctoral dissertation on the history of King's Inns, Dublin, published in 1992, he steered me to a level of research and expression that I might not otherwise have reached. I am indebted in that respect both to him and to its external examiners, Sir John Baker of St Catharine's College, Cambridge, and Dr Paul Brand, who subsequently became professor of legal history at the University of Oxford. I also acknowledge the liberalism of Dublin City University in supporting my research in the wider humanities, having recruited me from RTÉ in 1982 to help establish Ireland's first broadcasting and journalism courses at university level.

I wish to thank the archivists and librarians of Blackrock College in Dublin, the Bodleian Library in Oxford, the British Library, the Churchill Archives Centre (Churchill College, Cambridge), Dublin City University, King's Inns, the National Archives (UK), the National Archives of Ireland, the National Library of Ireland, the New York–Presbyterian Weill Cornell Medicine's Medical Center Archives, New York Public Library's General Research Division, RTÉ Archives, Trinity College Dublin, the Parliamentary Archives (Westminster), University College Cork, University College Dublin, the University of Birmingham, the University of Manchester and my local library in Bray, Co. Wicklow, which has a good Irish history section and which also when requested promptly summons up other volumes from branches of Ireland's public library system nationally. I am grateful for the space to push out the boat of research that John Dorney afforded me on his enterprising website *The Irish Story*. Thanks also to Tommy Graham, editor of *History Ireland*, which is a valuable forum in which to explore ideas, as is Cormac O'Hanrahan's annual *Cut & Paste*. Thanks also for their ideas to the independent scholars Brian Maye and Gerard Shannon and to Prof. Dan Edelstein of Stanford University—and to those worldly-wise members of certain groups (hillwalking, book-clubbing and Homer-reading) to which I belong who have challenging views on many matters, not least on Irish history.

As always, in the present and other cases when researching and writing, the support of my wife Catherine Curran and the encouragement of my sons Oisín, Conor and Sam are greatly appreciated. Last if perhaps least there is also Snowball, a feline acquaintance who reminds me daily that a cat may look at a king.

1

'CALL IT WHAT YOU LIKE'?

Commandant Rory O'Connor stood words on their head. He and some other anti-treaty members of the IRA seized Dublin's Four Courts at gunpoint in the early hours of Friday 14 April 1922. He demanded nothing less than the reversal of the recent treaty with Britain and the collapse of the provisional Irish government in Dublin. Asked by a special correspondent for the Press Association whether there were any possible grounds on which an arrangement for preserving peace could be made, O'Connor replied that 'Mr Griffith and Mr Collins would have to give an undertaking, and see that it was carried out, that the Provisional Government [of the Irish Free State] would not function'. He added that the only means he could see of averting civil war was the scrapping of the treaty.[1] O'Connor wanted the complete overthrow of the new state that was emerging from the Anglo-Irish treaty talks of 1921.

Next morning the *Belfast Newsletter* published an interview with O'Connor, conducted as he 'puffed meditatively on a cigarette'. Its reporter in Dublin wrote:

> 'The determination of the mutineers—they do not apparently object to this term—not to recognise any Government other than the republic was described to me yesterday in an interesting interview which I had with Roderick O'Connor, who is the power

> behind the irregular I.R.A., or the left wing of the "army", as he prefers to call it. He is a serious, ascetic, and somewhat cadaverous-looking man, with iron-grey hair. His clean-shaven face brings out very prominently his hard determined mouth and chin. Although he has been identified with the republican movement since 1916, no one had heard of this powerful middle-aged man until the split came over the "treaty".'[2]

Yet, notwithstanding O'Connor's demands, on 15 April 1922 the *Irish Times* and other papers were reporting that he denied that there was any question of a 'revolution' or '*coup d'état*'. He told the *Irish Independent* that 'There is going to be no revolution'. Had he not already admitted that there might be a military dictatorship if he got his way? 'You can call it what you like', he told the press.[3]

When and what was 'the Irish revolution' to which historians now refer? It was clearly not the fulfilment of what O'Connor sought, for his side lost the civil war that ensued. That definite article—the very word 'the' before 'Irish revolution'—glows on the title-page of history books. It shines brightly on the two words after it, like the sun rising above a laneway behind the Bank of Ireland in College Green and illuminating the façade of Trinity College. That little word 'the' gives to the chosen period of 'revolution' a distinctive and glorious hue, marking it out as a cut above earlier resistance to British imperialism in Ireland. Others tried to turn the wheel of fortune in Ireland, but we succeeded, it seems to say.

So what constituted 'the revolution' exactly? Was it a major advance in women's rights? Did the working class achieve great gains? Were the British in Ireland swept clean away? Did the entire green isle become a republic? Did small farmers advance much further than they had already advanced in the nineteenth century? Did rural labourers win much more than the new cottages already erected for them under a UK Act of Parliament? Was the growing power of the Catholic Church curtailed? The answer in all cases is 'no'.

While a revolution is not necessarily positive or negative in itself, the word can come to have a certain chic or radical ring to it that makes it appealing or exciting. So it was for English Protestants with their 'Glorious Revolution' of 1688–9, when William of Orange replaced King James II and confirmed Britain as a constitutional rather than an absolute monarchy.

Some revolutions—in Haiti or Russia or Cuba, for example—have been much more radical than others in respect of social and economic structures. In Marxist theory, as the *Oxford English Dictionary* reminds us, 'revolution' involves the violent overthrow of the ruling class and the seizure of power through control of the means of production by a class to whom such control was previously denied. This was not the nature of 'the Irish revolution'. A national independence movement does not require that level of class upheaval. When proclaiming 'the provisional government of the Irish Republic' at Easter 1916, rebel leaders did not even use the abstract noun 'revolution' and included the adjective 'revolutionary' just once. That was in reference to the past training of Ireland's manhood (*sic*) 'through her secret revolutionary organisation, the Irish Republican Brotherhood', founded in the 1850s. The rebels simply 'asserted the right to national freedom and sovereignty' and noted that 'six times during the past three hundred years' Irish people had done so in arms.

In a fresh study, Dan Edelstein of Stanford University explains how the idea of a revolution changes. In general, he writes, 'from the Peloponnesian War to the American Revolution, revolution retained a sulfurous odor. With few exceptions, revolutions were widely condemned as destructive events, to be avoided whenever possible. The primary sources for this period, accordingly, are almost entirely negative.' He adds that one finds that, during 'the American revolution', it is the case that

> 'The Americans don't really talk about "revolution". The expression "American Revolution" is very rare in the first decade of what we now call "the American Revolution". It's something that gets retrospectively applied to it. They're not writing to each other saying "Hey, this revolution that we're doing is pretty awesome, isn't it?" If anything, they still seem to view the word "revolution" as a bad thing.'[4]

This is a useful reminder for historians of the need to define clearly what one means if applying the term 'revolution' to distinct developments in the early twentieth century in Ireland that may otherwise be regarded as having constituted a glorious independence movement rather than an attempt at the wholesale revolution of social relations. In a notable speech in Dáil Éireann on 1 March 1923, Minister for Home Affairs Kevin O'Higgins TD identified some of the possible revolutionary actions that Sinn Féin did *not* espouse prior to the foundation of the state and declared: 'I think we were probably the most conservative-minded revolutionaries that ever put through a successful revolution'. Irish people wished to see Ireland take a seat alongside other constitutional states in Europe, but there is no evidence that many wished to follow Russia into an uncertain Bolshevik future. Was the subsequent assassination of O'Higgins part of 'the Irish revolution'?

Ernie O'Malley, who has come to be seen as a significant anti-treaty member of the IRA, was among those who occupied the Four Courts in 1922 alongside Rory O'Connor. He is today regarded with some respect because of the 'literary' style of his memoirs. He admitted in them quite frankly that 'The [IRA] Volunteer spirit in essentials was hostile to Labour, afraid that any attention to its needs or direction would weaken the one-sided thrust of force'. O'Malley, son of a solicitor's clerk, had dropped out of medical school to join the Volunteers full-time in 1918. Ostensibly reflecting a patronising nationalist mentality of that time towards socialist agitators, he later recalled 'my annoyance at the convictions of purely revolutionary workers who stood outside the nationalist movement and a certain amusement at their arguments'.[5] In a recent essay on O'Malley in the *Atlas of the Irish Revolution*, Nicholas Allen observes that the 'revolution' in which O'Malley took part was in fact 'barely worth the name in social terms, being a collapse of British political will by force of guerilla warfare, an achievement no less remarkable for that'.[6]

The practice of historians calling whatever they wish in the early twentieth century 'the Irish revolution' is the very act of myth-making. It reassures the Republic of Ireland's political establishment that it stands on a firm foundation of progress and success. We shall see later how historians in fact differ when describing the scope of any Irish revolution and ask what that means for Irish people's image of themselves today.

What if Rory O'Connor's assertion was correct and there was then in fact 'no revolution', or just a partial one?

Commandant Rory O'Connor was 'a serious, ascetic, and somewhat cadaverous-looking man' (*Belfast Newsletter*, 15 April 1922). He is seen here addressing members of the Dublin City Brigade, IRA, at Smithfield, Dublin, on 2 April 1922. (photo by W.D. Hogan; courtesy of the National Library of Ireland, NPA POLF220.)

2

'PURE SPANISH BLOOD'?

Some of his most enthusiastic supporters believed it. Éamon de Valera was surely descended from Spanish nobility. There was even mention of a family connection to the French emperor, Napoleon III, and another to a republican government minister in Mexico. That little boy who stepped ashore, aged two and a half, from an ocean liner at Cobh in 1884 to visit Ireland for the first time was not just any child of an Irish maid.[1] To his warmest admirers de Valera might as well have been Bonnie Prince Charlie finally crowned king, or one of those proud Gaelic earls who had fled Ireland in despair, returned at last as leader of a force of emigrant Irish 'Wild Geese' on board a Spanish armada. Between 1919 and 1933 his own supporters were heard singing a new street ballad called 'We'll crown de Valera king of Ireland'.

A sympathetic biography of de Valera, published in the 1940s, opens with the author quoting James Clarence Mangan's classic 1847 English translation of a much older poem in Irish addressed to a female personification of Ireland: 'And Spanish ale shall give you hope, My dark Rosaleen'.[2]

In my recent character study of de Valera I dealt at length with the long search for his roots over the years, including various aspects of records that do exist and those that do not. I shall not repeat many details of that story here.[3] It is, however, worth

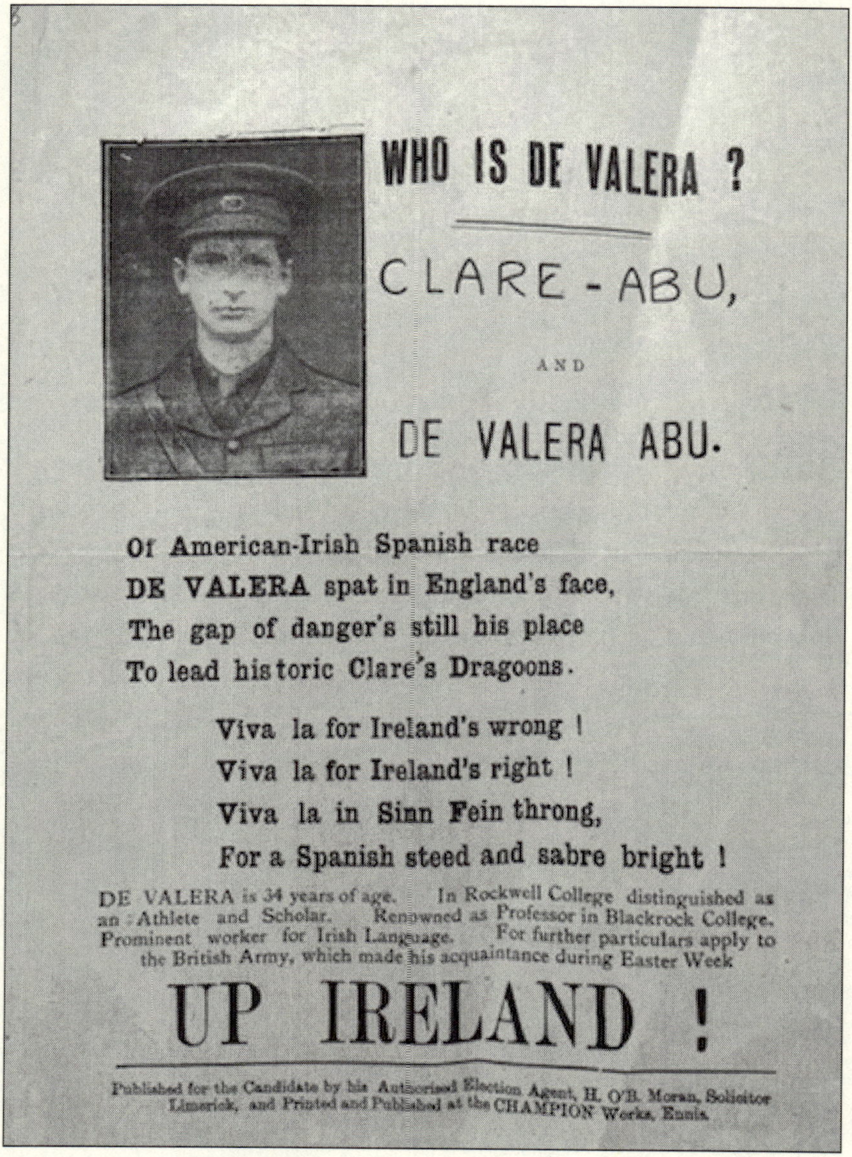

WHO IS DE VALERA ?

CLARE - ABU,

AND

DE VALERA ABU.

Of American-Irish Spanish race
DE VALERA spat in England's face,
The gap of danger's still his place
To lead his toric Clare's Dragoons.

Viva la for Ireland's wrong !
Viva la for Ireland's right !
Viva la in Sinn Fein throng,
For a Spanish steed and sabre bright !

DE VALERA is 34 years of age. In Rockwell College distinguished as an Athlete and Scholar. Renowned as Professor in Blackrock College. Prominent worker for Irish Language. For further particulars apply to the British Army, which made his acquaintance during Easter Week

UP IRELAND !

Published for the Candidate by his Authorised Election Agent, H. O'B. Moran, Solicitor Limerick, and Printed and Published at the CHAMPION Works, Ennis.

Leaflet issued on behalf of de Valera during the East Clare parliamentary by-election in 1917. He campaigned in his Volunteer uniform. De Valera tutored at Blackrock College, where he was a student, but was never on staff there (courtesy of the National Library of Ireland, MS LOP116/68).

repeating a few when considering the myth of his noble Spanish ancestry.

On the first page of their official biography of de Valera, Frank Pakenham (Lord Longford) and Thomas P. O'Neill make some inconclusive statements about his background that are unreferenced, like much of Pakenham's earlier book on the Anglo-Irish treaty. One of de Valera's sons, Terry, convinced himself of the family's noble ancestry and laid out a lineage in his 2004 memoir. He insisted in particular that his father's antecedents and background were not 'Cuban, or other than pure Spanish'—conscious, perhaps, of claims that de Valera's father was a Jew and of other racist innuendoes, such as that attributed to Ernest Blythe suggesting that de Valera was 'some class of a mulatto called Demerara [a light-brown sugar]'.[4] Terry wrote that one Spanish family relative had fought the Moors, that another was the 'Charles Dickens' of Spain, another served in the Spanish navy and another was a leading sculptor (whose statue of Don Quixote today graces a Madrid square).[5] But Éamon de Valera himself was never satisfied by the results of research into his background, including suggestions that he was related to those people.

Does it matter who his father was? It did to him. His political opponents whispered during elections that he was a 'bastard', a word commonly used then to describe or demean people whose parents were not married. Because of de Valera's perceived role in fomenting civil war, his detractors regarded him as a malign influence and consciously or unconsciously desired to depict him as an outsider and an outcast. Some of his supporters, however, proudly sang his praises as a supposed scion of Spain. During the East Clare by-election in 1917, when de Valera was elected to parliament for the first time, his agent published for him a leaflet headed 'Who is de Valera?'. It answered its own question with these verses:

'Of American-Irish Spanish race
DE VALERA spat in England's face,
The gap of danger's still his place
To lead historic Clare's Dragoons.

Viva la for Ireland's wrong!
Viva la for Ireland's right!
Viva la in Sinn Féin throng,
For a Spanish steed and sabre bright!'[6]

For personal and political reasons de Valera wished to confirm that he was born in the United States and that his parents were married there, and that his father or grandfather had been born in Spain. Dev's birth in the United States, and thereby his US citizenship, was of particular concern to his family and his supporters in 1916, as it was thought that these circumstances might save him from being executed by the British for his role in the Easter Rising that year. When he was imprisoned instead of being shot, his US citizenship was subsequently invoked in a campaign to have his sentence reduced. There was no reason in law why his being a US citizen would protect him from punishment for crimes committed in the United Kingdom, but there was a political dimension to how his punishment was seen in the context of the role of Irish-Americans in domestic American politics and the impact of this on relations between Washington and London. His wife believed at the time that his US citizenship was decisive in saving him from execution in 1916, although he later came to deny that it was. She wrote to a friend in 1916: 'He would have shared the death sentence with the others only I got the American Consuls [plural] to interfere on his behalf. I had his baptism certificate showing he had been born in America and then he had never taken out naturalisation papers here. So he was an American citizen.'[7] His baptism and birth papers are unsatisfactory, however, and no formal church or state record of his mother being married to his father was ever found.

His inability to prove that he was not born outside marriage may have been a negative consideration in respect of his ever being permitted to become a priest, which for at least a decade he thought he might become but received little or no known encouragement from priests with whom he discussed his incipient vocation. He subsequently pressed Irish ambassadors in Spain to find him Spanish roots, as his father was said on de Valera's birth return to be 'Spanish', but they did not discover any.[8]

Notwithstanding considerable research by his family, friends and supporters, and by ambassadors and clergy and academic researchers, no evidence has been found that his mother was married when de Valera was born in 1882. No birth, marriage or death certificate has been discovered for the man said to have been his father, and various records now online—including for the US census every few years—show no person who appears to come close to fitting the details given to de Valera by his mother in respect of the man whom she said was his father.

There is in the register of the Nursery and Child's Hospital of Manhattan a reliable record of the admission of his mother ('Mrs Kate de Valero' [*sic*], 'Romanist', whose birthplace was 'Ireland' and whose brother was 'Edward Coll') for the purpose of giving birth there in October 1882.[9] There is also a birth return from that hospital to New York state authorities recording that a first child named 'George de Valero' (not 'Edward' or 'De Valera') had been born there to his mother, 'Kate de Valero', on 14 October, and that this child's father, 'Vivion' (not Vivian) de Valera, had been born in Spain.[10] There is also at St Agnes's church in Manhattan a subsequent entry, 'corrected' by hand, for the baptism of Kate's son, by then named Edward.[11]

Since my book on the early life of de Valera was published in 2024, one author has raised questions even about the authenticity of de Valera's New York birth return and baptismal certificate.[12] A few people wrote privately to me to claim that de Valera's father was in fact Irish (sometimes giving his putative father's name, but not all giving the same name), and to suggest that his mother was pregnant before she went to America. No source is given for an unlikely suggestion that de Valera's mother worked in County Wicklow and married there a man called de Valera before she emigrated.[13]

In any event, de Valera never found reliable information about his father, who was said to have left his mother and himself in Manhattan in order to go west for the improvement of his health before dying soon afterwards. His mother Kate sent him to Ireland, aged under three, to be raised by members of her family. She later married in New York a Protestant Englishman with whom she had two other children.

Uncertainty about his background as well as his stark upbringing by a bachelor uncle in a labourer's cottage near Bruree in rural County Limerick may be viewed as formative influences on de Valera's personality. The books that he later recalled reading as a boy included notably both Daniel Defoe's *Robinson Crusoe*, literally a tale of insularity, and Abbott's biography of Napoleon, whom he admired in some ways and who died on the remote island of Saint Helena in the South Atlantic. De Valera once recalled that what he liked best when a boy was to go and play in the stream: 'I had an island in it. I could get away from everybody. I used to play Robinson Crusoe there … What I liked best was playing Robinson Crusoe.'[14]

When he was a student debating at Blackrock College, Éamon de Valera spoke in favour of a motion that 'the rule of the first Napoleon [Bonaparte] was beneficial to France', and in doing so 'dwelt on the horrors of the revolution and showed how necessary a Napoleon was to save France from scenes of Anarchy'.[15] When an adult, he quoted an observation attributed to Napoleon in exile on Saint Helena that, 'generally speaking, the truth of history' is a 'fable agreed upon'.[16] If he did not have a Napoleonic vision of his own destiny, he certainly shared Napoleon's awareness of the way in which myths are constructed in history and was long careful to police his own reputation.[17]

A leading contemporary French authority on Napoleon and his empire, Jean Tulard, recently described Napoleon in exile on Saint Helena as becoming '*presque un martyr, Prométhée sur son rocher*' ('almost a martyr, Prometheus on his rock').[18] It is a striking image that brings to mind a well-known Promethean-like statue of the Irish mythological hero Cú Chulainn chained to a rock, in the General Post Office in Dublin. It was de Valera who unveiled this statue in 1935, as a memorial to his former Volunteer comrades who took a stand in the GPO and elsewhere in the city during the Easter Rising of 1916. De Valera himself, on 25 October 1917, had described his first election to the political stage then as 'a monument to the brave dead' of 1916.[19]

He regarded himself as almost lost at the end of the Civil War but, unlike the fatally injured Cú Chulainn, was able to free himself from the bonds of adversity. Released from prison after a few months, he emerged in 1924 to embrace destiny as the founder of Fianna Fáil, Ireland's leading political party of the twentieth century. De Valera's origin myth, that he had descended from pure Spanish nobility before sailing to Ireland on the ocean green, has never been entirely abandoned by some of his admirers. It has been neither proven nor disproven as fact.

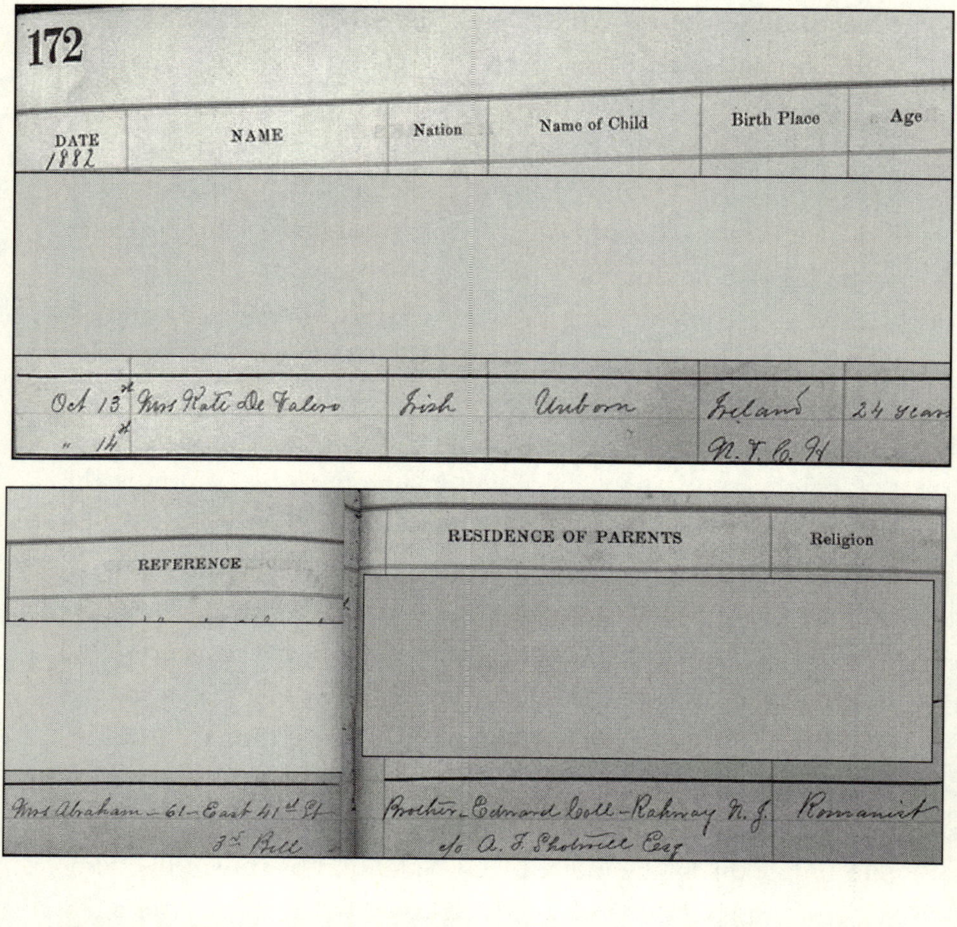

172

DATE 1882	NAME	Nation	Name of Child	Birth Place	Age
Oct 13th " 14th	Mrs Kate De Valero	Irish	Unborn	Ireland N.Y.C.H	24 years

REFERENCE	RESIDENCE OF PARENTS	Religion
Mrs Abraham – 61 – East 41st St 3rd Bell	Brother – Edward Coll – Rahway N. J. c/o A. T. Shotwell Esq	Romanist

The entry for de Valera's mother's admission in the register of the Nursery and Child's Hospital, Manhattan (in two parts for clarity, side by side in original). Her son was born there on 14 October 1882 (courtesy Presbyterian Weill Cornell Medicine's Medical Center Archives, New York City).

3

GRIFFITH WAS A MONARCHIST?

Griffith had no love for kings. He was at heart a republican, but he was also a realist. What he wanted first and foremost was the greatest possible measure of independence for Ireland, however that might come. Nothing should stand in its way. All other demands could wait. On 22 February 1902 Griffith wrote in his *United Irishman* paper that 'possibly Sir Horace Plunkett may come to believe with us that the permanent remedy for Ireland's disease is separation.' Nearly two years later he published in the *United Irishman* an unfavourable review of R.J.Smith's new book *The Irish Renaissance*. This review included a declaration that, 'For our part, we care little whether our government be republican or monarchical so long as it be Irish, independent and just'.[1] The following year he published *The Resurrection of Hungary*, first as a serial in his paper and then as a best-selling booklet. Inspired by Hungarian patriots named Lajos Kossuth and Ferenc Deák, he advocated in it that Ireland follow Hungary's path within the Austro-Hungarian Empire to ensure the greatest possible freedom for its people:

> 'Sixty years ago Hungary realised that the political centre of the nation must be within the nation. When Ireland realises this obvious truth and turns her back on London the parallel may be completed … Kossuth was imbued with French revolution-

ary principles, and dreamed of the Universal Republic. He hated Austria, and his secret ambition was to see Hungary an independent Republic. Deák did not share the principles of the French Revolution. Neither did he hate Austria, only Austrian oppression. He was willing to see Hungary linked with Austria, provided the link were one of friendship not of steel. Here is Deák's programme in Deák's own words:

"Hungary is a free country, independent in its whole system of legislation and administration. It is subordinate to no other country. We have no wish to oppose the interests of our country to the unity of the Monarchy or the security of its existence; but we consider that it is contrary to law or justice that the interests of Hungary should be made subordinate to those of any country whatsoever ... We will never consent that it shall be sacrificed to the unity of the system of government. Our Constitutional life is a treasure which we cannot sacrifice either to foreign interests or to material advantages, howsoever great. Our first duty is to preserve and strengthen it."[1]

Although Griffith's nickname within his family was 'Dan', he was inspired when younger by John Mitchel at least as much as by Daniel O'Connell. In 1901 Griffith declared that 'all my life I have worshipped [John] Mitchel'. He described him as 'the proud, fiery-hearted, electric-brained, giant-souled Irishman who stood up to the might of the whole British Empire'.[2] Griffith's *United Irishman* was named after Mitchel's paper of the same title. Griffith republished in it and elsewhere many articles that Mitchel had written. Today, retrospectively, Mitchel's reputation is clouded by his later association with the US Confederates and their racism, but that was not the Mitchel whom Griffith had come to admire. And the Griffith who admired the feisty Mitchel was the Griffith who worked with James Connolly and whom Connolly came to describe as an 'old friend'.

When in 1905 Griffith founded Sinn Féin the chance of Ireland becoming a republic was remote. He was an advanced nationalist on the fringes of politics, a prophet crying in the wilderness. The electorate had demonstrated no desire to adopt an advanced nationalist policy. Even the more conservative objective of Home Rule for Ireland within the United Kingdom, being pursued by Irish MPs in parliament at Westminster, was elusive. Few people then thought an Irish republic likely, which is too often forgotten now. Brian Maye made it clear in 1997, in his ground-breaking biography of Griffith, that Griffith's willingness to accept a ceremonial monarch jointly with Britain was a limited, pragmatic and 'worthy compromise' with unionists as the price of gaining freedoms and avoiding partition.[3] Griffith accepted monarchy only where the Irish constitution would guard jealously the independence of Ireland. As he had written in the *United Irishman* at the outset, on 22 April 1899, 'though I am a believer in republican systems of government, I am ready, as I believe is every other Irish nationalist, to accept any form of native government in preference to alien rule'.

Griffith formed 'the National Council' to further his objectives. At the First Annual Convention of the National Council held in the Rotunda, on 28 November 1905, its chairman Edward Martyn said that the meeting had been called 'to endorse the sinn féin policy', which was

> 'National self-development through the recognition of the duties and rights of citizenship on the part of the individual, and by the aid and support of all movements originating from within Ireland,

> instinct [*sic*] with national tradition, and not looking outside Ireland for the accomplishment of their aims.'

He believed that the Irish people were 'a free people, and must continue to possess the rights of a free people until, of our own free will, we renounce them. Any external power that attempted to control, or did by force control their free action, was a tyranny, and it was the first duty of the citizen to oppose and seek to end that tyranny.'[4]

Griffith envisaged a new Irish parliament different from that extinguished in 1800 by the Act of Union, for that had been a parliament for which Catholics could not be candidates. The extension of the eligibility ('emancipation') to Catholics and to a broader social class meant that the policy of a new Irish parliament would reflect a very different electoral perspective.

Griffith also resented English people meddling in Irish affairs, whether they were soldiers, politicians or trade unionists. This was perhaps most evident during the treaty debates, when in response to Erskine Childers on 10 January 1922 he declared that 'I will not reply to any Englishman in this Dáil (applause)'. He repeated the sentiment but more coarsely a moment later as Childers addressed him again: 'I will not reply to any damned Englishman in this Assembly'. This time no applause was recorded. Griffith was, in the opinion of the anti-treaty Ernie O'Malley, 'a man who seldom stooped to personal abuse' but others judged his outburst that day less kindly. Maye describes it as 'uncharacteristic'.[5]

The fact that Griffith's weekly papers received Irish Republican Brotherhood funding and that he was invited to attend the exclusive top-level meeting convened by the IRB in 1914 and later described at length by Seán T. O'Kelly (below) shows where his true sympathies lay. He served for Sinn Féin as acting president of Dáil Éireann through much of the War of Independence and continued to subscribe to the evolving policy and principles of that party, the very name of which is in the Irish language a declaration of independence (meaning 'we ourselves').

If Griffith is sometimes personally represented as ultimately wishing in principle to retain the British monarch's role in Ireland, that is due to a misunderstanding or to malice.

4

DE VALERA NEVER ACCEPTED PARTITION?

The prospect of the partitioning of Ireland was already on the horizon when Éamon de Valera ran as a Sinn Féin candidate in a parliamentary by-election in County Clare in 1917. His election literature then promised, firstly, that 'every vote for de Valera is a call for justice to the Council of the Nations'; secondly, it was 'a vote for Ireland as a nation'; thirdly, it was 'a vote against conscription'; fourthly, 'a vote against partition'. The list reflected the public's wishes—principally that there should be no conscription (against which a tract by de Valera was published at the time) and that any international peace conference held when the great war being fought in Europe ended would somehow recognise Ireland's independent nationhood. His list of promises did not refer to a republic but to a united Ireland.[1]

Yet de Valera had explicitly accepted the principle of partition by 22 August 1921 at the latest. This was just a few weeks after a truce had been agreed in the War of Independence, and he had then met alone with Prime Minister Lloyd George in London. The truth comes as a surprise to those who think that 'the split' and the Civil War of 1922–3 were mainly about the partition of Ireland, and that in this respect the peace delegates ('plenipotentiaries') who went to London must have somehow let down those who sent them there on behalf of the new Sinn Féin parliament in Dublin.

The partition of Ireland was an unprecedented tear in the political psyche of many Irish people—including, indeed, of some unionists—and this appears to have fuelled a suspicion that only treachery could explain why the plenipotentiaries signed an agreement that did not somehow achieve what the War of Independence itself had failed to achieve. The agreement did not reverse the United Kingdom's legislation of 1920 splitting Ireland into two political units.

It has been suggested that, precisely because de Valera became 'a near mythic figure in Irish political history' who 'projected his actions not on the silver screen of the possible but against the hard wall of principle', one needs to answer the question 'Was he a Republican?' and, indeed, that question gains force from a consideration of his concessions on Ulster.[2] It might, however, be fairer to ask 'Were not all the Sinn Féin members of Dáil Éireann "republican" in their own ways?', even if many of them saw a need to compromise in practice in 1921 in the light of democratic realities.

It has too seldom been recognised that Éamon de Valera himself accepted the principle of partition months before the plenipotentiaries started negotiations for a treaty agreement in London. He did so in an unambiguous speech in Dáil Éireann, which met that day in Dublin's Mansion House, the official residence of the city's lord mayor. It was Monday 22 August, and his speech made a considerable impact. Indeed, John Bowman in his study of de Valera and 'the Ulster Question' writes that de Valera's speech then was 'met with dissatisfaction, apprehension and confusion'.[3] Even during the bitter treaty debates four to five months later, de Valera acknowledged the deep division between unionists and nationalists and accepted the principle of partition, while asserting that the rest of Ireland should be a republic. Thus his objective was not necessarily the all-island republic envisaged either by his comrades

At Dáil Éireann in Dublin's Mansion House, in the autumn of 1921: de Valera (left) in an armchair, Griffith beside him on a settee (centre), and Collins standing (foreground) to address Eoin MacNeill TD in the chair (courtesy of the National Library of Ireland, KE220).

who died in the Easter Rising of 1916 or by others who had stood as Sinn Féin candidates in the general election of 1918. For his part, Arthur Griffith was ultimately prepared to settle in the short term for a form of separation from Britain less than that of a republic if such a compromise brought peace and British recognition of what was termed by the Irish negotiators the 'essential unity' of Ireland.[4]

That greater attention has not been paid to de Valera's words on this issue in August 1921 and January 1922 is partly because key speeches were made during private sessions of Dáil Éireann, when it met behind closed doors. Written accounts of the private sessions of the treaty debates in December 1921 and the debates in August and September 1921 before the negotiations in London began 'were locked in a safe and remained private for another fifty years'.[5] The record of these contributions disrupts simplistic narratives of 'the Irish revolution' and is easier to ignore than to try and square it with subsequent events, including the Civil War.

On the morning of 22 August 1921 the Dáil assembled for such a private session in the Mansion House to discuss possible peace negotiations, the terms of which were still being arranged with the British. Ceann Comhairle Eoin MacNeill TD took the Chair. Deputy J.J. Walsh asked de Valera for a full and clear definition of his policy with regard to Ulster, and the official parliamentary report records that de Valera, president of the Dáil, explained that 'they' (Sinn Féin ministers) 'had not the power, and some of them had not the inclination, to use force with Ulster':

> 'He did not think that policy would be successful. They would be making the same mistake with that section as England had made with Ireland. He would not be responsible for such a policy. Ulster's present position was that she claimed the Six Counties as a constitutional right given to her constitutionally through the Realm

> and did not want to be under the domination of the rest of Ireland whose sentiments, ideals and religion were different. They said they would not give away their established rights and that they were prepared to die for them. The question was how they were to deal with Ulster—peace or war conditions. At the present the [Sinn Féin] Ministry proposed to act as they had done before under war conditions. He could not definitely say further than that their object at present was to get in contact to see what exactly Ulster wanted. The moment contact was established they were up against a big difficulty. Ulster would say she was as devotedly attached to the Empire as they were to their independence and that she would fight for one as much as they would do for the other. In case of coercion she would get sympathy and help from her friends all over the world … For his part, if the Republic were recognised, he would be in favour of giving each county power to vote itself out of the Republic if it so wished. Otherwise they would be compelled to use force … His attitude would be that the minority in Ulster had a right to have their sentiments considered to the utmost limit. He believed the minority in this country were devotedly attached to certain connections and it was their duty so far as they could to go the utmost limit without sacrificing the interests of the majority.'

De Valera at this point does not appear to have regarded the oath to the republic that deputies had earlier taken as members of the Dáil as a barrier to conceding generously that Ireland could be partitioned on a county-by-county basis. It is reasonable to infer on the basis of his speech that he was willing to see Ireland partitioned if Britain permitted the new state to be a republic, free of all symbols and any power of the Crown. Mansergh, however, refers to de Valera's avoidance of the noun 'republic' in correspondence with Lloyd George in 1921 and thinks that he also then 'conveyed an impression of a wary readiness to consider adjustment of his stance if, but only if, that would bring in the minority in the North' to a united Ireland.[6] A 'united Ireland' might take various forms.

The Irish cabinet secretary's note of a crucial but fractious meeting of the Sinn Féin cabinet that took place in Dublin just a couple of days before the signing of the agreement for a treaty in London in December 1921 records Éamon de Valera making a statement in the course of a long discussion that on first sight appears to contradict his earlier statement about individual Ulster counties being permitted to opt out of a republic. He now said, according to the record, 'He personally could not subscribe to the Oath of Allegiance nor could he sign any document which would give N.E. Ulster power to vote itself out of the Irish State'. However, 'N.E. Ulster' (a common way for government ministers in Dublin to refer to Northern Ireland then) signified a combined unit of six counties. To give it a block vote would mean the largely nationalist counties of Fermanagh and Tyrone being outvoted. Giving individual counties the right to opt out, which is what de Valera had proposed in Dáil Éireann in August 1921, was a different matter. Moreover, his high-flown declaration at the cabinet meeting is immediately followed by a significant qualification, that 'With modifications, however, it [the proposed treaty] might be accepted honourably, and he would like to see the plenipotentiaries go back and secure peace if possible'.[7] So partition might be acceptable to him in certain circumstances, for example if the Free State was to be a republic and not a dominion under the Crown and if Tyrone and Fermanagh were explicitly free to join it. Griffith was willing to accept for now Ireland being a Dominion like Canada and not to insist on a republic but on a meaningful boundary commission, seeing this as a stepping-stone to greater independence later.

The agreement for a treaty that the plenipotentiaries signed in London on 6 December 1921 and that was endorsed by a majority of the Irish cabinet (de Valera being in the minority) and by

Dáil Éireann envisaged a continuation in some form of the partition of Ireland that had been created by the United Kingdom's Government of Ireland Act 1920, and the continuation of the parliament in Belfast set up under Article 12 of that Act.[8]

None of the plenipotentiaries liked the provisions of Article 12 that allowed partition to stand. All were advanced nationalists or republicans of some kind, and all had hoped for a better outcome from the War of Independence. But they were not going to get at a table in London what they could not extract from the British by force of arms, and compromises are inevitable in such circumstances.

It is noteworthy that when, during the treaty debates in Dáil Éireann, de Valera brought forward his own proposals for an alternative treaty between Ireland and the British Commonwealth, he was prepared to include an addendum again recognising the reality of 'North East Ulster'. Appendix 18 of the records of Dáil Éireann for 10 January 1922 show that this addendum was prefaced with some high-flown words, but its terms ultimately accepted that Northern Ireland would continue to enjoy 'privileges and safeguards not less substantial than those provided for in the … "Treaty"'.[9]

Within months de Valera would be involved in an insurrection aimed at overthrowing the Anglo-Irish treaty, but this was not because of its terms relating to Northern Ireland. In his case it had far more to do with his strong opinions on the oath to the British monarch that was required of members of Dáil Éireann and with the position of that monarch as constitutional head of the Irish Free State.

5

'*ULSTER* WILL FIGHT AND *ULSTER* WILL BE RIGHT'?

The rallying cry 'Ulster will fight and Ulster will be right' is thought to have been coined by the British unionist Randolph Churchill (father of Winston) in the 1880s. Did it? Will it? The answer depends on what one means by 'Ulster'.

Ulster is one of the four ancient provinces of the island of Ireland. It is home to the cycle of mythology that includes a great warrior hero, Cú Chulainn.

Some Ulster Unionists opposed the United Kingdom's Government of Ireland Act 1920 precisely because the UK administrative area of Northern Ireland that it created encompassed only six and not all nine counties of the province of Ulster. For their part, Irish nationalists thought that the British in 1920 engineered the new Northern Ireland to include a large Unionist majority in order to keep Ireland divided and thus to retain a secure foothold on the island.

In 1921 the great majority of Irish Protestants, many descended from British settlers and immigrants, favoured a continuing union between Ireland and Britain. When that ceased to be a possibility, they looked at other options. Creating a new Northern Ireland entity coterminous with all nine counties of Ulster would have meant its having a smaller proportion of Protestant inhabitants than the Northern Ireland of six counties that actually came into existence was to have. The former, as a political unit, would have been more unstable (politically and militarily) than the Northern Ireland created by the United Kingdom Government of Ireland Act 1920.

Cultural identity and chauvinism have often won out over geographic precision when it comes to the term 'Ulster'. Since 1920 the word 'Ulster' has been used emotionally by unionists to give Northern Ireland a cultural and political coherence, being frequently adopted as an alternative designation for the six Irish counties of the United Kingdom. Through ignorance or carelessness, many British commentators and politicians have frequently employed the term 'Ulster' to mean 'Northern Ireland'. It sounds more inspiring to cry out 'Ulster will fight and Ulster will be right!' than to shout 'Northern Ireland will fight and Northern Ireland will be right' or 'The Six Counties' etc.

On 17 October 1921, during the treaty talks in London, Arthur Griffith handed to the British for inspection certain maps drawn to illustrate the comparative strength of Protestants and Catholics in the whole of Ulster and also in the six counties of Northern Ireland. His figures, as recorded by the UK cabinet secretary, included the following:

Whole of Ulster	
Protestants	*Catholics*
890,000	700,000
Six Counties [Northern Ireland]	
Protestants	*Catholics*
820,570	429,161

The Protestant population of Northern Ireland being made up as follows:–

Presbyterians	395,039
Episcopalians	327,076
Methodists	45,942
All others	52,513

Lloyd George told him: 'The logical unit would have been Ulster [i.e. all nine counties]. Your predecessors [Irish MPs at Westminster] said that was unfair because of the homogeneous Catholic population in North-West Ulster. We made a compromise; no compromise is logically defensible.'[1]

Michael Collins complained to him in reply that 'The present six counties implies coercion; South and East Down, South Armagh, Fermanagh and Tyrone, will not come in Northern Ireland [because of Catholic majorities] and it is not fair to ask them to come in. We are prepared to face the problem itself—not your definition of it.' Lloyd George replied, 'It is not our definition, but our compromise, after much discussion with your predecessors. (All Irish history did not begin with Sinn Féin.)' He added: 'Don't father this compromise on us ... it is no use making peace with you if we are going to have civil war with Ulster'. When Collins said 'You are not putting up historic Ulster', Lord Chancellor Birkenhead retorted, 'It is a logical unit'.[2]

Relying particularly on election results that showed majorities voting for nationalist candidates in Tyrone and Fermanagh, Collins and Griffith believed that the boundary commission for which broad provision was made in the Anglo-Irish treaty would be obliged by circumstances to exclude those two counties from Northern Ireland and that this in turn would render the remaining four counties unworkable as a unit. However, there were no agreed terms of reference for the boundary commission and the extent of its powers were uncertain.

The Dáil had barely voted to accept the agreement for a treaty when Michael Collins met James Craig, premier of Northern Ireland, to discuss what might happen next. When they sat down again on 2 February 1922 the meeting was reportedly almost entirely confined to the subject of the boundary commission, and it did not go well, according to reports:

> 'Owing to the fact of Mr Collins's stand on the Boundary Commission and the Irish Delegation Agreements with Mr Lloyd George and the large territories that were involved in the Commission, and not merely a boundary line as Sir James Craig was given to understand privately by several British Ministers, and from statements of Mr Lloyd George in the House of Commons, no further agreement was reached, and a very serious situation has consequently arisen'.[3]

As has emerged clearly only quite recently—thanks to the research of Kevin Matthews, and as I have discussed elsewhere—it appears that in fact Lord Chancellor Birkenhead was of the view that in law the boundary commission could only in practice deal with minor changes to a narrow 'boundary line'. Private correspondence of Birkenhead with others involved on the British side that has quite recently come to light suggests that he may have had a bad conscience or at least political remorse about the way that British ministers had not clearly disabused the Irish of their alternative interpretation at the time.[4] Although what Craig reportedly claimed he was 'given to understand' thus has a ring of authenticity about it, in February 1922 Collins was eager to scotch any suggestion that the boundary commission would make little difference to the new border. On a file of Irish cabinet papers of 1922 is a typescript of thirty-two pages referring to the negotiations between Michael Collins and James Craig that, among other things, sets out in late April or early May various statements that have been made demonstrating what Collins and Griffith believed had been agreed with the British in respect of a boundary commission. Thus, for example, Collins told press representatives on 3 February 1922 that

> 'Everybody on the British and Irish Delegation perfectly understood that the Boundary Commission would mean the loss of Tyrone and Fermanagh to the North-East Parliament [i.e. their exclusion from Northern Ireland]. The Commission … would naturally give effect to the wishes of the inhabitants of places like East and South Down, South Armagh and large portions of County Derry. It was well known what those wishes were.
>
> At no time was there any question of being misled by Mr Lloyd George. I never went on any opinion of his on the subject. It was a matter for the inhabitants of the areas involved and for them only. The maps presented by the Irish Delegation to the British Delegation are clear and unquestionable. The maps are marked on five different bases:- (a) Counties (b) Constituencies (c) County Council Areas (d) Poor Law Areas (e) Parishes according to religion. Our claim was clear. Majorities must rule, and in any map marked on that principle under the above headings we secure immense anti-partition areas.'[5]

Griffith was eager to assure Ulster unionists that the government in Dublin had no intention of forcing unionist areas into the Free State, but he was clearly worried. On 3 February he made a statement saying that if unionists in the north, as a minority on the island, voted themselves out of a new Irish state, then

> 'the Irish Free State, although it would logically possess the right, would not forcibly exert its powers to prevent that vote having effect. It is a matter, not of logic, but of practical politics. It is governed by that letter of President de Valera to Mr Lloyd George [presumably that of 10 August 1921] in which he declared he would not coerce Unionist Ulster. We shall not coerce Unionist Ulster, but equally we shall not permit Nationalist Ulster to be coerced.'[6]

Griffith realised the seriousness of the situation. He sent a message to Collins on 15 February 1922: 'If British Government stands firmly on this [then the] situation will be saved. Otherwise disaster.'[7]

There followed disaster. The British certainly did not stand firm on the Irish interpretation of what was agreed, and for this and other reasons Sinn Féin continued to split, civil war ensued and within a few months both Collins and Griffith were dead. Their hopes and expectations for the boundary commission were dashed. Six counties of Ulster remained in the United Kingdom, while three of its counties became part of the Irish Free State. As Donegal was one of these, it meant that the most northerly point on the island of Ireland was in what many in Northern Ireland would come to call 'the South'!

CITY SPECIAL

SUNDAY INDEPENDENT

VOL. 16. NO. 45. DUBLIN, SUNDAY, NOVEMBER 6, 1921. PRICE 2d.

PROBLEM"

der to Sir Craig

E BLUNDER"

ments, Sir James Craig did actually come into touch with the British Premier yesterday, and the resulting consultations were protracted, indicating that vital matters were under discussion.

Mr. Desmond Fitzgerald's rejoinder to Sir James Craig's statement yesterday, subsequent to his conversations with Mr. Lloyd George, hits off the situation pretty clearly, and is the subject of much comment in the British Press.

THE ONLY OBSTRUCTION.

MORE

Ten From E
Nine F

DUBLIN A

Nine more Dublin men and a Kilk
man arrived in the city last ni
having been released from B
kinlar. The releases were un
ditional with one exception, th
ternee in question, who is from
kenny, being allowed out on pa

Enthusiastic scenes were witnesse
the railway terminus, wh
despite the heavy rain, a l
crowd gathered to receive the
who were loudly cheered on lea
the train.

Ulster will bite! *Sunday Independent*, 6 November 1921.

6

COLLINS LED THE TREATY TEAM, FOUNDED FG?

The impression is sometimes given in popular accounts, on TV or elsewhere, that Michael Collins led the treaty negotiations. Indeed, in Neil Jordan's film *Michael Collins* it is explicitly stated that he did so. Cutting a heroic figure at the time of armed hostilities, not least for organising the assassination of British spies, Collins has continued to fascinate people down through the decades. His daring escapades and tragic death are the stuff of hero-worship, material for a foundational myth.

As the Irish minister for finance in late 1921 and a leading figure of the War of Independence, Collins was a key participant in the negotiations in London, albeit reluctant to go there initially. Yet Griffith was chairman of the team, being both minister for foreign affairs and deputy president of Dáil Éireann. In fact, by the time he went to London for the talks, Griffith had acted as president of the Dáil longer than de Valera himself had.

Only one other player on the team of five that represented Dáil Éireann in London was in the Irish cabinet, that being Robert Barton, minister for economic affairs. The other two plenipotentiaries, Edmund/Éamonn Duggan and Gavan Duffy, were simply members of the Dáil. Within the Irish group there was a hierarchy based on their respective political standing. On the British side the UK prime minister led his team, whereas Ireland's prime minister,

Éamon de Valera, was absent, and all other British negotiators were also ministers. Even before they sat down to talk in London the Irish had been weakened by divisions within the cabinet in Dublin, and this meant that they did not field the most senior team possible for the Downing Street sessions.

Collins generally deferred to and respected Griffith, who drove forward the difficult negotiations. Yet Griffith is frequently not given due attention in media references to them. It was Griffith who convinced Collins in London to participate in the final session of the negotiations when Collins indicated to him that he was too fed up to care about the talks any longer. Griffith in turn was generous in his praise of the role played by Collins in the War of Independence. In Dáil Éireann on 7 January 1922 Griffith described him as 'the man who won the war':

> 'I said it, and I say it again; he was the man that made the situation; he was the man, and nobody knows better than I do [Griffith was acting president of Dáil Éireann for eighteen months during de Valera's absence in America from June 1919 until December 1920] how, during a year and a half he worked from six in the morning until two next morning. He was the man whose matchless energy, whose indomitable will carried Ireland through the terrible crisis (applause); and though I have not now, and never had, an ambition about either political affairs or history, if my name is to go down in history I want it associated with the name of Michael Collins (applause). Michael Collins was the man who fought the Black-and-Tan terror for twelve months, until England was forced to offer terms (cheers).'

The relationship between Collins and Griffith was not always straightforward. It suffered strains before and after the treaty was

Arthur Griffith, followed by Michael Collins, leads the Irish treaty team out of 10 Downing Street, 1921 (courtesy of the National Library of Ireland, NPA MKN33).

signed, not least when during the six months leading up to the ousting of anti-treaty forces from the Four Courts in June 1922 Collins struggled to balance the terms of the treaty with what he saw as the need for the northern IRA to protect Catholics who were experiencing murderous sectarian attacks. He did not want Northern Ireland to function until the boundary commission gave nationalists in certain areas of it a chance to join the Free State.[1]

*****

On 27 January 2019, the main BBC television news bulletin carried what it described as 'a rare interview' with Ireland's prime minister/taoiseach, Leo Varadkar. During its introduction Varadkar was shown walking through Government Buildings in Dublin with the BBC's political editor, Laura Kuenssberg. They stopped and gazed up at a large portrait of Michael Collins. Varadkar told her, 'This is Michael Collins, one of the founding fathers of the country and the founding father of my party'.

There are at least two problems with the claim that Collins was a founding father of Fine Gael. First, Collins died on 22 August 1922 and the official Fine Gael website states that 'Fine Gael was founded in 1933'. Second, Collins was dead before even a new Cumann na nGaedheal was founded in March 1923, and in any event the latter organisation alone did not go on to constitute Fine Gael. As Fine Gael's website notes, Fine Gael was founded 'following the amalgamation of a number of groups: the pro-treaty Cumann na nGaedheal of W.T. Cosgrave, the Centre Party under Frank MacDermot, and the National Guard' (of Eoin O'Duffy). One might add that it is by no means certain that, had they lived beyond 1922, Griffith and Collins would have walked the same path as those who went on from March 1923 to create or find a home in Cumann na nGaedheal and Fine Gael. It is quite possible that the pair would have taken a much stronger position on the boundary commission, for example, and that Griffith at least would have been socially more progressive.

Why does Fine Gael prefer to claim Collins as its founder rather than Arthur Griffith, or even W.T. Cosgrave? Griffith actually founded not only Sinn Féin (from which Fine Gael and Fianna Fáil both emerged) but also, with William Rooney, the first and earlier Cumann na nGaedhael, in 1900. He was president of Dáil Éireann when he died in 1921 and was then reportedly described by Collins himself as 'father of us all'. Is the hard-man military veneer of a 'Mick' Collins or 'Ernie' O'Malley more popular, more sexy, than such political credentials? It seems that Griffith, unlike O'Malley, is not one of those 'characters created by the Irish troubles'.[2] Why were so many events during the recent 'Decade of Centenaries 2012–2023' concentrated on violent aspects of the struggle for independence?

Especially since Pakenham's *Peace by Ordeal* appeared in 1935, fundamentally blaming Griffith for shortcomings in the treaty, it may have suited Fine Gael to distance itself from Griffith so that he might posthumously bear the weight of responsibility for that compromise agreement and so unburden the old pro-treaty party to face in new ways a resurgent de Valera and his self-styled 'republican party'.

Who fears to speak of the complex Griffith and his personal sacrifices aimed at avoiding division on the island and within the independence movement? Do his key contributions to the creation of this state discomfort people? His pen is not mightier than the sword of Michael Collins when it comes to honing a myth.

7

THEY DISOBEYED THE CABINET?

In 1921 the Irish cabinet consisted of the seven most senior government ministers (then also termed secretaries of state). One was Éamon de Valera, president of Dáil Éireann and therefore also head of the cabinet. He proposed to Dáil Éireann that it pick three ministers (Arthur Griffith, Michael Collins and Robert Barton) and two other members of the Dáil who were not ministers (Éamonn Duggan and George Gavan Duffy) to go to London to negotiate an agreement for a treaty. Dáil Éireann then approved the five as its 'plenipotentiaries'. The three senior cabinet ministers remaining in Dublin with de Valera were Cathal Brugha, W.T. Cosgrave and Austin Stack. Brugha and Stack were highly suspicious of, and even openly hostile to, the peace talks.

References to the Irish cabinet having given 'instructions' to the Irish team of five plenipotentiaries at the London treaty negotiations in October to December 1921 are somewhat misleading and confusing. While de Valera proposed and appointed the plenipotentiaries he did so as president of Dáil Éireann which as a body actually approved and ratified them. It was not a power or decision of the cabinet alone. The Dáil vested in these men full power, as de Valera himself put it, to 'negotiate and conclude on behalf of Ireland with the representatives of his Britannic Majesty, George V, a Treaty or Treaties of settlement, association and accommodation between Ireland and the community of nations known as the British Commonwealth'. De Valera had told the Dáil 'They should have full powers because if they go over they needed to have the moral feeling of support of the position to do the best they could for Ireland.' That day he even rejected a plea by one of the five deputies about to be appointed a plenipotentiary, George Gavan Duffy, that he and the other four delegates not be called this as it would give Lloyd George 'a present of plenipotentiaries with full powers'.[1] It may be noted that the English word 'plenipotentiary' is made up directly of two simple Latin words meaning 'full power', as no doubt well understood by de Valera and others at a time when Latin was widely taught in Catholic schools.

Thus the cabinet had no legal power to instruct the team in London to do anything, regardless of the cabinet's wishes or policy and even if de Valera was concerned that in his absence the five might make decisions that he would not like. Nevertheless, on 7 October 1921 he sent what purported to be 'instructions' to the Irish team. While the letter communicating these 'understandings' contained a clear acknowledgement of the fact that 'The Plenipotentiaries have full powers as defined in their credentials', it was headed 'Instructions to plenipotentiaries from the Cabinet', although the word 'instruction' does not appear in the body of what seems to be a cabinet resolution. If the men going to London had 'full powers', which they did, then nobody had a legal power to bind them by ancillary 'instructions'. De Valera's 'instructions' read in full as follows:

'(1) The Plenipotentiaries have full powers as defined in their credentials.
(2) It is understood however that before decisions are finally reached on the main questions that a despatch notifying the intention of making these decisions will be sent to the Members of the Cabinet in Dublin and that a reply will be awaited by the Plenipotentiaries before the final decision is made.
(3) It is also understood that the complete text of the draft treaty about to be signed will be similarly submitted to Dublin and reply awaited.
(4) In case of break the text of final proposals from our side will be similarly submitted.
(5) It is understood that the Cabinet in Dublin will be kept regularly informed of the progress of the negotiations.'[2]

The ambiguous term 'it is understood', rather than 'it is agreed/decided', for example, is used here three times and implied too by the word 'similarly' in 'instruction' no. 4. It is unclear from the letter how many members of the cabinet had an opportunity to discuss these 'instructions'. The letter may have been approved by no more than the four members of cabinet remaining in Dublin. It did not explicitly demand prior cabinet approval of decisions by the plenipotentiaries as such but 'understood' that 'the Members of the Cabinet in Dublin' (presumably the four senior ministers who were not plenipotentiaries) would have proposals submitted to them for their opinions to be ascertained. In Dáil Éireann on 14 December 1921 de Valera insisted that 'I was the strongest advocate that they should have full powers of discussion. There was no use in sending them if they were to be figureheads. There was no question of withdrawing powers.' Dáil Éireann had in fact given them full powers 'to negotiate and

Constance Markievicz in uniform, kneeling against a studio prop, c.1915 (courtesy National Library of Ireland) KE 82. None of the plenipotentiaries proposed by de Valera or chosen by Dáil Éireann was a woman.

conclude' an agreement and not simply powers of 'discussion'. In this context, not all academic and political observers have clearly distinguished between such words as 'plenipotentiary', 'understood' and 'instructions'.

De Valera decided not to be part of the team, becoming a hurler on the ditch when it came to the game being played in London. He might strive to control the flow of discussions, but he had to recognise that the plenipotentiaries were 'fully empowered' to make their own decisions. There was a further cabinet minute made on 13 November that 'the plenipotentiaries should have a perfectly free hand but should follow original instructions re important decisions'.[3] The original instructions, as seen already, were not and could not ultimately be actual enforceable 'instructions' but remained 'understandings', and this new minute did not alter their nature. Some members of the cabinet who had chosen not to be delegates might yearn to 'instruct' those in London who were, but the five men meeting Lloyd George and his team were answerable directly to Dáil Éireann for the exercise of their power. Dáil Éireann had given them full authority to do what they saw fit.

Constance Markievicz (née Gore-Booth), a hard-line republican, had been a senior minister in the 1st Dáil (1919–21), being the cabinet's sole female member and the first female government minister in western Europe, but de Valera demoted her ministry to junior status on the formation of the 2nd Dáil and she was not included in the delegation for the Peace Conference. Speaking against the treaty in Dáil Éireann on 3 January 1922, she claimed that the plenipotentiaries had been 'tricked', and some deputies laughed when she added that 'my people came over here in Henry VIII's time and by that bad black drop of English blood in me … I know the English personally better perhaps than the people who went over on the delegation'. The Dáil report records an unidentified deputy intervening to ask, 'Why didn't you go over?' She retorted, 'Why didn't you send me?' Here was a glimpse of the gap between rhetoric and everyday reality for women and others involved in 'the Irish revolution'.

The Anglo-Irish Gore-Booth ostensibly became the aristocratic 'Countess Markievicz' through her passing marriage to a Polish landlord in Ukraine. Every 'revolution' has its icons and she provided one by posing in a studio in her Volunteer uniform in radical chic or romantic mode, stroking a revolver. According to the National Library, who hold a copy of that picture, it was taken about 1915–even before a rebellious shot had been fired in anger.

No sooner had shots ceased being fired after a truce in the War of Independence was called in the summer of 1921 than men of the IRA's second North Cork Brigade turned up at the Dublin Metropolitan School of Art to be painted by Seán Keating as they gazed dreamily and manfully into the future. He portrayed them grouped together and gripping their rifles, with a suitably attractive rural landscape provided as backdrop rather than a glimpse out some studio window of a nearby Guinness hop store or Nelson's Pillar. So iconic has this particular artistic fiction become, the editors of the *Atlas of the Irish Revolution* chose it for the front cover of their massive tome.[4]

Although the cabinet could not usurp the full powers granted to the five plenipotentiaries by Dáil Éireann, and the five men remained free to decide ultimately on the best course of action to take in London, there is no reason to think that any of the five wished to avoid complying with the cabinet's 'instructions' if possible—not least because three of the five were members of the cabinet and no doubt would have welcomed full cabinet approval for any deal done in London if that deal was to come into effect.

From the outset, the plenipotentiaries and their secretarial team sent back a stream of communications to Dublin, including personal letters from Griffith to de Valera relating to the major points of discussion in his private meetings with Lloyd George. Formal documents such as drafts of the proposed agreement were also forwarded. Cabinet members in Dublin had an opportunity to express their opinions on such drafts.[5]

Plenipotentiaries also returned to Dublin from time to time, not least for a particular cabinet meeting requested by Griffith and held on 3 December 1921, just two days before what transpired to be the last session of the negotiations in London. The plenipotentiaries' journey back for this meeting took place after a round of very demanding meetings with the British and involved tiring travel by rail and sea. This even included some delegates having to return to Holyhead for hours following a collision between the mail-boat on which they travelled and a small vessel.[6]

Griffith had written urgently to de Valera on the evening of 29 November 1921: 'It is essential a Cabinet meeting should be held. I shall return to Dublin on Friday morning and hope to see you on that evening. Please have a Cabinet meeting arranged for Saturday morning, when we shall be all there. I intend to return to London on that evening.'[7] The purpose of the meeting, in the spirit of the cabinet 'instructions', was to discuss the latest text of the draft treaty as it stood, just two days before a vital session of negotiations in Downing Street. Yet the timing of the meeting appears to have irked de Valera, who had to come back from the west of Ireland to attend it, for he told Joe McGarrity later that month that 'I was suddenly summoned to Dublin to meet Griffith and the plenipotentiaries who had returned'. He had been away visiting groups of IRA Volunteers in the west of Ireland to boost their morale, and to warn them off irresponsible drinking. Many were new recruits who had not taken part in the War of Independence.[8] Although negotiations were at a crucial point then, de Valera again left Dublin after the cabinet meeting ended. The inadequate official notes of that confused meeting indicate some affirmation of, but no change to, the cabinet 'instructions' of 7 October 1921.

Back in London on 4 December Griffith and his team won further changes to the draft agreement, including to the wording of the 'oath of allegiance'. Again during these final talks Griffith indicated clearly to the British that he wished to return to Dublin for his cabinet colleagues to consider the position. It was not to frustrate any cabinet 'instructions' before signing the agreement that Griffith and his colleagues did not again at that point cross the Irish Sea. It was to avert the immediate resumption of war in Ireland that the British were suddenly threatening unless the Irish signed that very night. According to Robert Barton, who was present then,

> 'Griffith sought repeatedly to have the decision between war and peace on the terms of the treaty referred back to Dáil Éireann but this proposal Lloyd George directly negatived'.[9]

When Griffith and the others finally signed the agreement under duress in the early hours of 6 December 1921, they did so conscious of the fact that the agreement itself still contained a provision requiring it to be approved by elected representatives in London and Dublin before it could come into effect as a treaty. Thus each Irish senior minister still had an opportunity to express his opinion on it, both at cabinet and in the Dáil. By four votes to three, members of the Irish cabinet in fact approved the agreement as signed rather than face great uncertainty and quite possibly renewed fighting by trying to face down the British at that point. Dáil Éireann was to make the same decision in January 1922. A majority of cabinet members and of Dáil deputies felt that the British were then unlikely to yield significantly more and thought that the plenipotentiaries had won enough to allow further political advances by the new Irish Free State as it developed in due course. This turned out to be the case.

8

THEY 'SIGNED THE TREATY'?

The plenipotentiaries did not actually sign the Anglo-Irish treaty in 1921 but rather a conditional agreement. A friend has suggested to me that this is 'maybe a bit Jesuitical'. Wasn't the Belfast or 'Good Friday' Agreement of 1998 itself subject to parliamentary approval? And isn't it an internationally binding treaty? Did Bertie [Ahern] not first sign it as such? These are fair questions. Indeed, even those who put their signature to the document of 1921 sometimes spoke of 'signing the treaty' that night, despite the fact that what they signed was an agreement requiring the members of Dáil Éireann to approve it before a treaty could come into effect.

Leaving aside complex jurisprudence about what constitutes the moment at which a treaty is binding in international law, it can be said that the document signed by the plenipotentiaries was headed '*Proposed* Agreement *for* a Treaty' (my emphasis). The word 'proposed' was subsequently crossed out at some time. The plenipotentiaries had full authority from Dáil Éireann to draw up with the UK an agreement for a treaty. This did not take away the right of the Dáil in Dublin and of parliament at Westminster to reject the agreement and to refuse to enact it into law. In normal circumstances it might be unusual for plenipotentiaries to have a proposal rejected, but the circumstances were quite abnormal in December 1921, not least owing to the British threat of immediate and terrible war. It is a basic principle of law that contracts entered into under duress are void or voidable. On that last night the Irish wished to return to Dublin to consult their fellow ministers before signing but the British threatened war if they did so.

At the cabinet meeting that took place on 3 December 1921 in Dublin at Griffith's request, two days before the final session of talks began, de Valera made clear his opposition to aspects of the proposed agreement as it stood that day. It may be noted that the agreement subsequently signed in London in the early hours of Tuesday 6 December 1921 was not precisely the same as that discussed at the chaotic cabinet meeting in Dublin on the previous Saturday. Nevertheless, the differences between the draft discussed at cabinet in Dublin and the document signed in London were not weighty enough to say with confidence that de Valera, or any other Irish minister remaining in Dublin who so far had been against terms of the proposed agreement, would definitely have changed his mind had he known in advance the precise terms of the agreement signed by the plenipotentiaries in London on 6 December.

De Valera had told Dáil Éireann on 14 September 1921 that he understood any agreement reached in London would be subject to ratification. He rose in the Dáil on 14 December 1921, at the outset of the treaty debates, and again made it clear that as president of the Dáil he accepted that the signed agreement was indeed conditional. He said in the opening speech:

> 'Really there is nothing extraordinary in the division of opinion, for this reason, that when the plenipotentiaries would report, it was obvious the Cabinet would have to take a policy. Either the whole Cabinet would have to go over if the possibility of division was to be eliminated, the whole Cabinet should take responsibility for the negotiations, which was a thing that would not be desirable for

> other reasons. Even if they did there might be divisions. You could scarcely eliminate differences of opinion. It was necessary then either that the plenipotentiaries should be a whole Cabinet or that there should be other persons than members of the Cabinet. What we did was, we selected three members of the Cabinet with two others and it was obvious if these plenipotentiaries were to be in a position to do the work given to them they should have full powers of negotiation. At the two meetings of the Dáil at which they were appointed I made it quite clear that my own point of view, and the point of view of the Cabinet as a whole [—] at least I took responsibility for saying it was the view of the Cabinet [—] was that the plenipotentiaries should have full plenary powers to negotiate, with the understanding, however, that when they reported, the Cabinet would decide its policy, and whatever arrangement they arrived at, it would have to be submitted to the Dáil for ratification. The question of committing the country completely without ratification by the Dáil was of course out of the question. This assembly would not have sent any five men to negotiate a treaty which would bind the nation without some chance of a larger body of representatives of the nation having an opportunity of criticizing and reviewing it, and, I would say under the circumstances, of the nation itself reviewing it. Now, that was quite a commonsense understanding. They had to have the plenary powers in order to be able to do their work. If there was a definite difference of opinion, it was the plenipotentiaries had the responsibility of making up their own minds and deciding on it. We had ourselves the right of refusing to agree with them, if we thought that was right.'

Indeed, Article 18 of the agreement explicitly recognised the need for parliament at Westminster and the Irish assembly in Dublin to approve 'the instrument', namely the agreement for a treaty signed in London on 6 December 1921:

> '18. This instrument shall be submitted forthwith by His Majesty's Government for the approval of Parliament and by the Irish signatories to a meeting summoned for the purpose of the members elected to sit in the House of Commons of Southern Ireland and *if* [emphasis added here] approved shall be ratified by the necessary legislation'.

In these circumstances it seems reasonable to state that the plenipotentiaries did not sign a treaty but a conditional agreement *for* a treaty. Once a majority of both the cabinet and the Dáil then voted to accept the agreement, the final statutory document giving the treaty agreement the force of law was framed and passed, and the treaty took effect on 6 December 1922.

Referring to a discussion amongst themselves on that fateful last night in London when he and his four colleagues were faced with the dreadful British ultimatum to sign or face immediate war, Robert Barton told Dáil Éireann on 19 December:

> 'Arthur Griffith, Michael Collins, and Éamonn Duggan were for acceptance and peace; Gavan Duffy and myself were for refusal—war or no war. An answer that was not unanimous committed you to immediate war, and the responsibility for that was to rest directly upon those two delegates who refused to sign. For myself, I preferred war. I told my colleagues so, but for the nation, without consultation, I dared not accept that responsibility. The alternative which I sought to avoid seemed to me a lesser outrage than the violation of what is my faith.'

This looks like an effort to blame Griffith, Collins and Duggan for doing what Barton himself dared not do, walking out and taking full personal responsibility for the consequences if the British were not bluffing about immediately renewing hostilities in Ireland. By leaving London without signing Barton could have brought down the whole house of cards. That Griffith, Collins and Duggan may have believed that they had reached the point where Sinn Féin had achieved as much as it could in London, while Gavan Duffy and Barton ostensibly did not believe this, was irrelevant in the immediate context. The British insisted all must sign for a deal.

Turning to de Valera in the Dáil on 19 December 1921, Barton added that he had not been prepared to decide whether to commit his nation to immediate war 'without you, Mr President, or the Members of the Dáil, or the nation having an opportunity to examine the terms upon which war could be avoided'. He had earlier pleaded with de Valera to come to London.

It was quite clear to the British that the final decision rested with Dáil Éireann, and that the signature of the plenipotentiaries was thus provisional or conditional. The conservative *Morning Post* newspaper of London critically acknowledged as much, a fact to which the plenipotentiary Gavan Duffy referred sarcastically on 21 December 1921 when he gleefully quoted it in Dáil Éireann. He told the house:

> 'I cannot help enjoying such a statement as that which I find in the *Morning Post*—the best friend that Ireland ever had in England—of yesterday. It begins its leading article:
>
> > Like humble suppliants on the doorstep waiting for an answer to their plea for charity, the [UK] Government and people of this once proud and powerful country are now hanging expectant on the discussions of an illegal assembly, self-styled Dáil Éireann,

> to know whether or not that body will graciously condescend to accept their submission.
>
> I think it is difficult for any of us to look at this matter perfectly fairly, because when you feel jubilant your feelings are apt to run away with you. I tried to look at it fairly, and it must be realised that the Irish people have an achievement to their credit in this respect at least, that this Treaty gives them what they have not had for hundreds of years; it gives them power, it puts power of control, power of Government, military power in the hands of our people and our Government.'

At the end of the day the acceptance of the treaty depended on a majority of the elected members of Dáil Éireann.

George Gavan Duffy, plenipotentiary. By John Lavery, 1921. Collection & image © Hugh Lane Gallery.

9

DURESS AND *IMMEDIATE* WAR?

Perhaps not 'immediate' war in practice, but compared to the fact of any renewed hostilities the precise timing made little difference. Neither side was under any illusion about the consequences of a breakdown in negotiations in London. Each held out the prospect of renewed fighting as a lever to extract concessions from the other, and to that extent there could be said to be duress on each side. Both sides understood, however, that Sinn Féin and its armed wing faced a mighty struggle in the face of armed Ulster loyalists and a British Army freed from the European constraints of World War I. If many IRA members were prepared to continue fighting, their military capacity to do so effectively was severely limited at this point. If they did so, the consequences for Irish society would be severe.

What happened on the last night of talks in December 1921 was that the British ratcheted up their duress, making it personal by impressing on the five Irish plenipotentiaries that if they did not agree unanimously that very night to sign the agreement there and then and subsequently propose it to Dáil Éireann, then Britain would on the next day resume battle. The Irish negotiators gave in, knowing that the Dáil itself still had the option of accepting the proposed treaty or rejecting it. They felt that the five of them in London—especially in the absence of de Valera—should not precipitately plunge the island of Ireland into further bloodshed.

Whether the British would actually have resumed hostilities that very night was not the point. The problem was that the Irish plenipotentiaries were put in the intolerable position of being made responsible for that possibility, knowing that war was in any event likely to follow a breakdown at some stage. For one thing, the British still had soldiers south of the Irish border and might quickly reinforce these with its best regiments.

Lloyd George had told his cabinet secretary that he did not wish to coerce the Irish—provided, of course, that from his perspective the Irish behaved reasonably. Nevertheless, he had red lines that he had made clear to de Valera in the months before delegates met in London in October to December 1921, and he told his cabinet secretary that 'If they are not coming into the Empire, then we will make them'.[1]

The Irish plenipotentiaries had feared that if talks broke down they themselves would be in danger of immediate arrest and imprisonment, or even worse. For that reason, in case of emergency, Michael Collins had a small aircraft on standby in London to take them to County Dublin. It was thought to hold just enough fuel to let them make a landing on Leopardstown racecourse.[2] The five were sensitive, however, to any suggestion that they signed because of any threat to them personally. It was the threat to Ireland that made them sign the agreement for a treaty, they insisted. The British ultimatum on the last night clinched it for them. In Dáil Éireann on 21 December 1921 one of the delegates, Gavan Duffy, was to quote what he called 'a semi-official denial' and 'ingenious attempt' by the British government to spin 'the monstrous iniquity' of their giving the delegates on the last night 'the grim choice between acceptance and immediate war'. The British denial had been issued to the Press Association and its terms seem patently disingenuous:

> 'The statement by Mr Robert Barton, one of the Irish Peace Treaty signatories, that the agreement was signed under duress, and that Mr Lloyd George "threatened" war in the event of a refusal occasioned no undue surprise in authoritative quarters in London to-day. It was pointed out that the Irish Envoys, who, it must be remembered, were Plenipotentiaries, had negotiated during the preceding weeks with full knowledge of the alternative in the event of a final rejection of the terms.
>
> "They accepted the proposals under duress of circumstances or duress of their own minds and not because of any eleventh hour declaration on the part of the Prime Minister," declared an authority this (Tuesday) evening. "In so far as it was well known that the alternative to acceptance was war, there is an element of truth in the statement".'

Gavan Duffy commented on this: 'The [Irish] complaint is not that the alternative to signing a Treaty was war; the complaint is that the alternative to our signing that particular Treaty was immediate war; that we who were sent to London as the apostles of peace—the qualified apostles of peace—were suddenly to be transformed into the unqualified arbiters of war; that we had to make this choice within three hours and to make it without any reference to our Cabinet, to our Parliament or to our people'.

Earlier in the treaty debate, on 15 December 1921, Daniel O'Rourke TD had asked Arthur Griffith as chairman of the delegation 'what would have been the result if the treaty was not signed':

> MR ARTHUR GRIFFITH
>
> It was the impression of every member of the delegation they [the British ministers] were replying to Ulster that night and it was a question of whether they would break off with us or not, and from

their attitude we knew that probably before we got back to Dublin war would have broken out here; not war in the proper sense but somebody was going to be shot on our side, probably someone on their side and the same thing started again. I had absolutely no doubt in my mind the issue there was peace or war.

MR KEVIN O'HIGGINS

Did Mr Lloyd George single Mr Barton out as the left wing of the delegation and did he say, 'The man who is against peace may bear now and forever the responsibility for terrible and immediate war'?

MR R.C. BARTON

I want first of all to say we were eight and a half hours on that Monday in conference with the English representatives and the strain of an eight and a half hours conference and the struggle of it is a pretty severe one. When I am asked a question like that, 'Was it or was it not?', I cannot give you an answer. But as regards particular aspects of that question, which I cannot take on oath, I can only give you my impression. It is in my notes that the answer is given, and it is there because it was my impression of that conference. It did appear to me that Mr Lloyd George spoke to me and I had an impression that he actually mentioned my name; but I could not swear on oath that he mentioned my name, or actually addressed me when he spoke. It appeared to me that he spoke to me. What he did say was that the signature and the recommendation of every member of the delegation was necessary, or war would follow immediately and that the responsibility for that war must rest directly upon those who refused to sign the treaty (applause).

Barton's references to his being unable to 'swear on oath' to his 'impression' of what happened at the final session of the talks on 5-6 December 1921 is testimony to his state of mind then.

De Valera himself said in the Dáil on 29 December 1921 that 'in Downing Street the proposals to which we could unanimously assent in the Cabinet were practically turned down at the point of the pistol and immediate war was threatened upon our people. It was only then that this document was signed, and that document has been signed by plenipotentiaries, not perhaps individually under duress, but it has been signed, and would only affect this nation as a document signed under duress, and this nation would not respect it.' Kevin O'Higgins remarked in the Dáil on the same day:

> '"The man who is against peace," said the English Premier in presenting his ultimatum, "must bear now and for ever the responsibility for terrible and immediate war." And the [Irish]men there knew our resources and the resources of the enemy, and they held in their own hearts and consciences that we were not entitled to plunge the plain people of Ireland into a terrible and immediate war for the difference between the terms of the treaty and what they knew a united Cabinet would recommend to the Dáil. Ireland, England, and the world must know the circumstances under which this Treaty is presented for your ratification. Neither honour nor principle can demand rejection of such a measure in face of the alternative so unequivocally stated by the English Prime Minister. Neither honour nor principle can make you plunge your people into war again.'

It was Kevin O'Higgins too who would later famously describe the provisional Irish government of early 1922 as simply young men 'standing amidst the ruins of one Administration, with the foundations of another not yet laid, and with wild men screaming through the keyholes'.[3] But in Britain also in 1921 and 1922 they had their own wild men screaming through the keyholes, albeit perhaps more politely. These included, not least, conservative and unionist back-benchers who intensely disliked Sinn Féin and feared that Lloyd George's attempted peace deal posed an existential threat to the United Kingdom and the 'British Empire'. Domestic political forces such as these, and in a different sphere organised labour, bore down on Lloyd George's coalition government during the period of peace talks and are too easily overlooked in Ireland. They were to dislodge the Welsh prime minister before long.

Nevertheless, Mary MacSwiney TD and some others against the treaty were certain that the plenipotentiaries had been fooled. On 14 December 1921 she confidently informed the Dáil that 'We know and they know now that they were bluffed. When he said to them at 3 o'clock, "You will sign or we will declare war", they should have said, "Very well do your worst".' In his profile of Lloyd George for the Oxford *Dictionary of National Biography*, Kenneth O. Morgan appears to agree. He claims that while Lloyd George 'threatened the Sinn Féiners with an immediate resumption of hostilities unless they accepted the terms already agreed', this was 'a colossal bluff'. All the terms were not in fact 'already agreed' to the desired extent, however, and where was the 'bluff' in such a threat unless the British had no intention of ever resuming hostilities in Ireland, which there is no reason to believe was the case? Would MacSwiney or Morgan really have refused to sign in the circumstances?

Griffith, Collins and Barton represented Ireland at what turned out to be the final session of talks, with Duggan and Gavan Duffy staying back at the delegates' house in Hans Place. The very fact that it was not a plenary session suggests that the Irish did not expect to be given that night a terrible ultimatum between the terms of the agreement as they then stood and immediate war. Aghast, the three returned to Hans Place to share the news with their two colleagues and the back-up team. On 21 December 1921 Gavan Duffy told deputies:

> 'Our delegates returned to us to inform us that four times they had all but broken and that the fate of Ireland must be decided that night. Lloyd George had issued to them an ultimatum to this effect: "It must now be peace or war. My messenger goes tonight to Belfast. I have here two answers, one enclosing the treaty, the other declaring a rupture, and, if it be a rupture, you shall have immediate war, and the only way to avert that immediate war is to bring me the undertaking to sign of every one of the plenipotentiaries, with a further undertaking to recommend the treaty to Dáil Éireann and to bring me that by 10 o'clock. Take your choice." I shall not forget the anguish of that night, torn as one was between conflicting duties.'

Writing in his *World Crisis: The Aftermath* (London, 1929), Winston Churchill described the mood: 'In the end, after two months of futilities and rigmarole, scarred by outrages in Ireland in breach of the truce, unutterably wearied Ministers faced the Irish Delegates, themselves in actual desperation and knowing well that death stood at their elbows'. British officials briefed the press that the situation was 'most critical'. By their bullying the British had greatly increased the risk—albeit an unusual one in practice when treaties are negotiated and agreement is reached—of having Dáil Éireann reject what its delegates had earlier signed.

In the case of this agreement in London in 1921 there was also a real possibility that Lloyd George's own government and parliament at Westminster would reject the deal. Lloyd George—head of the minority party in a British coalition—faced hostility to the deal within the parties that shared power in government in London. The diaries of Thomas Jones provide various examples of Lloyd George and other British ministers expressing concern not just to the Irish but also to people on their own side about the political pressures they were under from their colleagues in the coalition government.

On 14 October 1921 the Conservative Party leader, Austen Chamberlain, said to Michael Collins: 'You are not aware of the risks we are taking with our whole political future. We are bound to do it, as a coalition, but do not believe it is plain sailing.' On 17 October he told Griffith: 'My position gets more difficult day by day and my authority less and less [within the Conservative Party]'. On 21 October Lloyd George told Collins that 'We are taking great political risks. The life of the government is put in issue by our proposals.' Chamberlain told Jones on 29 October that, as regards the Irish, '"In my opinion they are just playing with us, just fooling us" and he bade me tell the Irish that we were being fooled'. At Waterloo Station on 17 November Lloyd George complained to Jones about 'the unfriendly part' that Bonar Law, who would eventually supplant Chamberlain as Tory leader, had played: 'He felt that Bonar had meant to make a bid for the leadership of the Conservatives and a break up of the Coalition'.[4]

Having signed the agreement, all five plenipotentiaries did the honourable thing and proposed and voted for it in Dáil Éireann, while also explaining the objective circumstances. None had been physically forced to sign it. Reading the first speech of each of the plenipotentiaries during the treaty debates in December 1921 and January 1922, one finds each at pains to point out in different ways that the agreement they had signed was and would be the best available in the circumstances and that there was nothing to be gained by risking immediately renewed warfare.

As regards any question of bad faith, Birkenhead—who was on the British treaty team as lord chancellor—later confided to a cabinet colleague that he had doubts as to whether the British had acted honourably in terms of how they framed and presented to the Irish the boundary commission article in the treaty. Lloyd George had led Griffith along, promising him but not securing a reply from Craig on certain crucial matters concerning the proposed settlement, right up to the matter being raised on the last night. If the British were exasperated, so too was Griffith.

Michael Collins was in no doubt that, ultimatum or not, the choice was ultimately between renewed warfare in some form ('immediate' or not) and the terms on offer on 5–6 December 1921:

> 'It has been variously stated that the treaty was signed under duress. I did not sign the treaty under duress, except in the sense that the position as between Ireland and England, historically, and because of superior forces on the part of England, has always been one of duress. The element of duress was present when we agreed to the Truce, because our simple right would have been to beat the English out of Ireland. There was an element of duress in going to London to negotiate. But there was not, and could not have been, any personal duress. The threat of "immediate and terrible war" did not matter overmuch to me. The position appeared to be then exactly as it appears now. The British would not, I think, have declared terrible and immediate war upon us. They had three courses of action open to them. First, to dissolve the parliaments and put their proposals before the country [i.e. to call a general election as a form of referendum on what Ireland was then being offered by the British]; second, to resume the war by courting openly and covertly

breakages of the Truce (these breakages of the Truce might easily have come from either side); thirdly, to blockade Ireland, and at the same time encourage spasmodic internal conflict. The first course of action seemed to me to be the most likely, and, as a result of a political win on our side either No. 2 or No. 3 would have been very easily managed by the British. A political reverse [i.e. Irish voters in a general election voting for candidates who accepted the British deal] would have been more damaging to us [i.e. Sinn Féin] than either 2 or 3. The threat of immediate and terrible war was probably bluff. The immediate tactics would surely have been to put the offer of July 20 [i.e. the original proposals of the British government for an Irish settlement, sent by Lloyd George to de Valera in July 1921], which the British considered a very good offer, before the country, and, if rejected, they would have very little difficulty in carrying their own people into a war against Ireland. Another thing I believe, is, that on resumption of hostilities the British would have been anxious to fight with us on the basis of belligerent rights. In such circumstances, I doubt if we would have been able to carry on a conflict with the success which had previously attended our efforts. I scarcely think that our resources would have been equal to bearing belligerent rights and responsibilities. I am not impressed by the talk of duress, nor by threats of a declaration of immediate and terrible war. Britain has not made a declaration of war upon Egypt, neither has she made a declaration of war upon India. But is the conflict less terrible because of the absence of such declaration? We must not be misled by words and phrases. Unquestionably the alternative to the Treaty, sooner or later, was war, and if the Irish Nation had accepted that, I should have gladly accepted it. The opponents of the Treaty have declared over and over again that the alternative to the Treaty was not war. In my judgment, this was misleading the Irish Nation. The decision of the Irish Nation should

> not be given on a false basis. That was, and is, my own attitude, and if, indeed, it be true, as the antagonists of the Treaty say, that the alternative to the Treaty was not war, where, then, is the heroism [of people proclaiming their willingness to reject the agreement, presumably]? Where, then, is the necessity for the future sacrifices that have been talked of so freely? To me it would have been a criminal act to refuse to allow the Irish Nation to give its opinion as to whether it would accept this settlement or resume hostilities. That, I maintain, is a democratic stand. It has always been the stand of public representatives who are alive to their responsibilities.'[5]

Those who had not attended the talks in London might assert that the British would have yielded more, gone further than they had before they decided to deliver an ultimatum to the Irish, but the plenipotentiaries who were present certainly did not think so. If the threat of 'immediate war' in December 1921 was a bluff that became part of a myth, the likelihood of a political and military defeat of Sinn Féin if Irish delegates had walked away without signing on 6 December was very real.

In the heat of the moment, little attention was to be paid to the achievements of negotiators, such as the winning of fiscal and financial sovereignty for the Irish Free State, or to last minute changes to the British draft proposals that saw, for example, the oath of allegiance to the king moderated to an oath of faithfulness.

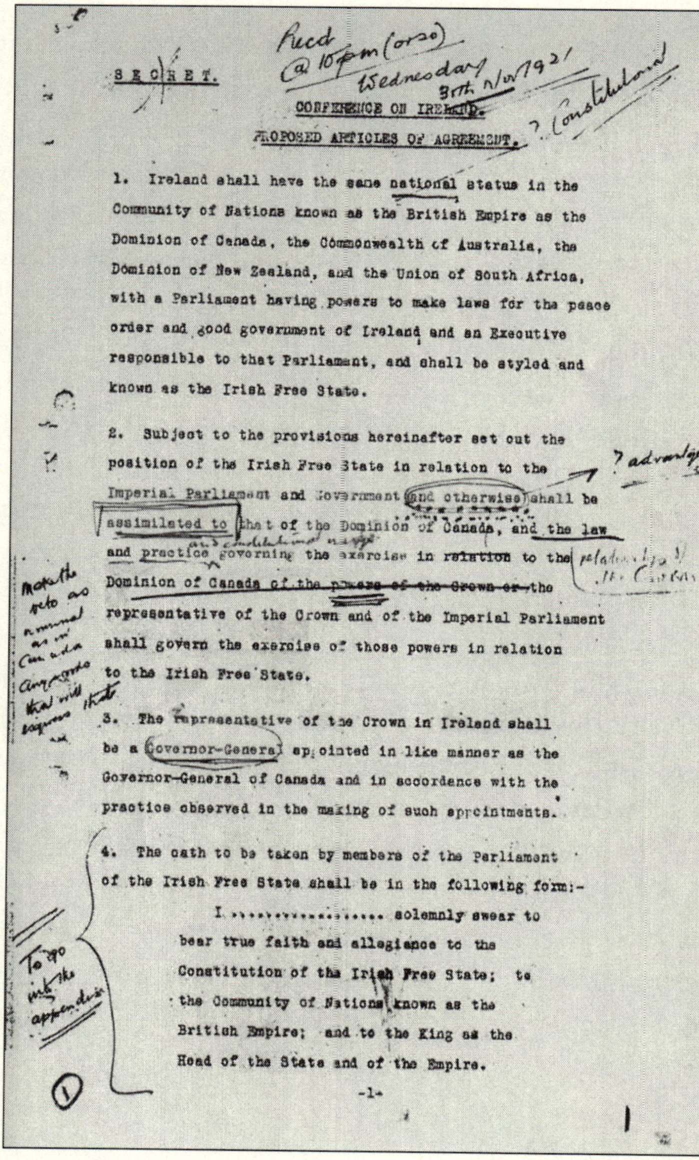

SECRET.

CONFERENCE ON IRELAND.

PROPOSED ARTICLES OF AGREEMENT.

1. Ireland shall have the same national status in the Community of Nations known as the British Empire as the Dominion of Canada, the Commonwealth of Australia, the Dominion of New Zealand, and the Union of South Africa, with a Parliament having powers to make laws for the peace order and good government of Ireland and an Executive responsible to that Parliament, and shall be styled and known as the Irish Free State.

2. Subject to the provisions hereinafter set out the position of the Irish Free State in relation to the Imperial Parliament and Government and otherwise shall be assimilated to that of the Dominion of Canada, and the law and practice governing the exercise in relation to the Dominion of Canada of the powers of the Crown or the representative of the Crown and of the Imperial Parliament shall govern the exercise of those powers in relation to the Irish Free State.

3. The representative of the Crown in Ireland shall be a Governor-General appointed in like manner as the Governor-General of Canada and in accordance with the practice observed in the making of such appointments.

4. The oath to be taken by members of the Parliament of the Irish Free State shall be in the following form:-

> I .... solemnly swear to bear true faith and allegiance to the Constitution of the Irish Free State; to the Community of Nations known as the British Empire; and to the King as the Head of the State and of the Empire.

-1-

Article 4 of a draft treaty: The oath of allegiance proposed by the British to be taken by members of Dáil Éireann, 30 November 1921. The draft is shown here annotated by the Irish side. The wording was to be changed in the final agreement for a proposed treaty (NAI DE 2/304/1).

10

THE TREATY PARTITIONED IRELAND?

One hears people in discussion refer to the treaty as if it somehow created or endorsed the border on the island of Ireland, but the British under Prime Minister Lloyd George had already divided Ireland by the Government of Ireland Act 1920. The Irish team of five plenipotentiaries who negotiated the agreement for the treaty insisted in fact on the 'essential' unity of Ireland.

The Government of Ireland Act 1920 had been passed at Westminster in the absence of most of the elected Irish members of parliament, for the latter were also by then members of Sinn Féin and had deserted Westminster to convene Dáil Éireann in Dublin for the first time in early 1919. The Act created a 'Parliament of Northern Ireland' (known later as 'Stormont'). But that was not all. The statute's first section had provided that

> 'On and after the appointed day there shall be established for Southern Ireland a Parliament to be called the Parliament of Southern Ireland consisting of His Majesty, the Senate of Southern Ireland, and the House of Commons of Southern Ireland, and there shall be established for Northern Ireland a Parliament to be called the Parliament of Northern Ireland consisting of His Majesty, the Senate of Northern Ireland, and the House of Commons of Northern Ireland'.

THE KINDEST CUT OF ALL.

Welsh Wizard. "I NOW PROCEED TO CUT THIS MAP INTO TWO PARTS AND PLACE THEM IN THE HAT. AFTER A SUITABLE INTERVAL THEY WILL BE FOUND TO HAVE COME TOGETHER OF THEIR OWN ACCORD—(*ASIDE*)—AT LEAST LET'S HOPE SO; I'VE NEVER DONE THIS TRICK BEFORE."

Lloyd George as the 'Welsh Wizard', *Punch* magazine 10 March 1920. The United Kingdom Government of Ireland Act 1920 first partitioned Ireland, more than a year before the Anglo-Irish Treaty was agreed. The cartoonist has shaded all nine counties of Ulster and not just the six counties of Northern Ireland. (*Punch*, 1920).

That Act came into force on 3 May 1921, but the envisaged Parliament of Southern Ireland was dead on arrival. Its elected MPs now sat as TDs in Dáil Éireann as the representative assembly for the twenty-six counties of Ireland that were not in Northern Ireland. Members of the Parliament of Southern Ireland convened as such just once, in January 1922, to approve the agreement for a treaty, after Dáil Éireann had done so.

Elected members of the Parliament of Northern Ireland did, however, meet regularly (after King George V had come and opened it with ceremony). It had sat even before July 1921 when a truce was declared in the Irish War of Independence. Moreover, as seen above, months before Irish plenipotentiaries signed the Anglo-Irish treaty agreement in London, de Valera told the Dáil in 1921 that, from his perspective, individual Ulster counties could be allowed to vote themselves out of an Irish republic.

Crowds in Belfast to greet the king and queen on their visit to open the parliament of Northern Ireland, June 1921 (courtesy National Library of Ireland, HOGW 184).

11

OATHS OF 'ALLEGIANCE' AND A BROKEN 'PLEDGE'?

On 30 November 1921, during the last week of extended negotiations in London for the Anglo-Irish treaty, Prime Minister Lloyd George sent to Arthur Griffith the terms of a draft treaty that he said his government was prepared to submit to parliament in Westminster for approval. Among its provisions was an oath of allegiance to the king that the British expected deputies of Dáil Éireann to swear. At the fraught Irish cabinet meeting on 3 December, which was requested by Griffith to discuss the draft and for which the five plenipotentiaries returned to Dublin, it was 'decided unanimously that the present Oath of Allegiance could not be subscribed to' as worded in that draft.[1]

Lloyd George's proposed wording of the oath to be taken by Irish members of parliament was in fact changed shortly before the agreement for a treaty was signed in London in December 1921, as part of a final deal that also yielded the new state a large measure of financial and economic autonomy. The oath of *allegiance* to the king was then replaced by an oath of *faithfulness*. It was the latter that was in the final agreement signed by Griffith and the four other plenipotentiaries.

Neither the *Oxford English Dictionary* nor the *Merriam-Webster Dictionary* defines 'allegiance' as 'faithfulness', although some thesauruses give the two words as synonyms. One may argue that there is no great difference between 'allegiance' and 'faithfulness', and some have done so and have continued to refer to the oath to the king in the treaty as an 'oath of allegiance.

Yet the oath to the Irish Republic that Griffith had strongly supported all members of Dáil Éireann taking in August 1919, when he was acting president during de Valera's long absence in America, included both 'faith and allegiance' (as does the oath of office of US senators) and such wording implies a difference:

> 'I do further swear (or affirm) that to the best of my knowledge and ability I will support and defend the Irish Republic and the Government of the Irish Republic, which is Dáil Éireann, against all enemies, foreign and domestic, and I will bear true faith and allegiance to the same, and that I take this obligation freely without any mental reservation or purpose of evasion, so help me, God.'[2]

This oath to the 'Irish Republic' of 1919 was itself later a stumbling block for deputies who felt in conscience that it was incompatible with and would be broken by taking any new oath to the king.

Opponents of the treaty's oath to the king who long persisted in referring to it even in its amended form as an 'oath of allegiance' and ignored the fact that it had been altered to an oath of faithfulness were making a propaganda point. It is still common for members of the public to believe that there was an oath of 'allegiance' to the king in the treaty as signed. This is what Garvin has called 'a marvellous lie of silence that has become institutionalised in Irish popular culture'.[3] The matter was ultimately not one of language or grammar but of sentiment, with any oath involving the king in England being offensive to Irish nationalists generally.

There is in fact an 'oath of allegiance', so described, in the final treaty itself, as agreed in London on 6 December 1921, but it is to the constitution of the Irish Free State and not to the king. Article 4 gives the form of oath prescribed for members of the Dáil from 1921:

> 'The oath to be taken by Members of the Parliament of the Irish Free State shall be in the following form:– I —— do solemnly swear true faith and allegiance to the Constitution of the Irish Free State as by law established and that I will be faithful to HM King George V, his heirs and successors by law, in virtue of the common citizenship of Ireland with Great Britain and her adherence to and membership of the group of nations forming the British Commonwealth of Nations'.

The new term 'commonwealth' was increasingly preferred to 'empire' by self-governing dominions such as Canada (if not by British Tories) and is said to have been first used officially in the agreement of 1921, although the term 'British Empire' is also still used in it.[4] The use of the word 'commonwealth' was a conciliatory gesture to the Irish as well as recognition of the evolving status of the Australian and Canadian dominions in particular.

Some critics of the final form of oath grasped at straws, claiming that the provision in the treaty did not actually require Dáil deputies to swear an oath but merely agreed a form of oath if they wished to take one. This became known as the 'whiskey argument', akin to a club stating that its members did not have to drink alcohol but if they did so on the premises then they had to drink Jameson's. No court, and particularly the privy council as ultimate arbitrator of disputes about the treaty, was likely ever to construe the words 'the oath to be taken by members' as other than imperative or mandatory and as requiring all deputies to take it.[5]

The changes to the terms of the oath in the treaty as signed on 6 December certainly did not conciliate de Valera or his cabinet colleague Cathal Brugha. They were to claim that Griffith had promised them at the cabinet meeting on 3 December that he would not sign then any treaty in London. Griffith disagreed.

It was explained above that de Valera had issued 'instructions' to the delegates in October 1921 but that these could not bind them, as their authority came from Dáil Éireann and not from himself or even from the cabinet. He himself could have gone with them to negotiations with the British prime minister but he chose not to go, even when cabinet colleagues asked him to do so. Part of his reasoning appears to have been that in June 1921, just a few months earlier, he had met alone four times with Prime Minister Lloyd George and knew precisely the point beyond which the British would not go. The British insisted that the king, or 'Crown', must be part of any deal.

Minister Cathal Brugha, a militant who strongly opposed any settlement less than a republic, claimed that he and de Valera had extracted a promise from Griffith when they met for the cabinet meeting on 3 December.[6] The minutes of that cabinet meeting record no attempt by the cabinet to issue 'instructions' again, presumably for the same reason that the 'instructions' listed in de Valera's letter of 7 October 1921 could not bind the team in London, for the team had full powers from Dáil Éireann to do what it thought fit.[7] However, it seems that before Griffith left the meeting on 3 December to return overnight by boat and train to London he agreed explicitly then with Brugha and de Valera not to sign in London the proposed treaty as currently drafted by the British and as discussed at the meeting just ended, a meeting that had in any event already unanimously decided to reject the form of oath in that draft. The draft was subsequently changed by agreement with the British in a few ways at the final session of talks on 5–6 December. Even with those changes, Griffith still wished to defer signing and to bring the amended version back again to cabinet. He and his four colleagues only signed it when confronted with the British threat of immediate war if they did not do so.

Detractors later tried to use Griffith's unrecorded conversation with Brugha and de Valera as he left the cabinet meeting of 3 December, a conversation not identified in the notes of the cabinet meeting that day, in order to discredit him. Thus Seán Etchingham TD from Wexford rose in the Dáil on 10 January 1922:

> 'Arthur Griffith cannot deny that he pledged his word to the President of the Republic [de Valera] and the Minister of Defence [Brugha] in the Mansion House, Dublin, on December 3rd, that he would not sign any document until he returned .... He said he has pledged his word.
>
> MR GRIFFITH:
> That is not so; it is a deliberate misrepresentation—and you know it.
>
> MR ETCHINGHAM:
> I never heard it contradicted before—that the Chairman of the Delegation did not pledge his word in the Mansion House. It is on record.
>
> MR CATHAL BRUGHA:
> Does Mr Griffith deny that he gave his word to us that he would not sign anything? Does he deny that?

MR GRIFFITH:
I gave my word that I would not sign that document [presumably the draft before cabinet on 3 December].

MR DE VALERA:
We must be clear on this. Nobody here will be able to accuse me of at any time telling any untruth. I say it is a solemn truth that the Chairman of the Delegation, on leaving us at the Cabinet meeting—otherwise things might have been different—gave an undertaking that any document which involved allegiance to the Crown, and involved our being British subjects would not be signed until it was submitted to Dáil Éireann.'

The secretary's notes of the cabinet meeting do not record such a general 'undertaking' by Griffith about 'any document which involved … our being British subjects' and suggest something more nuanced, for they explicitly record Griffith as saying that 'The country would not fight on the question of allegiance and there would be a split. He would not recommend the Government to accept [the draft] but would say that the Plenipotentiaries should sign and leave it to President and Dáil to reject.' De Valera's intervention in the Dáil riled Griffith, who replied:

'I have sat here and I have listened for weeks to misrepresentations. At the Private Session we had all this up, and we are having it at the Public Session now. The first line of attack on us was that we had exceeded our powers. President de Valera admitted that we had not. On that Saturday after I came back I was at the Cabinet meeting, and I told them I would not break on the Crown. I asked President de Valera himself to go to London if he wished [Robert Barton pleaded with de Valera to do so]. When I was going away the

President asked me to try and get the thing back to Dáil Éireann. I tried, and I tried all I could, to get the matter kept back for a week. I could not succeed. I was faced with the responsibility of signing or not signing. The responsibility was placed on me and I signed. I protest against the misrepresentation that I was a man who pledged his word to something. The Deputy for Wexford also charged me with something—he intended to convey to the Irish people that I, in some way, connived with Lloyd George. That is a damnable lie and he knows it.'

The 'damnable lie' was to be honed by Frank Pakenham when he surmised in 1935, in his book *Peace by Ordeal*, that Griffith made some kind of 'secret' deal with the British about the terms of the final treaty weeks before the agreement was signed. This accusation will be examined in unprecedented detail and rebutted later below.

12

'GRIFFITH WAS A PACIFIST'?

Griffith was prepared to use armed force if he thought it necessary, as graphically illustrated by Fianna Fáil's Seán T. Ó Ceallaigh (O'Kelly) when later President of Ireland, who recalled a remarkable meeting organised in 1914 by the Irish Republican Brotherhood (below). Griffith was no absolute pacifist. Nevertheless, influenced by the old Fenian John O'Leary, who was his mentor when young, he disliked stunts that might rebound on the population at large and on the poor in particular. He was hesitant to see violence used lightly.

Griffith was among those who collected his rifle when arms were run to the nationalist Volunteers at Howth in 1914, and he drilled with it thereafter.

Griffith's absence from the Easter Rising of 1916 did not signify opposition to such an insurrection in principle, but he was concerned about its timing and was kept out of the fighting. His eyesight was poor, and he was seen as having long-term value as a propagandist. When the British interned him immediately after the Easter Rising, he wrote to a friend, the artist Lily Williams. On 29 November 1916 he told her that 'England can never enforce conscription if Ireland fights, and Ireland must fight conscription with tongues, pens, sticks, stones, pitchforks, guns and all the resources of civilization'. This was consistent with the decisions of a significant meeting attended by Griffith in 1914, as recalled by Ó Ceallaigh (below). When de Valera was absent in America during most of the War of Independence in 1919–20, Griffith was acting president of Dáil Éireann and in that capacity did not in general recoil from military action by the Volunteers when he felt that it was merited.[1]

Griffith distinguished between necessary and ineffective armed struggle. As he himself said in Dáil Éireann on 19 December 1921,

> 'During the last few years a war was waged on the Irish people, and the Irish people defended themselves, and for a portion of that time, when President de Valera was in America, I had at least the responsibility on my shoulders of standing for all that was done in that defence, and I stood for it (applause). I would stand for it again under similar conditions. Ireland was fighting then against an enemy that was striking at her life, and was denying her liberty, but in any contest that would follow the rejection of this offer Ireland would be fighting with the sympathy of the world against her, and with all the Dominions—all the nations that comprise the British Commonwealth—against her.'

Ó Ceallaigh kept no notes of the meeting that he attended in 1914, recalling it three and a half decades later for the Bureau of Military History when president of Ireland. Most of the people who did attend it were executed in 1916. The fact that Griffith attended such a meeting should be borne in mind, because suggestions that he was a pacifist are not only incorrect but may be used to discredit and diminish his role in 'the Irish revolution'. His widow later told the Bureau of Military History: 'My husband was a member of the IRB and of the Volunteers and had been present at the Howth gun-running with his Unit'.[2]

Above: Arthur Griffith, with glasses and moustache, drills with his rifle collected from guns run into Howth harbour in July 1914. The man on his 'photo left' without a hat is thought to be Padraic Colum (courtesy National Library of Ireland MS 13,174/7/1, Bulmer Hobson Papers).

Right: Close-up of Griffit and Colum, from the same image.

Ó Ceallaigh described in detail the meeting that he convened for the IRB in 1914, at which it seems that all IRB members present hung on the words of Arthur Griffith. It was, said Ó Ceallaigh,

> '... an important meeting which was called at the suggestion of some members of the IRB Supreme Council. I was consulted by [Thomas] Clarke and [Seán] MacDermott as to whether it would be convenient for me to allow an important meeting, which was proposed should be held to consider the new situation created by the war in Europe [World War I began on 28 July 1914], to take place in my office at 25 Parnell Square. They explained that they wanted a meeting of representatives of the different National bodies whom they regarded as anti-War, and they wished this to take place as secretly as possible, and they thought that the Library of the Gaelic League which I used as an office would be a suitable place if I consented to have it held there. I agreed, and they asked me at once if I would consent to attend the meeting. I asked what the purpose of the meeting was, and they said to try to get the heads, or at any rate the influential leaders amongst their sections of progressive National organisations together to consider what action could jointly be taken by them in view of the outbreak of the European War. From my conversation with these two members of the Supreme Council of the IRB, I gathered that it was their intention to try to organise the progressive—or as others might call them the extreme Nationalist—element to work together to promote certain activities that they had in mind towards achieving independence while the war continued.
>
> ... I remember well Clarke and MacDermott being present, also Arthur Griffith and Major John MacBride. Pádraig Pearse also was present as was Thomas McDonagh and Joseph Plunkett [Clarke, MacDermott, Pearse, McDonagh, Plunkett and Connolly

were six of the seven signatories who signed the proclamation of the Easter 1916 rebels on behalf of 'the provisional government of the Irish Republic', Éamonn Ceannt being the seventh]. I certainly remember William O'Brien being present, but I am very hazy as to the presence of James Connolly whose name is mentioned by Mr O'Brien as having been present at the meeting. There was one other man whose name is not mentioned by Mr O'Brien and that is a man named Seán Tobin. Tobin was, I think, then Chairman of the Centres' Board for Dublin of the IRB. I have an idea that Seán McGarry was also present. The meeting was a long one and as I try to recollect it now it was opened by a statement made by Tom Clarke. Clarke went on to describe the world situation at the moment, Gt Britain being engaged in a war and efforts being made by her to recruit young men into her Army to fight for her and for her allies, and the necessity for the Nationalist forces to take united action, to prevent recruiting, and finally the steps that should be taken to use the war situation to endeavour to secure the independence of Ireland. Clarke then invited discussion and asked everyone present to express his opinion on what should be done to take the best advantage of the situation Everyone in turn gave his views, and as I remember, all agreed that a joint effort by all the progressive Nationalist organisations that favoured independence should be made before the end of the war to do everything possible to secure independence. All present fully accepted this policy.

All the IRB people present were most anxious to hear what Arthur Griffith would say, and Griffith expressed full agreement with the policy of getting all the progressive Nationalist forces to work together to win complete independence before the end of the war…'

Having noted this manifestation of respect for Griffith, Ó Ceallaigh further recalled that,

> 'After protracted discussion—speaking now from recollection—the meeting unanimously agreed that an effort must be made to win complete independence for Ireland before the European War was brought to a close. It was agreed also that it would be necessary for the forces at that meeting to work together to bring about the expulsion of the British from Ireland by force if necessary. It was agreed, as I recollect it, that all the forces and all the organisations with which the members present were associated should get all the organisations they represented or all those whom they could influence to fight conscription if the British attempted to enforce conscription in Ireland at any time during the War. It was agreed that the British should be resisted with force if they attempted to disarm the Volunteers.
>
> It was agreed that if the Germans made a landing in Ireland the bodies represented at the meeting should work with the Germans provided a formal and satisfactory statement could be got from the Government of Germany pledging themselves if they landed in Ireland only to land then so as to help the Irish to expel the British from Ireland and to win complete independence. It was agreed that if such a declaration could be got from the German Government a German armed force should be welcomed in Ireland to help to end British domination. It was certainly agreed that on no account would the Germans be helped unless an open declaration was received from them through their Government that they did not intend to land in Ireland in order to occupy it permanently. Lastly it was agreed that should it appear that the war was coming to an end and that so far none of those other things already mentioned had happened, an effort should be made by all the organisations

> represented at the meeting to organise insurrection in Ireland to drive the British out and end British government in the country. Thus we should become combatants in the war, and could claim as combatants a hearing at the Peace Conference that must follow when the war came to an end.'[3]

Ó Ceallaigh had become friendly with Griffith when they were members of the Celtic Literary Society in the late 1890s, and they knew each other from the reading room of the National Library of Ireland too. Ó Ceallaigh was also a founding member of Sinn Féin and of the Irish Volunteers. During the Easter Rising of 1916 he was aide-de-camp to Pearse. He took the anti-treaty side in the Civil War and later became a senior member of Fianna Fáil. Had he thought that Griffith shirked a commitment to the Irish revolution he could and would have said so. Any description of Griffith as a pacifist either is an error, based on a simplistic understanding of his position, or may be maliciously intended to distance him from more militaristic heroes of the time.

13

DE VALERA 'KNEW NOTHING' ABOUT POLITICS?

De Valera knew nothing about politics until the treaty was signed—or so he said in Dáil Éireann on 6 January 1922. It was an astonishing admission coming from one who had seized the presidency of Sinn Féin in 1917, ranged all over the United States in 1919 and 1920 during the Irish War of Independence while representing Dáil Éireann, met Lloyd George four times alone in London in July 1921 to arrange treaty talks later in 1921, and then avoided joining those same talks as one of the Irish delegates. He represented himself as an innocent at large, a man who did not dirty his hands dealing in the soiled currency of public affairs: 'It is because I am straight that I meet crookedness with straight dealing always, and I have beaten crookedness with straight dealing', he told the Dáil.

Lloyd George certainly appears to have thought little of de Valera's political abilities. Having met him for four sessions of talks about talks in London in July 1921, the British prime minister was pleased to confide in his cabinet colleagues that the Irish leader was 'an unskilled negotiator'.[1]

The first time de Valera even saw politics in action, or so he said, was when the five Irish plenipotentiaries signed the agreement for a treaty in London. He told the Dáil on 6 January: 'I am sick and tired of politics—so sick that no matter what happens I would go back to private life. I have only seen politics within the last three weeks or a month. It is the first time I have seen them and I am sick to the heart of them.' Had he gone to London, would things have been much different? Notwithstanding his inexperience of politics, he seems to have thought so, for he also told deputies: 'I know what others didn't know: where the verge of the precipice was, and nothing would have pulled me beyond it—not even Lloyd George and all his Empire could have brought me over it'.

Three days later he returned to the same theme: 'I knew nothing about political tactics until the question of this Treaty came up. I have seen too much of them, goodness knows, since, and I hope to heavens I will see no more of them, no matter how we finish this.'[2]

Arthur Griffith too had been speaking of getting out of politics, but in his case privately, following nearly two decades of political strife since he founded Sinn Féin and struggled thereafter to keep his political papers in production. The negotiations in London had taken an enormous toll on Griffith. James Joyce in his novel *Ulysses* has a character famously remark that Griffith 'has no go in him for the mob', and Griffith had sought others who agreed to take on the role of president of the movement that he established. He was reported to have yielded gracefully to de Valera when the militants arranged for the latter to seek the presidency of Sinn Féin in 1917. Padraic Colum, to whom Griffith's widow spoke for his biography of her husband, said that her Arthur told her on the night the treaty was signed in London in December 1921 that 'You will have your wish … In August I will be out of politics.'[3] The prediction proved tragically accurate, for he collapsed and died eight months later.

De Valera had indeed had little experience of politics before he became president of Sinn Féin. In fact, he does not appear to have been earlier even a member of that party, or of any other. His interest in politics was minimal before he joined the Irish Volunteers in his thirties. His ambition had been to become a university professor of mathematics. His learning the Irish language then was advisable in the context of such a career, at least as much as it was a commitment to nationalist ideals. His decision to risk his life in the Easter Rising was messianic rather than political, because he believed that he would die. However, imprisoned after the 1916 Rising, he displayed an incipient vocation for politics when he insisted that those internees who had joined the rebellion honour and respect those, such as the Irish Volunteer leader Eoin MacNeill, who had decided against doing so immediately but who ended up interned nevertheless. This won de Valera a reputation for being able to unite people of opposing viewpoints that he was to lose in 1922. Elevated to the presidency of the Sinn Féin political party after surviving 1916, he found himself swept to election on a tide of emotion following both the executions of the leaders of the Easter Rising and public reaction to the possible introduction in Ireland of conscription into the British Army. His status as the most senior surviving commandant was akin to that of a high priest of political orthodoxy as much as to that of a democratic leader. In 1921 the general election was uncontested, and Sinn Féin monopolised Dáil Éireann. Hence his rueful appeal in the Dáil on 9 January 1922, at the end of the treaty debate, that 'We were one party before this occurred and, in God's name, let us be one party after it, in the Dáil anyway'.

Yet the treaty negotiations were not his first taste of real politics, for he had experienced at first hand the tensions of Irish-America while lodged at the Waldorf Hotel in Manhattan in 1919–20, and admitted as much in the Dáil on 6 January 1922: 'What has sickened me most is that I got in this House the same sort of dealing that I was accustomed to over in America from other people of a similar kind. He had had a number of bruising experiences across the Atlantic, not least when he mishandled a comparison between Cuba and Ireland. He was concerned about the impact of such political dealing on the reputation of Dáil Éireann 'because, holding the position that I do, I don't want to see it tarnished'.

Here was the key to understanding his ambitions: it was that phrase that he used, 'holding the position that I do'. He saw himself standing above the fray as the personification of Ireland, a symbol, a monument, a monarch in all but name, no mere politician. He had enjoyed being leader of a united, single party that supported its president. It had not even insisted that he descend into the pit of politics when Britain's prime minister saw fit to lead his ministers into talks on the independence of Ireland. He saw this as a strength but, in reality, his political decisions in 1921 and 1922—which included passing up the chance to begin peace talks in Scotland earlier in 1921, refusing to go to London even when the Irish plenipotentiaries asked him to go, and miscalculating his role in respect of the anti-treaty IRA and civil war—arguably damaged and were potentially catastrophic for the emerging state.

In 1917 de Valera described himself as 'a monument to the brave dead' of the Easter Rising, and in the autumn of 1921 as 'the symbol of the republic'.[4] He was often hailed as 'President of Ireland' or 'President of the Republic of Ireland' when he toured the United States in 1919–20 (and not just 'president of Dáil Éireann', which was the actual title of the office that he held). Notably, on 26 August 1921, when Seán Mac Eoin TD and Richard Mulcahy TD nominated him for re-election to the office that he already held and the title of which had not been changed, they proposed him explicitly to be 'president of the Irish Republic'. The treaty, however, forced him to abandon any hopes that he had of fulfilling in the foreseeable future the symbolic role of head of an Irish independent state, for the constitution of the Irish Free State retained the residual role of the British monarch as head of state. He had opposed that provision more strongly than he opposed partition.

From 1919 at the latest de Valera's supporters, and even children in the street, were singing a popular ballad entitled 'The King of Ireland' (ending 'We'll crown de Valera King of Ireland'). On 2 October 1921 the song was part of the programme of the Cork Pipers' Band at the Drimoleague Aeridheacht, just days after de Valera accepted a formal invitation from Lloyd George to begin treaty negotiations. It would continue to be sung by his supporters throughout the 1920s. In his memoir published in 1983, the former Fianna Fáil senior minister and proud republican Kevin Boland recalled how in 1926, after founding Fianna Fáil, 'the Soldiers of Destiny' marched from Dublin's La Scala theatre chanting this ballad. Describing it as a 'lusty song', *TIME* magazine notably reported hearing it sung at the end of a meeting of 25,000 of de Valera's followers in Dublin during the general election campaign of 1933 that saw him and his Fianna Fáil party elected to Dáil Éireann with an overall majority for the first time.[5]

Symbolism got de Valera nowhere politically. By 1933 he had undoubtedly learnt the art of politics. His rationalisation of the decision by himself and his colleagues to take an oath on admission to Dáil Éireann that had hitherto seemed a stumbling block on his road to power was a political somersault of the highest order. It gave him access to political power. As a politician he was to become Ireland's most notable taoiseach of the twentieth century. If he really was 'sick and tired of politics' in 1922, that did not prevent him from become Ireland's leading politician in the twentieth century.

14

THE PLENIPOTENTIARIES BOUND IRELAND?

Dáil Éireann was only locked into the treaty when in 1922 a majority of its members voted to accept it and then passed legislation to enact it. Although the delegates or 'plenipotentiaries' who negotiated the agreement in London later used as a kind of shorthand the expression 'signed the treaty' to describe their final formal action there, it is important to bear in mind that what they actually signed was just an agreement *for* a treaty, one conditional upon approval firstly by the cabinet in Dublin and secondly by a majority of members of Dáil Éireann. This is not just a legalistic quibble. By portraying Griffith as betraying republican ambitions, his detractors could distract from the fact that the agreement was subsequently approved in short order by the Irish cabinet and by Dáil Éireann and was effectively endorsed by the decisive result of the Irish general election in June 1922.

The British always accepted that the proposed treaty might have to be approved by Dáil Éireann. For example, on 19 October 1921 Michael Collins and one of the secretaries to the plenipotentiaries, Erskine Childers, presented a memorandum to the British negotiators that led to a private discussion of the Irish constitutional standpoint among the British. The UK cabinet secretary, Thomas Jones, noted in his official diary that one two-tier suggestion as to how the British might accommodate an Irish perspective was considered inadequate by the British: 'This proposal was rejected, however, on the ground that Dáil Éireann might accept the first and reject, or subsequently repudiate, the second instrument'. A second proposal was rejected on similar grounds.[1] The British preference was for an agreement that would have to be accepted in total or not by a single vote of the Dáil.

At the fractious cabinet meeting in Dublin on 3 December 1921, Griffith had said that he did not like the draft agreement as it stood but did not think it dishonourable: 'He would not recommend the Government to accept but would say that the Plenipotentiaries should sign and leave it to President and Dáil to reject'. In the end, on the last night of talks a couple of days later, all five plenipotentiaries signed an amended draft on that basis when threatened with immediate war if they did not.

When he opened the treaty debate in Dáil Éireann on 14 December 1921, Éamon de Valera said:

> 'It would be ridiculous to think that we could send five men to complete a treaty without the right of ratification by this assembly. That is the only thing that matters. Therefore it is agreed that this treaty is simply an agreement and that it is not binding until the Dáil ratifies it. That is what we are concerned with.'

He could not deny that they had been given the power to do what they did but needed a way to discredit it. He was aware of the respect in which the public held Griffith and was careful to acknowledge Griffith's good intentions while condemning his actions in London. Referring to the fact that the plenipotentiaries had signed the agreement for a treaty, de Valera told Dáil Éireann on 19 December 1921 that

> 'I hold that it was in their excessive love for Ireland they have done what they have. I am as anxious as anyone for the material prosperity of Ireland and the Irish people, but I cannot do anything that would make the Irish people hang their heads. I would rather see the same thing over again [i.e. suffer another war of independence, for most of which he himself had been absent from Ireland] than that Irishmen should have to hang their heads in shame for having signed and put their hands to a document handing over their authority to a foreign country. The Irish people would not want me to save them materially at the expense of their national honour.'

It would soon transpire at the polls that the Irish people did not share his framing of the dilemma facing them and did not see a need to be 'saved' from the treaty that their elected representatives had already been given a chance to vote on and had accepted.

In the fratricide about to be played out, when the mythological republican Eden was lost, Cain must find some way to slay Abel. De Valera's reference in 1921 to 'excessive love' echoed a couplet in 'Easter 1916'—that well-known poem by W.B. Yeats published in 1918—in which the poet asked of the martyrs of the 1916 Rising, 'And what if excess of love Bewildered them till they died?' If Griffith and Collins could not be attacked head-on as devious or traitorous, they might be depicted regretfully as well intentioned but bewildered fools duped by the bluffing of Lloyd George, that 'Welsh wizard', as he was already then nicknamed in England. If they bound Ireland, which was a convenient thesis if one wished to ignore the subsequent debates and votes in both the Irish cabinet and Dáil Éireann, then it was all the more effective to shake one's head and acknowledge that they meant well.

In his 'classic' and influential account of the treaty negotiations, Frank Pakenham in 1935 likewise purported to respect Arthur

Griffith even as he shafted him to provide a motivation for the subsequent behaviour of Éamon de Valera, a man whom Pakenham admired greatly. The future Lord Longford assured his readers that

> 'No misunderstanding must be allowed to arise from our account of Griffith's doings that day [i.e. 12 November 1921, when Griffith is alleged by Pakenham to have given 'some kind of assent' secretly to certain 'Ulster proposals' of the British government, weeks before the end of talks in London]. No one with any knowledge of his character needs telling that he concealed nothing, and would never under any pressure have concealed anything from his colleagues, that he judged of material importance'

—not even those 'startling and secret concessions' and 'some kind of assent' that Pakenham himself claimed that Griffith made during negotiations in November?[2] It was a damaging claim that will be considered and rejected later below but that continues to be cited as if the Bible says it's so. Pakenham's version brings to mind Alexander Pope's once well-known 'Epistle to Dr Arbuthnot', where in 1734 the English poet disdains people who

> 'Damn with faint praise, assent with civil leer,
> And without sneering, teach the rest to sneer;
> Willing to wound, and yet afraid to strike,
> Just hint a fault, and hesitate dislike'.

As an English schoolboy and Oxford scholar, Pakenham may have learned those lines off by heart, as the present Irish author was expected to do in Ireland as late as 1967.

15

NOT ALL FIVE SIGNED OR VOTED FOR THE TREATY?

The Irish delegates argued in London about whether or not they should sign the agreement for a treaty, with Barton and Gavan Duffy putting up some resistance, but in the end all agreed that they would do so in the circumstances. They also voted as TDs to accept it. Owing to statements that two of them made after Dáil Éireann approved the treaty, an impression arose that they had not acted unanimously. After one talk that I gave recently, a member of the public was most adamant that the five had split when it came to the vote on the treaty in Dáil Éireann, but the record is clear.

It is unfair to those who first reached that decision to state, as Kenneth O. Morgan does in his entry for Lloyd George in the *Dictionary of National Biography*, that 'By 3 to 2, the Sinn Féiners accepted terms'. In fact, all five accepted the same terms in the end, even if each had reservations to various degrees and disagreed with each other on certain aspects. All went along with the deal to avoid a new war. All of them were adults and each of them chose to sign it. It was intrinsically no easier for one than for another to make such a decision. In the absence of their own head of government and in the face of a sustained threat of immediate and outright war from the British, how could they not do so? And why would they not do so when the whole deal would still require a vote of the full cabinet in Dublin and of the Dáil for it to be effective?

As Gavan Duffy told the Dáil on 21 December 1921, 'I am going to recommend this Treaty to you very reluctantly, but very sincerely, because I see no alternative'. Barton said that he had broken his oath of allegiance to the Republic when he signed the agreement but did so 'because I judged that violation to be the lesser of alternative outrages forced upon me, and between which I was compelled to choose'. The greater outrage was a return to war with Britain and the very real possibility of military defeat and devastation now that the British Army was free from World War I. Having originally supported de Valera's decision not to lead the team in London, Barton had lately pleaded with him to come to Downing Street, but his plea fell on deaf ears.

In Dáil Éireann on 19 December 1921, during debates on the proposed treaty, Barton tried to clarify what the nub of the matter had been in London in the end. He said: 'The English Prime Minister ... declared that the signature and recommendation of every member of our delegation was necessary or war would follow immediately ... The issue before us was whether we should stand behind our proposals for external association [outside the British Empire/Commonwealth], face war and maintain the Republic, or whether we should accept inclusion in the British Empire and take peace.'

When Barton said 'maintain the Republic', he was referring to the ideal or notional republic that the rebels had declared during the Easter Rising of 1916 rather than one that actually existed yet. There is no question but that such a republic was in 1916 intended to include the whole island. That still went without saying on 20 August 1919 when members of the first Dáil Éireann agreed that each of its members should swear allegiance to the Irish republic and the Dáil in the following form:

'I, A.B., do solemnly swear (or affirm) that I do not and shall not yield a voluntary support to any pretended Government, authority or power within Ireland hostile and inimical thereto, and I do further swear (or affirm) that to the best of my knowledge and ability I will support and defend the Irish Republic and the Government of the Irish Republic, which is Dáil Éireann, against all enemies, foreign and domestic, and I will bear true faith and allegiance to the same, and that I take this obligation freely without any mental reservation or purpose of evasion, so help me, God.'[1]

Arthur Griffith at that time was acting president of Dáil Éireann in the absence in America of de Valera. Griffith told the Dáil that day in 1919 that he was 'astonished at finding that the Members had not taken an Oath of Allegiance when the Dáil first met earlier that year. Every person elected there should pledge his or her allegiance to the standing Government of Ireland.' Later, those who opposed ratification of the agreement for a treaty would make much of this oath in their efforts to prevent the provisional Irish government from giving effect to the treaty. As demonstrated above, however, by the time that substantive negotiations for the treaty actually began in London in October 1921 de Valera himself had already conceded that counties could vote to exclude themselves from an Irish republic.

De Valera again conceded the principle of partition during the treaty debates when, in an addendum to his Document No. 2 proposal for an alternative treaty, he allowed that Northern Ireland would continue to exist separately.[2] Some other anti-treaty republicans might not make such concessions and might cling to their hopes for an all-Ireland republic, but de Valera and others recognised this to be an unrealistic demand. If the 1919 oath was not a barrier to de Valera's concessions, it was not a barrier to the terms of the treaty in respect of partition.

Notably, in setting out in the Dáil on 19 December 1921 what had happened and what had been the crunch issue in London, Robert Barton did not mention partition. The status of the British monarch in a new Irish state was the burning issue for de Valera and for some of his supporters. Barton did not deny that delegates were threatened with immediate war if they did not sign, but he proceeded that day in the Dáil to make a statement that was certainly confusing if not disingenuous. He stated that

> 'Arthur Griffith, Michael Collins, and Eamonn Duggan were for acceptance and peace, Gavan Duffy and myself were for refusal—war or no war'.

On the face of it this seems to suggest some kind of narrow vote, with the real possibility that if one man had changed his mind the delegates would have refused to sign and gone home to prepare for further battle. It is clear, however, from Gavan Duffy's own key speech in the Dáil that month that in fact he decided to sign the agreement because he felt that nothing better would be achieved at that point. He does not endorse in any way Barton's statement that Gavan Duffy was 'for refusal—war or no war'. It also appears from an entry in the diary of Erskine Childers (a relative and friend of Barton's as well as a secretary to the plenipotentiaries) that Barton himself decided on the last night to sign for the sake of people back in Ireland.[3] Indeed, the rest of the speech that Barton made to the Dáil appears to bear that out and to contradict his assertion that he was for refusing to sign, war or no war. The very terms of Lloyd George's ultimatum, that all five delegates must sign, put every single member of the delegation in the position of being able to pull the plug on negotiations. Any of them might have. None of them chose to do so.

It was all very well for Barton to declare that he was for war and then vote the other way, but what did this really mean? He had been in the British Army at the time of the Easter Rising in 1916 and, although he later joined the Volunteers and was elected for Sinn Féin, he spent nearly all of the War of Independence in prison for making seditious speeches. Two members of the delegation who knew far more than he did about the fitness of the IRA Volunteers to resume fighting then were Michael Collins and Éamonn Duggan, the latter having been (as is too seldom noted in discussion of the talks in London) a senior member of the Irish Republican Brotherhood and the IRA's director of intelligence between May 1918 and November 1920. The fact remains that Barton voted for the agreement for the same basic reason that the other four plenipotentiaries voted for it: to spare Irish people further hardship in a renewed war with Britain.

Although he claimed that he somehow 'preferred war', Barton actually voted in Dáil Éireann for the agreement, so that de Valera—who had been absent in London, as Barton pointedly observed—as president of the Dáil and other members of the house could make the final decision as to whether or not to accept the proposed settlement:

> 'For myself, I preferred war. I told my colleagues so, but for the nation, without consultation, I dared not accept that responsibility. The alternative which I sought to avoid seemed to me a lesser outrage than the violation of what is my faith. So that I myself, and of my own choice, must commit my nation to immediate war, without you, Mr President, or the Members of the Dáil, or the nation

having an opportunity to examine the terms upon which war could be avoided. I signed.'

Barton pointed out to the Dáil that in the struggle that took place at the final session of talks in London 'Arthur Griffith sought repeatedly to have the decision between war and peace on the terms of the treaty referred back to this assembly. This proposal Mr Lloyd George directly negatived.' Here—less than a fortnight after the agreement was signed in London—Barton paints a picture of Griffith as certainly not predisposed or inclined to sign off quickly on a deal with Lloyd George that night.

In Hans Place, London, 1921: Plenipotentiaries Arthur Griffith (chairman), Éamonn Duggan, Michael Collins and Robert Barton are seated left to right. Standing centre is George Gavan Duffy. The delegates' secretaries Erskine Childers and John Chartres stand photo-left and photo-right of Gavan Duffy respectively. (Courtesy National Library of Ireland POLF 31).

16

PARTITION WAS THE CRUNCH ISSUE?

Partition was not at the nub of the debate about the treaty in Dáil Éireann and did not in itself cause the split in Sinn Féin in 1922. In fact, partition was seldom mentioned in the course of the debate, with the most bitter comments relating to the oath and king, the constitutional status of the new state and the status of certain Irish ports that the British Navy would be permitted to continue using. The fact that the plenipotentiaries expected the boundary commission to achieve great changes to the border partly explains why more was not said about partition.

The editor of a special 'Treaty Debates' section of the current Dáil's website notes that on the third day of debates (16 December 1921) 'Seán MacEntee, who was from Belfast and was a TD for Monaghan, spoke at length, his contribution notable for his focus on Ulster and partition, a subject that was largely absent from the debates before or after'.[1] Moore observes that the new parliament fiercely debated the proposed treaty but devoted only a small amount of time to the issue of partition, just about nine pages in total out of 338 transcript pages, while O'Connor Lysaght writes that only two anti-treaty deputies, Seán MacEntee and Seán Moylan, 'gave more than a sentence to the north'.[2]

Insofar as more might have been done to ensure that the boundary commission would have a significant outcome in terms of land transfers to the new Free State from Northern Ireland, and thus ameliorate the reality of partition, it is understandable that northern nationalists felt let down by their southern counterparts. On both sides of the Irish border after 1920 there were minorities who were not completely at home. Many if not most Protestants south of the border inclined towards a unionist point of view, whilst many Catholics in Northern Ireland would have preferred their districts to be included in the Irish Free State or an Irish republic. This was not to be, and the boundary commission that the signatories to the agreement in London in December 1921 hoped would make big changes to the line of the border never did so. The sense of abandonment north of the border was already evident in a letter that the officer commanding the 3rd Northern Division of the IRA sent south in September 1922, its tone as much one of resignation as of anger:

> 'After the death of the late general Collins it was encouraging to us to see that the Government were determined to carry out his policy. I took it that this meant his policy regarding Ulster also. A new situation has now arisen.'[3]

Nobody in the Irish cabinet, neither those members who were plenipotentiaries nor their colleagues, including de Valera, who stayed in Dublin, appears to have taken the necessary steps to ensure that the precise legal terms of the relevant treaty article on the boundary commission could produce a better outcome. In any event, whatever legal or moral strength that article had, there was no opportunity to hold the British to what the Irish thought it should mean, for by the end of the Civil War neither Griffith nor Collins was alive to argue the point, and valuable time had been lost owing to the recklessness of anti-treaty forces. The article in effect then became a bargaining tool for other objectives of the new state.

Robert Barton, one of the men who signed the treaty, had some bitter things to say when he made a witness statement for the Bureau of Military History in 1954. Although he had voted for the treaty in early 1922, he later ended up in Fianna Fáil and claimed in his 1954 statement (but not earlier in the Dáil during the treaty debates of 1921–2) that Griffith and Collins had said 'most terrific things' to him to persuade him to sign the agreement.[4]

When it came to the boundary commission provision, however, his comments were more nuanced; he even blamed Lloyd George for 'letting down' Griffith and Collins:

> 'Collins looked upon the treaty as being, as he said, a stepping-stone to complete independence. He believed in accepting it, working it as far as it suited us and doing what has happened since, using it as a means of getting more. I can understand that it might be claimed now that the position having been given away by the signature of the treaty, it would have been reasonable to accept the position as it then was and combine to get more as time went by. I think that that was probably where Griffith and Collins made their greatest mistake. They were completely caught. Griffith so often exclaimed, "Well, if the North refuses to come in, we will have a boundary commission, and they will lose half their territory, and they cannot stay out." Over and over again he made that statement.
>
> Of course, we had discussed the boundary position in the full conferences and the "boundary" had been described to us in very different terms from what it turned out to be. We even discussed the question of whether the option to vote territories in or out of Southern Ireland should be by the parish units rather than by rural district areas or by counties or Poor Law Unions. We agreed that islands, such as West Belfast, would vote themselves into Southern

> Ireland, and we agreed that it would be administratively impossible for such an area to come into Southern Ireland. Voting in or out would have to be by contiguous areas. What happened was the very opposite, merely the rectification of a boundary line without loss of territory or option to vote in or out.
>
> I rather imagine that Lloyd George did not intend to let Griffith and Collins down so badly, but who knows? As a negotiator he was unreliable. If the boundary clause had been clarified in the final document and if it had been stated in the boundary clause that voting for exclusion or inclusion in the Free State must be by specific areas, as agreed verbally, then it would have been impossible to throw overboard the proposed plebiscite and exclusion or inclusion of large territories. Here is where Griffith and Collins made their biggest mistake, and at a later date they must both have recognised it. Collins got himself into that position but, I think, he pressed his interpretation of the boundary clause upon Sir James Craig when he met him in Dublin. I think Collins was at that time almost prepared to go to war; he was no partitionist—nor for that matter was Griffith.'[5]

Collins surely deceived himself when he had a conversation alone with the British prime minister early on the morning of the last day of talks about the treaty in London in 1921. Even in his memorandum of that conversation, he did not seem to realise that Lloyd George had not actually 'assented' to him but rather he to Lloyd George when the latter simply affirmed that Collins had made a particular statement (as underlined here below):

> 'I said that I was perfectly dissatisfied with the position as regards the North East … <u>He remarked that I myself pointed out on a previous occasion that the North would be forced economically</u>

> to come in. I assented but I said the position was so serious owing to certain recent actions that for my part I was anxious to secure a definite reply from Craig and his colleagues, and that I was as agreeable to a reply rejecting as accepting [the proposition that Northern Ireland would be part of a united Ireland but with its own subsidiary political institutions, or else it would remain in the United Kingdom and be subject to a revision of its boundaries].'

Collins added that he had told Lloyd George that, if Northern Ireland opted to remain in the United Kingdom, the Irish Free State 'would save Tyrone and Fermanagh, parts of Derry, Armagh and Down by a boundary commission ...'.[6]

In the general election of 1918 there had been decisive nationalist majorities in the counties of Tyrone and Fermanagh. Collins and Griffith appear to have convinced themselves that any kind of boundary commission would have to render these counties into the new Irish Free State, along with some other largely nationalist areas close to the border. Had this happened, the later problem of some unionists in areas of those Ulster counties that were actually in the Free State but adjacent to the border demanding to be allowed to join Northern Ireland might not have arisen as starkly as it did. During negotiations on 17 October Churchill had indicated that what he called a 'piebald result' was not practicable, in that some smaller nationalist communities would inevitably end up inside the four Northern Irish counties with the largest unionist majorities and not every such community could be joined with the Free State. It appears from Barton's comments quoted above that the plenipotentiaries accepted that practical point. Barton may well have been right that Lloyd George intended to be generous. But by early 1922 Griffith was sufficiently concerned to tell Collins that 'If the British government stands firmly on this situation we'll be saved. Otherwise disaster.'[7] With the deaths of Griffith and Collins during the Civil War and the downfall of Lloyd George politically, the main negotiators on the Irish side were not around to argue the point.

Lloyd George himself expressed contempt for the existing borderline created by the Government of Ireland Act 1920. On 10 November 1921 he had written to James Craig, leader of the Ulster unionists, in striking terms to warn that, if Northern Ireland remained in the United Kingdom,

> 'Customs barriers would have to be established between Northern and Southern Ireland over a jagged line of frontier. The inconvenience of this arrangement would be considerably enhanced by the fact that there must of necessity be large elements of the population on both sides whose sympathies will lie across the border. The natural channels of trade would be arbitrarily obstructed. The difficulty of working any such arrangement would be unceasing, the cost considerable, and the vexation to traders continuous.'[8]

He soon added a further remarkable warning:

> 'The existing state of central and southeastern Europe is a terrible example of the evils which spring from the creation of new frontiers, cutting the natural circuits of commercial activity, but when once such frontiers are established they harden into permanence. Your proposal would stereotype a frontier based neither upon natural features nor broad geographical considerations by giving it the character of an international boundary. Partition on these lines the majority of the Irish people will never accept, nor could we conscientiously attempt to enforce it.'[9]

There was another obstacle to the boundary commission's making great changes to the border and it was a matter of the legal interpretation of such provisions. I have examined this at some length elsewhere—how the British framed the boundary commission in seemingly innocent language that Lord Chancellor Birkenhead believed was in fact capable of being interpreted in law only narrowly. In this context the role of the privy council within the British Empire or Commonwealth was expected to prove crucial, and Lord Birkenhead believed that London could depend on it to do the right thing from a British perspective. It appears that the barrister John O'Byrne warned Griffith of this danger a few days before the agreement was signed in London, but Griffith thought that it was then too late to revisit that article as already drafted.[10] Although the privy council was not mentioned in the treaty, it had a crucial role as arbiter of disputes between members of the commonwealth, an unspoken aspect of the treaty agreement. At a cabinet meeting on Monday 14 November Lloyd George expressed the view that 'We ought to make it clear that, if there is any difference between Imperial and Irish Parliament, decision would rest with the Judicial Committee of the Privy Council, whereupon F.E. [Lord Birkenhead] remarked: For twenty years the finest tribunal in the world.' Then, on 15 November, following a conversation with Lloyd George, who was on his way to Sir Philip Sassoon's house 'to have a private conversation with Griffith and Collins', Jones wrote: 'I believe the P.M. was going to suggest to the Sinn Féiners for the first time that any questions of constitutional interpretation would have to go before the Judicial Committee of the Privy Council in this country …'.[11] To what extent the Irish then understood the implications of this, especially in respect to the boundary commission, or were concerned about it is unclear. The cabinet secretary made a note of a private exchange that took place between members of the British team when discussing what would in December become Article 2 of the agreement for a treaty. This article did not explicitly name the privy council but stated coyly that 'the position of the Irish Free State in relation to the Imperial Parliament and Government and otherwise shall be that of the Dominion of Canada, and the law, practice and constitutional usage governing the relationship of the Crown or the representative of the Crown and of the Imperial Parliament to the Dominion of Canada shall govern their relationship to the Irish Free State':

> 'P.M. [Prime Minister Lloyd George] reading: 'The relation of Ireland to the Imperial Parliament and otherwise.'
> F.E.S. [F.E. Smith, Lord Chancellor] 'And otherwise.' Intended to import into the document the jurisdiction of the Judicial Committee [of the Privy Council].
> P.M. It has been explained to them. Don't put it in if you can avoid. Difficult to explain to public.
> F.E.S. I said I would be willing to constitute it with an Irish Judge [amongst others, but not necessarily a nationalist].
> Churchill. I would go into action on all parts of the document.'[12]

It will be shown below that there is some evidence that Birkenhead later acknowledged privately that the possible role of the privy council as a stumbling-block for Irish aspirations had not been clearly identified to Sinn Féin in 1921. One wonders what might have happened if Birkenhead's views on the necessary limitations of any review by a boundary commission had been exposed to the light and subjected to more careful legal scrutiny by the Irish government and Dáil Éireann in December 1921.

As Barton points out, neither Griffith nor Collins was a partitionist. Each saw the treaty as a stepping-stone to a united Ireland.

Indeed, the enthusiasm of Collins in early 1922 to have the IRA continue being actively engaged in fighting north of the border is widely recognised. Both believed that the boundary commission was going to be a meaningful body making significant changes and thus entirely consistent in spirit with the principle advanced by de Valera in Dáil Éireann four months earlier (above) when he said that northern counties might vote themselves out of a united Ireland. If the two men were deceived by the British or by their own wishful thinking or by both, others who also purported to care deeply about partition should have spotted the problem and raised it vocally and effectively at the cabinet table or in Dáil Éireann.

17

THE TREATY PASSED BY A NARROW MAJORITY?

A majority of seven is not always considered 'narrow' or 'small' in politics. A stable government may be formed on a slimmer margin. The result of the Dáil's vote on the proposed treaty in January 1922 was 64 in favour and 57 against. The pro-treaty margin of victory was proportionally three times that of Sinn Féin over its combined rivals in its election 'landslide' of 1918.

Furthermore, this margin of seven does not indicate that only 64 out of every 121 Irish voters supported the deal as opposed to continuing hostilities. For all but four of the 128 seats in the second Dáil were filled by members of Sinn Féin, returned unopposed in 1921. That election was certainly not a usual one. Many voters who would have cast their votes for representatives of parties other than Sinn Féin were effectively disenfranchised. Had they been represented by those other parties in Dáil Éireann in January 1922, the margin in favour of the treaty would have been bigger.

Before the Act of Union came into effect on 1 January 1801, Ireland had long had a parliament of its own in Dublin, albeit one ultimately subservient to London and one that by law for more than a century had been exclusively Protestant. From 1801 Irish MPs sat at Westminster. For decades before 1918 many of those tried to win 'Home Rule', which would have seen a parliament of limited powers restored in Dublin, but the British continually frustrated even that modest objective.

The general election of 1918 across Britain and Ireland was a milestone, coming as it did after the rebellion and executions in Dublin in 1916 and being held following the passing at Westminster of the 1918 Representation of the People Act, which for the first time gave the vote to all men aged over 21 and to women aged over 30 who met a property qualification. Before 1918 Sinn Féin had won just a few by-elections but it now triumphed in Ireland, sweeping away the old Irish Parliamentary Party. It won seventy-three of the 105 seats allocated to Irish MPs out of 707 seats in the House of Commons, and the Irish Parliamentary Party was reduced to just six. Unionists took twenty-six (including three Labour Unionists and one Independent Unionist). In accordance with their party's policy, Sinn Féin MPs now declined to sit at Westminster and in 1919 set up the first Dáil Éireann in Dublin. Because the electoral system of the United Kingdom was not one of proportional representation, Sinn Féin in 1918 won a considerably larger share of seats than it did of votes, and this should be remembered when assessing just how many Irish people supported the proposed treaty rather than the option of continuing struggle and warfare. In 1918 Sinn Féin won 497,107 votes, while the Unionists and the Irish Parliamentary Party notably won 478,151 (257,314 and 220,837 respectively).

Those who voted for Sinn Féin in 1918 did so for various reasons and it cannot be assumed that a strong desire for an immediate or long war of independence leading to a 32-county republic was their dominant motivation. They certainly wished to see Ireland represented in international discussions about the future of European nations, but even more pressing was their wish to ensure that conscription would not be introduced in Ireland. The importance of the latter issue was marked by the publication of a discrete pamphlet on it by Éamon de Valera.

In 1920 the United Kingdom parliament passed the Government of Ireland Act, thus partitioning Ireland by law and establishing parliaments in Belfast and Dublin inferior to that in London. Two separate general elections in Ireland were then arranged for May 1921. Sinn Féin took the opportunity to stand candidates on the basis that these would assemble not in the two new Irish parliaments created by the United Kingdom parliament in 1920 but as the second Dáil Éireann. Their candidates were unopposed by Labour and the Irish Parliamentary Party and unionists in the twenty-six counties of the southern parliamentary area. Hence the second Dáil Éireann consisted completely of 124 Sinn Féin deputies along with four Independent Unionists who represented the special constituency of the University of Dublin (Trinity College). From these facts alone it is quite evident that the second Dáil Éireann was not representative of the full breadth of Irish public opinion and was more militantly republican than the country as a whole. Even with this imbalance, Dáil Éireann in January 1922 still voted by a majority of seven to accept the proposed Anglo-Irish treaty.

It is clear, too, from reading newspapers of the time that the vast bulk of churches, trade unions and other influential organisations and media in Ireland preferred acceptance of the proposed treaty to continued warfare for a republic.

One remarkable aspect of the 1918 and 1921 elections is that the Irish Labour Party decided not to participate. In 1918 this was in order to give voters a clear choice on the national question between the objectives of the old Irish Parliamentary Party and of Sinn Féin, and in 1921 to hasten the achievement of independence so that social and economic matters might sooner take centre stage. The extent to which intimidation played a part in Sinn Féin candidates being unopposed in 1921 is uncertain, but it is not thought to have been a decisive factor generally.

Had there been an all-Ireland referendum on the treaty, the pro-treaty Sinn Féin members of the Dáil and their supporters are likely to have been joined in voting for it by very many non-Sinn Féin voters who rejected the further turmoil that was likely to be involved if fighting was resumed for an all-Ireland republic against the wishes of the majority in Northern Ireland and the British Army.

On the basis of voting figures in the 1918 general election in Ireland, any referendum on the treaty in the area of the future Irish Free State would have been passed by a substantial majority. If people's experience of the behaviour of British forces in Ireland during the War of Independence in 1919–20 made many more eager for an independent state, the experience of death and destruction brought home the reality of continuing warfare.

It was widely thought on both sides that the result of any referendum on the proposed treaty or of any general election at that time was likely to see the electorate endorse the decision of Dáil Éireann in January 1922 to accept the proposal agreed in London by the Irish plenipotentiaries the previous month rather than risk the threat of renewed hostilities. Indeed, the general election in the Irish Free State in June 1922 saw a significant majority of pro-treaty candidates returned, including those standing for the Labour Party on this occasion. Anti-treaty campaigners had called for that general election to be postponed in order to update the electoral roll—not least by giving women the right to vote on the same basis as men. However, with growing turmoil in early 1922, these calls were dismissed as delaying tactics by those who wished to see Irish people given an early opportunity to express themselves at the polls on the treaty.

18

THE OATH WAS 'ALMOST MEANINGLESS'?

The oath that the treaty required members of Dáil Éireann to take was symbolically of great importance, and the UK government's insistence both on it and on the British monarch's being head of state for Ireland underlined its significance for unionists and imperialists who wanted it kept, as well as for the many Irish who found it offensive.

Keith Middlemas, the editor of the published edition of UK cabinet diaries kept by the cabinet secretary Thomas Jones, allowed himself a number of rather lengthy interpositions that are sometimes explicitly based on Pakenham's *Peace by Ordeal*, and sometimes so based without reference. This was most unfortunate because, while the diaries are themselves invaluable, Pakenham's book is—as will be demonstrated later—a misleading and biased source at times.

Middlemas refers to what Jones described as the 'confused and inconclusive discussion in Irish Cabinet' on 3 December 1921 to which the plenipotentiaries made a dash by land and sea days before the final talks in London. Official notes of this meeting (such as they are) show that 'in the course of a lengthy discussion of the treaty the President [de Valera] gave it as his opinion that it could not be accepted in its then form. He personally could not subscribe to the Oath of Allegiance … With modifications, however [he added], it might be accepted honourably.' It was 'decided unanimously that [the] present Oath of Allegiance could not be subscribed to'. The inclusion here of the words 'then form' and 'present' meant that an alternative form of oath mentioning the king was not excluded.[1]

As noted earlier, the form of oath was in fact subsequently altered. This was something that the Irish plenipotentiaries insisted on after they returned to London that weekend, although it was altered not in the exact form that de Valera had suggested at the cabinet meeting which had been:

> '*I do solemnly swear* true faith and allegiance to the constitution of the Irish Free state, to the treaty of Association and *to recognise the King of Great Britain as Head of the Associated States* [emphasis added]'.

Such a form as that was compatible with de Valera's wish that the new state might be associated externally with the empire/commonwealth but not actually be within it.

In the final treaty agreement, as already noted, the only 'oath of *allegiance*' required was to the new constitution of the Irish Free State, but an oath of *faithfulness* was required to the king. The new form that was actually agreed by the plenipotentiaries and the British was as follows:

> '*I — do solemnly swear* true faith and allegiance to the Constitution of the Irish Free State as by law established and *that I will be faithful to HM King George V, his heirs and successors by law, in virtue of the common citizenship of Ireland with Great Britain and her adherence to and membership of the group of nations forming the British Commonwealth of Nations*' [emphasis added].

So the oath of allegiance to the king was gone, albeit some claimed that an oath of faithfulness was no different in practice and certainly not in principle. According to Middlemas, 'The best account of the Irish Cabinet debate [of 3 December 1921] is given in *Peace by Ordeal*, pp. 255–63', but Middlemas does not mention de Valera's refusal at that meeting to accept the oath or his refusal to accept the changes subsequently made to it at the last session of talks in London. Notwithstanding these refusals, Middlemas claims that, on the last day of talks,

> 'Much easier to settle was the question of the oath, where great efforts were made to assimilate the words to the susceptibilities of both sides. The result was a mishmash of legal verbiage, making the oath almost meaningless, satisfactory at the time, but not afterwards.'[2]

In fact, the matter was only 'settled' as part of a final *quid pro quo*, and then not 'settled' fully to the satisfaction of the Irish, for it did not take the form that the Irish cabinet as a whole wanted. Later on the day that the treaty was signed, Griffith reported to his fellow ministers that, returning to Downing Street as midnight approached after a break on the last session of talks on 5–6 December, the Irish had proposed some further amendments to the draft agreement:

> 'They accepted most of them when we said we spoke as a united delegation, that we were willing to recommend inclusion with the other states in the Empire [i.e. Ireland to stay in the 'commonwealth']. It was on this basis, by the way, that they

altered the oath of allegiance—earlier in the day. At 2.12 a.m. we signed the document.'[3]

The oath to the king has continued to this day to be referred to as an 'oath of allegiance', despite its having been changed to an oath to 'be *faithful* to HM King George V, his heirs and successors by law'. The word 'allegiance' had a more potent propaganda value than the word 'faithful' to the anti-treaty side.

Coupled with the required oath was the fact that the British insisted that Ireland remain within the British Empire as a member of the commonwealth—and therefore at least nominally under the king as the ultimate head of state. As Ned Broy later told the Bureau of Military History, 'The mere expression "British Empire" compressed into itself the concentrated hatred of Irish nationalists'.[4]

A long and unhappy relationship between England and Ireland also framed the British monarchy itself in a highly problematic way, given its association with religious, political and military oppression. Thus any oath that elected deputies of Dáil Éireann might have to take that honoured the king stuck in the throat of Sinn Féin members. In the Dáil, on 21 December, Gavan Duffy was to describe the king as 'a gentleman who necessarily symbolises in himself the just anger and the just resentment of this people for 750 years [...] If they had kept their King out of Ireland an honest settlement would have been easy.'

There was good reason for Irish people to resent these forced expressions of loyalty, not least when the monarch was head of the Church of England. Ireland was a largely Catholic country, and the British had long persecuted and discriminated against Catholics in various ways for practising their religion. The issue of the oath would indeed have been 'much easier to settle' had the British not insisted on it in 1921, but this was the price they intended to exact for the creation of an Irish state. It was not petty of de Valera and others to take exception to it, and those with a strong Catholic faith had understandable difficulties in coming to terms with its ultimate significance, either because they found it dishonest in conscience to take such an oath or because they feared that it could in conscience unreasonably constrain their political freedom.

The oath was a stumbling-block to participation in Dáil Éireann when the Irish Free State came into existence. Because they refused to take the oath, de Valera and his followers remained partly outside the democratic process until August 1927. Then, squaring the oath with their consciences by deeming it an empty formula that required them only to sign a book in a Dáil office, he and other elected members of his new party, Fianna Fáil, entered Dáil Éireann.[5] At that point, and not at the end of the Civil War, the democratic Irish state that had grown out of an independence struggle supported by armed Volunteers was effectively consolidated. In May 1933 de Valera's government used new powers granted to commonwealth dominions by the British and abolished the controversial oath.[6]

19

DANGERS OF BOLSHEVISM?

It is said that, in the wake of the Easter Rising of 1916, 'Lenin was quick to rebuke the Polish revolutionary Karl Radek for suggesting that events in Dublin amounted to no more than a bourgeois effort at a "putsch": only a pedant, Lenin argued, would vilify the Irish rebellion in these terms'.[1]

The word 'putsch' may signify any of a wide range of sudden efforts to overthrow a government, including the Irish 1916 Rising and the Russian Revolution of 1917. Radek wrote that 'the Irish question was an agrarian one'; people had been pacified by reforms, and the nationalist movement remained a 'purely urban, petty-bourgeois movement, which, notwithstanding the sensation it caused, had not much social backing …'. Lenin felt that Radek failed to give events in Ireland enough credit as a blow against imperialism.[2]

It does not necessarily vilify 'the Irish revolution' to define it as a national independence movement, principally seeking liberation from British rule rather than being more generally in pursuit of radical social or economic changes. It is not clear how much the Russian revolutionary Lenin knew about developments in Ireland, but he was perhaps informed of the Citizen Army's role in the Easter Rising under James Connolly. Connolly, however, was not typical of the leadership of that rebellion, most of whose members were not socialist, let alone communist. The Rising of 1916 and 'the Irish revolution' more generally were largely nationalist affairs aimed at independence from Britain rather than at the upending of social relationships. Given the continuing place and power of the Catholic Church in Irish society, they were not even very republican.

James Larkin had left the island after the frustration of his efforts as a social revolutionary in the 1913 Lockout in Dublin. By 1916 Larkin was aged 39 but had spent only seven of those years in Ireland. In 1907 he had been sent to Belfast from England as a trade union organiser and then moved to Dublin. He departed for the United States in 1914 and did not return until after the establishment of the Irish Free State. Emmet O'Connor has written that 'the defeat [in 1913] had a shattering effect on him',[3] but Larkin's depression can scarcely have been worse than that of workers and their families caught up in the confrontation that he sought but now left to their own devices. Some English trade unionists were hesitant to get involved in Irish matters, with national considerations complicating labour issues on both sides of the Irish Sea.[4]

Nevertheless, labour historians rightly point out interesting developments in the years immediately before independence, such as the creation of dozens of 'soviets' where Irish workers seized their places of employment and continued in production for very brief periods under new management structures that they devised. These soviets were an alternative to ceasing work in a strike but, in practice, they were usually aimed at winning concessions on wages and working conditions rather than possession of the means of production, and it was not long before owners were again in control of their premises.[5] Ireland was, after all, a conservative agrarian society with conservative Christian churches. In 1917, for example, Sinn Féin assured those who could vote for Éamon de Valera that 'It has been said that a Free Ireland means … Red Ruin and Revolution … These are the facts. A Free Ireland does not mean Revolution: It means peace and prosperity ... A Free Ireland means—not Red Ruin—but the salvation from Red Ruin.'[6]

In 1921, at the YMCA in Belfast, one James McCandless, 'who spent ten years in Russia', warned of the 'dangers of Bolshevism', which, he said, was the same as socialism and which 'was responsible for all the horrors occurring in Russia at present'.[7] Most Irish politicians wanted nothing to do with a form of revolution that might be like that of the Bolshevik revolutionaries in Russia. A few of the more marginal ones, such as Maud Gonne and Constance Markievicz, did claim that Russian revolutionaries and the Irish people shared common principles of 'democracy', 'universal peace' and 'liberty', but such values scarcely seem novel or especially radical.[8] Indeed, it was later alleged in an ITGWU newspaper that Markievicz, when minister for labour of Dáil Éireann in the autumn of 1921 (between the truce and the beginning of treaty talks in London), threatened to send in the IRA to evict workers from a 'soviet' in County Limerick unless those workers left the premises they had occupied of their own accord. Notably, this soviet was in the village of Bruree, near which Éamon de Valera—self-styled 'symbol' of the Irish republic and head of the government in which Markievicz then served as minister—had grown up as a child after his arrival in Ireland.[9]

On 23 November 1921, under a headline 'Instructive Incident in Co. Limerick', the *Belfast Newsletter* reported that 'There is trouble between the Sinn Féiners and the Bolshevists in Co. Limerick':

> 'A local branch of the Irish Farmers' Union refused to pay a harvest bonus demanded by the Irish Transport Workers' Union, which for some time past has been drifting apart from Sinn Féin, and, consequently, there was a strike of farm labourers in the district.

> Following this some disturbances occurred, and after the raiding of a farmer's house, Sinn Féin "police", in a desire to show their self-imposed "authority", kidnapped four of the strikers. Against this "arrest" the Transport Union protested, and demanded the release of the four men by Saturday last. The demand not having been complied with, a general strike was declared in Kilmallock, and a mob paraded the streets carrying a red flag. Local creameries are closed down.'

Insofar as there was anything resembling a spirit of Bolshevism in Ireland, it owed at least as much to other phenomena as it did to any spirit of revolutionary communism. These included trade unions organising in Ireland, an infectious spirit of militancy among workers in Britain after World War I, an increase in literacy and newspaper circulation that brought home to people across Ireland what was happening abroad and a general sense of comradeship with people struggling against imperialism. It also owed much to terrible social circumstances in parts of Ireland, as the Dublin Industrial Development Association was warned in 1921 when Mrs Maud Walsh, 'speaking of the wretched conditions of the tenement houses in Dublin, which constitutes the homes of the toilers', told the association that 'It was in such loathsome dwellings that the spirit of Anarchy and Bolshevism was bred'.[10]

Nothing quite illustrates the way in which social issues were marginal to 'the Irish revolution' than the stepping aside of the Irish Labour Party from the general elections of 1918 and 1921 in order to leave the field clear on 'the national question'. While Sinn Féin Volunteers fought British armed forces, the poor remained poor. On 10 January 1922, just three days after Dáil Éireann approved the treaty deal with Britain and some months before the eruption of outright civil war, a deputation from the Irish Labour Party and Trade Union Congress was given permission for its secretary, Tom

Tom Johnson (1872–1963), trade unionist and leader of the Labour Party in Dáil Éireann 1922–27 (courtesy National Library of Ireland, KE 193).

Johnson, to address the Dáil. The deputation purported to represent 300,000 organised workers and Johnson–who himself was to be elected to the Dáil in June–made it clear that there had been no revolutionary advances in the lot of poor workers:

> 'Our delegation represents all the various towns: Cork, Waterford, Limerick, Dublin and other towns, as well as some of the agricultural districts of the country. I said we had refrained from contesting elections in the interests, as we thought—as we know—of national solidarity in the face of the enemy; in the face of the enemy of Ireland and the enemy of the working class—the capitalist imperialism in operation in this country. We had reason to know—we had documentary evidence to prove—that in the minds of certain very high officials of the British Government there were hopes and beliefs, and their conduct was founded on those hopes and beliefs, that we would sometime in the struggle split off from the national movement. That was one of the factors—a very important factor which determined our action at the elections.'

Johnson told deputies that the executive of the Labour Party had followed the Dáil's debates on the treaty intently,

> 'and we could not but feel that with the stress of the war, the critical periods, and the difficulties of administration, both the Government and the Deputies seem to have forgotten—in the stress of political issues—to some extent, that there was a social problem at home. There are at this time probably one hundred and thirty thousand men and women walking the streets, unemployed. Tens, and twenties, and thirties of thousands of these have been only intermittently employed for the last year, or one-and-a-half years. In every country in Europe all such people have been forced

to agitate more or less violently against the powers that be. But the feelings of solidarity with the nation which permeate the working class in Ireland have tended to restrain any action which they would naturally take. We were in the position that we could not agitate with the British Government on such matters as social conditions. We dared not agitate because of the critical nature of the situation—we dared not agitate against the Irish Government. The times have developed; circumstances have developed. Those times have passed and we are in the situation to-day that a very large proportion of the population is at its wits' end to know how things are going to move. Thousands of children are hungry and naked, huddled together like swine in their so-called houses. In all parts of the country we hear cries of desperation, cries of: "What is going to be done for us?" These murmurs presage, in our minds, something like the tremors of an earthquake, and unless something is done rapidly—something effective—there will be a grave situation developing in this country that will be a problem for even an old-established government, let alone a new one. The working classes in Ireland have taken a full share in this national struggle (hear, hear). Individually and collectively the workers have borne their part (hear, hear). They are prepared to do it again when the need comes. But I would like to say that, in so far as they are conscious of their purpose—and that applies to the greater part of the men who went into this fight for freedom and for Ireland's nationality—they went into the fight for freedom for the men and women of Ireland individually (hear, hear). Freedom from bondage to wage slavery, freedom from bondage to the machine, freedom from bondage to capitalists and financiers in Ireland or in other parts of the world. We feel, and they feel, that there must be something done immediately to lessen this burden that they are suffering.'

Johnson thought that 'probably one million acres of land have gone out of cultivation during the last couple of years. A million acres of land gone out of cultivation!' He added:

> 'The patience of the workers, of the people, of the poor unemployed, and the wives of the unemployed, is becoming exhausted. We want to impress on you this: there is an insistent and immediate need for these problems to be tackled—the problems of unemployment, tillage, housing—and they will not brook delay. It will not do to allow them to wait on political exigencies. These are social problems that must be dealt with at once. We realise fully all the difficulties of the situation. We are fully aware of them, and are prepared to make every allowance for those difficulties. But we want to impress on you members of the Dáil—the Government of Ireland—that this is a problem which is your responsibility. You are responsible to see that this problem is dealt with and tackled effectually. If it is not so done the people will rise and sweep you away, as they would sweep any government away that failed to do its duty to the common people (applause).'

The Labour Party had taken a political risk in not contesting the previous two general elections. It would do relatively well in the next one, in June 1922. Meanwhile, Johnson's speech stripped away any pretence that 'the Irish revolution' was an all-round affair in which social and economic as well as political relations were upended. Indeed, far from responding promptly and imaginatively to Johnson's appeal, Dáil Éireann divided against itself and the new state became embroiled in a wasteful and damaging civil war. One of the legacies of that conflict would be a political system long polarised not to the right and left, as in many European countries, but predominantly along the axis of Civil War bitterness. The

Labour Party has been rarely able to repeat, let alone improve on, its performance in the general election of June 1922.

A "Shemus" cartoon from the *Freeman's Journal*, 13 May 1922. Entitled 'If Winter Comes', it reflected fears about the impact of civil strife on the economic and social state of Ireland in early 1922. Its sarcastic caption read "Mr [Erskine] Childers: 'The country is racked with the desire for material comfort.' " (Courtesy National Library of Ireland, PD 4309 TX 127.)

20

DEV 'HEARTILY DISAGREED WITH [RORY] O'CONNOR'?

Later efforts by his supporters to distance Éamon de Valera from the actions of the anti-treaty IRA, who in early 1922 seized the Four Courts and other buildings and pledged themselves to destroy the treaty and the emerging Free State, were undermined by de Valera's own actions and words both then and throughout the Civil War. Who wanted a civil war if it could be avoided? Its avoidance was not a matter of fate but of choice. The real question is what price or ransom was demanded by those in the minority in return for laying down their arms and accepting what most members of the Dáil and of the public agreed was necessary.

In 1953 Florence O'Donoghue wrote: 'My personal impression is that he [de Valera, or 'Dev' as he became widely known] was opposed to Civil War all the time, but, like Cathal Brugha, who also opposed it, he felt it to be his duty to participate when it started'.[1] That this was not the only option is illustrated by O'Donoghue's own decision. From March to June 1922 he was adjutant-general of the anti-treaty IRA and a member of its army executive, 'and was a leading figure in unsuccessful efforts to reunite the pro- and anti-treaty IRA factions prior to the civil war'. In June 1922 he resigned from the anti-treaty IRA, opposing plans to interfere with the 1922 general election, and remained neutral during the subsequent Civil War.[2]

In March 1922, as seen above, the IRA commander Rory O'Connor made very strong statements about the nature of IRA resistance to the treaty, and expressed indifference to a journalist who suggested that O'Connor was espousing military dictatorship. O'Connor made those statements at a press conference for international journalists held at 23 Suffolk Street, the building in which de Valera's new political organisation, Cumann na Poblachta, and de Valera himself had their headquarters. De Valera's official biographers, in their book of 1970, claimed that O'Connor's presence there that day 'was a painful embarrassment for him [de Valera] when he heartily disagreed with O'Connor's action and outlook'. Indeed, at the press conference O'Connor reportedly 'admitted that at the Dáil Mr de Valera asked the army [IRA] to still obey the Dáil Éireann Ministry of Defence, but they would not obey him [the Minister for Defence] and accept his view, because he had violated his agreement with them'.[3]

Some contemporaries appears to have been more sceptical then about de Valera than were his later biographers. One of de Valera's biographers, Mary Bromage, has written that the ageing nationalist Timothy Healy went to the offices in Suffolk Street to see de Valera:

> 'He received his caller coolly and kept [Harry] Boland by him while Healy warned that if he—Dev—lent himself to the use of force he would be a sorry man within a year. "I don't think so," de Valera curtly replied. He had nothing to do with the Army, he emphasized to his visitor. In another room upstairs sat Rory O'Connor and fellow officers.'[4]

Within months, embroiled in an uneasy relationship with the anti-treaty IRA as the Civil War raged, de Valera would indeed be sorry—as Healy had predicted—and was by then referring privately to 'Rory O'Connor's unfortunate repudiation of the Dáil, which I was so foolish to defend'. In the same letter, intercepted by the government and subsequently leaked to newspapers, de Valera identified that repudiation as being 'now the greatest barrier that we have'.[5]

De Valera's withdrawal from Dáil Éireann had itself been an inflammatory and provocative action. On 23 August 1921 in Dáil Éireann, when still its president, he had envisaged the possibility of 'sharp differences' over the result of treaty talks in London but had sketched a scenario in which the continuation of government would depend on a majority and not on unanimity. In January 1922, however, shocked to find himself in the minority in Dáil Éireann, he refused to serve and walked out.

It is the case that de Valera would have preferred to achieve his objectives peacefully and through political action, but his objectives were such that this was never a realistic prospect, as their achievement would have required the government to abandon the treaty agreed with the British and risk returning to outright war in Ireland. He formed Cumann na Poblachta with Austin Stack, Cathal Brugha and Mary MacSwiney, militants who were highly unlikely to compromise on the treaty, and he frankly described prospects of a compromise to Stack as 'a dream pure and simple'.[6]

Week after week de Valera also travelled throughout the country to state the anti-treaty case, as his official biographers have noted, and to issue what they describe as 'awful warnings'.[7] Charles Lysaght has written recently that 'De Valera campaigned against the treaty, warning presciently that its adoption would lead to bloodshed between supporters of the treaty and those loyal to the republic and unwilling to remain within the Empire'.[8] Its adoption by a majority of deputies in Dáil Éireann did not in fact 'lead to bloodshed' until a minority attempted by force of arms to overthrow that decision. It is not difficult to understand why many people saw at least some of de Valera's 'warnings' as threats. On 17 March 1922, for example, the *Irish Times* reported de Valera as saying, 'If you don't fight today you will have to fight tomorrow, and I say, when you are in a good fighting position, then fight on'. Referring to de Valera's tactics at this point, Bromage cites an old Irish proverb, 'There's no crime in the blow that has not been struck',[9] yet one can see from contemporary reports why some thought that he was inciting others to strike. In Carrick-on-Suir, Co. Tipperary, where he was accompanied by armed IRA members, he reportedly told a crowd of 2,000 people that 'If Ireland accepts the treaty then full freedom can be got only by civil war in Ireland'. He added, as the *Cork Examiner* reported on 18 March:

> 'If the treaty is accepted the fight for freedom will still go on, and the Irish people, instead of fighting foreign soldiers, will have to fight the Irish soldiers of an Irish Government, set up by Irishmen. If the treaty is not rejected perhaps it is over the bodies of the boys and young men he [de Valera] saw around him that day the fight for Irish freedom may be fought.'

On 18 March, too, the *Irish Independent* noted that de Valera had proceeded to nearby Dungarvan, Co. Waterford, where he proclaimed that 'It was only by civil war after this they could get their independence', and in Thurles the following day he said that if the treaty was accepted then the Volunteers of the future would 'have to wade through Irish blood, through the blood of soldiers of the Irish Government, and through, perhaps, the blood of some of the members of the Government in order to get Irish freedom'. His subsequent 'denial' of one of these reports was actually a denial of the validity of its interpretation of his words and not of the accuracy of its account of his statements.[10]

By early April de Valera was telling the Manchester *Guardian* that, as far as he knew, the aims of those armed forces that opposed the treaty were 'identical' to his own political aims and claiming that 'an overwhelming majority' of Irish people agreed with what the anti-treaty section of the IRA desired: 'If the army could save the nation from the calamities which are bound to follow the acceptance of these Articles of Agreement [for a treaty], I think it justifiable for it to use its strength to do so', including by preventing elections 'in the last resort'. On Friday 14 April 1922 Rory O'Connor and his men occupied the Four Courts in Dublin, with O'Connor reportedly saying that day that they 'had the greatest respect for Mr de Valera' and 'were the Army ever to follow a political leader, Mr de Valera was the man'.[11]

Protesting frequently that he wanted peace, de Valera played for time during the first six months of 1922 but failed to achieve the postponement of a general election beyond June of that year. He and Michael Collins sought a way forward that might please both sides, perhaps by means of a formula that could reconcile the irreconcilable by allowing the treaty to go ahead but at the same time devising a republican constitution for the new state and/or sharing power between republicans who accepted the treaty and those who rejected it. These ideas were unrealistic and doomed. The two men did conjure up a remarkable voting pact that saw both sides in the split agree to select Sinn Féin candidates for the general election of June 1922 in numbers proportionate to their respective strength in the outgoing Dáil, so that Sinn Féin could continue to dominate if not monopolise that chamber while including within it many anti-treaty deputies. To work, this pact depended partly on other interested parties standing aside from the coming general election as they had in 1921, but this did not happen. Candidates standing from other parties this time included members of the Labour Party, despite clear disapproval by Sinn Féin of their doing so. It was also the first Irish general election to be held under the system of proportional representation whereby constituencies returned more than one member of Dáil Éireann, so that the pact required not only a high level of transfers from one Sinn Féin side to the other but also a very low vote for candidates not belonging to Sinn Féin in order for it to succeed as planned. Transfers worked quite well in practice, but they were not enough to achieve the result intended. De Valera was bitter about a speech by Collins on the eve of polling in which he urged people to 'vote for the candidates you think best of'. Anti-treaty republicans later claimed that this amounted to 'a direct repudiation of the pact'—to calling it off, in effect—but Gallagher argues that newspapers in general at that time did not report it as being intended that way, even if it clearly encouraged people to think outside 'the pact'.[12]

Griffith had disliked the pact and saw it as a means of frustrating the democratic process, and the extent to which Collins himself was playing de Valera along or really believed that there was some way to square the circle that was the treaty remains uncertain. There were grounds for de Valera to feel deceived and further angered by the provisional government's delay in publishing the full text of the proposed Irish Free State Constitution until the last minute before voters went to the polls, but there is also little reason to believe that the militant anti-treaty republicans would have settled ultimately for anything less than the destruction of the treaty as agreed in London and accepted by Dáil Éireann in January 1922. Likewise, complaints that the voting register was out of date and that Dáil Éireann acted in breach of legal or constitutional powers and duties during 1922 were more propagandist than persuasive when it came to the central question of what the public wanted done at this point. There was little appetite for fighting on.

The result of the general election of 1922 showed clearly that the anti-treaty side did not command majority support. Thereafter de Valera worked openly with the anti-Treaty IRA, even bearing (if not using) arms on occasion, and taking steps to advance its cause. If his statements were on occasion couched in the ambivalent or ambiguous language that was characteristic of his quite tortured political style, historians should not be coy about frankly identifying his key role in precipitating or prolonging the disaster that was the Civil War. His own official biographers described his position frankly, and as thus put it does not sit easily with their claim that he heartily disagreed with Rory O'Connor in early 1922:

> 'De Valera was in no way happy about the military situation. All along he found a reluctance on the part of the [anti-treaty IRA] men to fight … Yet while there was any chance of success, de Valera plunged whole-heartedly into the war. As he saw it, the Republican Army was throwing itself "across the stampede of the nation".'[13]

De Valera's official biographers have written that, when the pact failed, 'The Republican politicians dropped their hands by their sides and said to themselves, through pure inability to prevent it, this thing has to be. So, having to choose, they preferred to stand with those who, whatever the differences on other matters, were yet true to their pledges and professions and to the traditional national faith.'[14] That sly phrase 'through pure inability to prevent it' denies agency on the part of de Valera and his associates for their actions in taking up arms against politicians who were in fact also republicans but who accepted the treaty as a step in the right direction. The quotation also affords those who favoured military dictatorship a moral high ground, as does the title of the same biographers' chapter on the treaty debate, namely 'Peace v. Principle', and their citing of de Valera's own words when he proclaimed that 'In Rory O'Connor and his comrades lives the unbought indomitable soul of Ireland'.[15] One notes what the *Cork Examiner* of 20 March 1922 reported de Valera as saying at Killarney, that 'The people had never a right to be wrong. He was certain that the same pluck which had carried them so far would enable them to finish (cheers).'

The question of exactly how the War of Independence might have been 'finished' against the 'wrong' choice of voters to accept the treaty was never put to the test. There were many indications that most people were sick of hostilities. Collins and other key figures had grave concerns about IRA resources too. The anti-treaty IRA was beaten in the Civil War. Had the latter side 'won' and brought down the provisional government, could it have gone on successfully to take on Ulster unionists and the British Army and beat them into submission and perhaps even into leaving Ireland? There are few if any grounds for believing that to have been a likely outcome.

While acknowledging that de Valera and others may have acted bravely on their principles, there is no good reason for intellectuals such as academics, journalists or politicians to avoid a realistic assessment of the destructive Civil War and of de Valera's responsibility for exacerbating and rationalising it. To say this is not to refight the Civil War or to take sides politically between de Valera and Griffith/Collins, or to judge individuals definitively as being true or not to what de Valera's official biographers called (above) 'the traditional national faith'. The latter concept in their case appears to evoke once more the recurrent trope of a glorious martyrdom for old Ireland, when in fact there were better options.

21

'THE CIVIL WAR STARTED ON 28 JUNE 1922'?

To pick 28 June 1922 as the 'start' of the Civil War is a choice that stacks the cards in favour of those who paint the elected government of the emerging Free State as some kind of an aggressor for responding to a threat. It is too simplistic a choice of date and historians should hedge it around with major qualifications. These include reference to:

- a series of earlier military actions by the anti-treaty IRA before June 1922;
- the armed occupation of the Four Courts in Dublin from early April 1922, and the storage of high explosives there and in the neighbouring Record Office;
- threats by the anti-treaty IRA not to desist from further action until the government of the Free State collapsed;
- refusal by those occupying the Four Courts to leave peacefully when asked;
- a desire by anti-treaty forces to see the British drawn again into fighting;
- widespread fears that an IRA military dictatorship might be set up.

One frequently reads categorical statements such as the following one on the website of the Royal Irish Academy: 'The Irish civil war began on 28 June 1922 when the National Army attacked the forces of the IRA Army Executive at the Four Courts in Dublin'.[1] Indeed, in a time-line included in my own biography of Arthur Griffith in 2020, I gave 'civil war begins' under that June date. Yet anti-treaty forces had decided long before then that they would persist with their armed resistance to the lawful authorities of the emerging Irish Free State until victorious. Events on 28 June were a logical consequence of their actions, and one that they embraced.

'They started it' is a familiar assertion in children's playgrounds but it is not the most helpful way to approach this question. Is it really true that the proposition 'That the Anti-Treatyites Started the Twenty-Six County Civil War' can be accepted 'only by accepting the argument of certain Treatyite supporters that the war began when the Anti-Treaty Volunteer Executive occupied the Dublin Four Courts some months before Treaty and Anti-Treaty supporters agreed their electoral pact'? So wrote O'Connor Lysaght, who went on to state:

> 'It is doubtful whether even the majority of Treatyite heirs would agree with this. They would be part of the broader majority that recognizes that the Treatyite attack on the Four Courts (like Britain's refusal to negotiate with the Dáil in 1919) turned what had been a state of disorder into full-blown war. The initiative came from the Treatyite Dáil Cabinet in the mistaken belief that the Four Courts garrison represented only one wing of an opposition divided against itself.'[2]

One observer's 'state of disorder' is another's declaration of war, whether 'full-blown' or not. Members of the anti-treaty IRA shot at pro-treaty soldiers of the Irish government from early 1922 onwards (in Limerick, Kilkenny and elsewhere). On the evening of 2 March

1922, Captain Bill Stapleton of the National Army—formerly a very active member of Michael Collins's assassination squad—was shot and wounded by anti-treatyites in Limerick. Stapleton was in charge of John Street Barrack. He was entering a hotel in the city, unaccompanied, when he was 'followed by five civilians into the coffee room where the order "Hands up" was given'. He turned around, 'whereupon a revolver shot was fired point blank at him, the bullet passing through the muscle of the left arm. He staggered and was overpowered by two of the civilians who relieved him of his revolver and disappeared.'[3] If this was the first shot of the Civil War, it did not lead to immediate widespread hostilities, yet tensions were rising.

Later in March 1922 the anti-treaty leader Rory O'Connor made clear the unbending intentions of the anti-treaty IRA. Defying an order of the government not to convene a meeting of the IRA, he also held a press conference for Irish, American and English journalists on 22 March 1922 (at which he claimed that he represented 80% of IRA members). The next morning's newspapers reported his 'remarkable statements', which included:

> '"There were times when revolution was justified and the army had overthrown the Government in many countries in that way."
>
> Asked: "Is there any government in Ireland today to which your army gives allegiance?" he replied emphatically "No" … "In effect, the holding of the convention means that we repudiate the Dáil. If a Government goes wrong it must take the consequences." …
>
> "If the people," he was asked [by a 'lady journalist'[4]], "vote for the treaty will you force a Republic upon them—that is to say, if a majority choose the treaty are the army and Mr de Valera going to force them into bloodshed and murder in order to get obedience to the ideal of a Republic?" "That is a matter of policy for the Executive of the Army to consider."

"Do we take it we are going to have a military dictatorship, then?" "You can take it that way if you like".'[5]

In the first week of April 1922, armed men broke up railway tracks in County Wicklow to prevent Michael Collins and others from attending a meeting in support of the new state and may have intended to derail Collins into the River Avoca. Collins said that 'it looks as if civil war can only be averted by a miracle', and he expressed his fear that the British would return 'to restore the order which we would have shown ourselves as having been unable to preserve'.[6]

During the second week of April, O'Connor's forces took over the Four Courts in Dublin. Hundreds of armed members of the anti-treaty IRA seized the legal complex, along with the adjacent Public Record Office and Four Courts Hotel. Not the start of the Civil War? Their assault, two days before Easter, during which the assailants held policemen at gunpoint and fired shots, was presumably intended to echo the rebellion of Easter 1916, when republican Volunteers had taken control of the General Post Office and the Four Courts, amongst other key buildings. Now the occupation in April 1922, led by Rory O'Connor, paralysed legal business but also challenged the authority of the Provisional Government and Dáil Éireann. Other buildings, including the Masonic Hall and Ballast Office, were also seized by anti-treaty forces in Dublin, and there were heavy exchanges of gunfire in the city as anti-treaty forces tried to extend their control.

The occupiers of the Four Courts were armed and intended to use gunfire to resist removal. Asked how many people were occupying the Four Courts, O'Connor said, 'Quite enough to defend it'. He promised that 'every care would be taken to preserve all documents', but high explosives were stored in one block of the complex and part of the Public Record Office itself was used as a munitions factory. The occupiers dug up soil to fill sacks, with the *Irish Independent* reporting that 'All the windows overlooking the principal thoroughfares were sandbagged, and numbers of law books and what appeared to be bags of papers were also utilised for defensive purposes. Armed sentries were stationed at all vantage points.' Some locals left their homes, 'fearing trouble'. A bakery had its bread taken to feed the garrison. Rory O'Connor, 'Chief of the Executive Council of the seceding forces', told the *Irish Times* that 'He did not know what Mr de Valera's exact policy was, but he was safe in saying that were the Army ever to follow a political leader Mr de Valera was the man'. He 'declared emphatically' to the *Irish Independent* that the occupation 'should not be taken in any way as a *coup d'état*', but his denial clearly underlined the reality of the threat to the emerging state. His claim that his IRA brigade just needed premises bigger than its current headquarters at 44 Parnell Square ('We simply wanted the place and came here and took it') was not credible.[7]

Asked by the Press Association whether there were any possible grounds on which an arrangement for preserving peace could be made, O'Connor was adamant, reported the paper, that 'Mr Griffith and Mr Collins would have to give an undertaking, and see that it was carried out, that the Provisional Government would not function. He added that the only means he could see of averting civil war was the scrapping of the treaty.' He also said that 'the responsibility of civil war will rest upon the shoulders of those who are supporting the treaty ... we shall never allow Mr Collins, the Provisional Government, or any other Government to replace the Republic'.[8] If those words in themselves were not a declaration of war, what words would be?

Following the occupation of the Four Courts in 1922, the Provisional Government sent troops to the Shelbourne Hotel and certain other buildings in Dublin, 'as a precautionary measure against possible developments during Easter Week'. Speaking of the Four Courts, one unnamed 'eminent lawyer' complained that 'An enormous number of cases have been pending for many years and are still undisposed of'. This highlighted the disruption caused to commercial and social life by continuing troubles. He made a brave but flawed prediction that 'the Irish administration could take the place by force, but he was certain that they would not do so'. He thought that 'they would be ill-advised in attempting to do so'.[9]

In her biography of de Valera, Mary C. Bromage describes the atmosphere in Dublin at this time, made no less fraught by de Valera's answers to questions posed by a special correspondent of the *Manchester Guardian* that she quotes:

> 'Dublin streets at night were laced with bullets when rebel machine-guns opened fire from roof-tops on the offices of the provisional government in Merrion Square. The Telephone Exchange, the City Hall, the Bank of Ireland, Beggars Bush Barracks became targets of the Republican snipers. Dev feared that an election would not be really representative of the people, and when newsmen pressed him to say whether the use of force was justified, slowly and hesitatingly he gave his answer, "The Army, as the last defence of the nation, is entitled to prevent elections such as those proposed …". The men inside the Four Courts were waiting to hear that. "If the Army could save the nation from the calamities which are bound to follow the acceptance of these articles of agreement," Dev decided, "I think it justifiable for it to use its strength to do so."'[10]

There were also shootings during April 1922 from and at various vehicles carrying armed men in the city. On Easter Sunday night,

An Irish Free State National Army armoured car, with effigy of Rory O'Connor, in Henry Street, Dublin. (Courtesy of the National Library of Ireland, NLI HOG 134).

a clash involving an armoured car of the National Army was followed by a statement from the anti-treaty side protesting 'definitely and emphatically' that 'an attack on Mr Michael Collins was not in any way intended or contemplated. He happened to be in the vicinity during the incidents at Parnell Square and thus became implicated in the events there'.[11]

On 26 April the Catholic hierarchy warned that Ireland was 'on the brink of ruin' and called for matters to be settled by an election and by reason, not by firearms. The bishops said: 'Like the great bulk of the nation, we think that the best and wisest course for Ireland is to accept the treaty and make the most of the freedom it undoubtedly brings us'.[12]

At the start of May there was a fierce two-day gunfight in Kilkenny city, after anti-treaty forces occupied Kilkenny Castle and the tower of St Canice's Cathedral, among other positions. The National (Free State) Army drove them out.[13] 'This certainly looked very much like civil war' observes one historian who has produced with government support a podcast about 'the battle of Kilkenny'.[14] Indeed the very term 'truce' that was widely used in the press and elsewhere to describe a welcome ceasefire agreed between pro-treaty and anti-treaty factions of the IRA early that same month tells its own story. One does not usually speak of a 'truce' being necessary in peacetime. Later in May, Collins and de Valera agreed the electoral pact that would see anti-treaty candidates permitted to stand on the Sinn Féin ticket in June's general election, proportionate to their strength in the outgoing Dáil relative to deputies who had voted to accept the treaty. The anti-treaty IRA did not respond to this pact by leaving the Four Courts or other buildings that it had occupied.

Events in Belfast were also putting pressure on the Provisional Government. On 24 March, a group of Northern Ireland's special police had murdered in cold blood Owen McMahon (a prominent Catholic businessman) and his four sons. Now, on the weekend that the Four Courts was occupied, the lead story in Saturday's *Evening Herald* was not about Dublin but about 'another orgy of bloodshed in Belfast' that had seen five people killed in sectarian violence since Thursday, as well as four members of the Special Constabulary shot, a Catholic church bombed and a Catholic congregation come under fire. It was hard to control the IRA in such circumstances. That weekend, too, Arthur Griffith went to Sligo to honour a speaking commitment, despite serious tensions in the town owing to the presence of pro-treaty and anti-treaty IRA units in close proximity to one another. A Sligo alderman who favoured the treaty said that 'The people would either have to support Dáil Éireann or a military dictatorship'. It was just one of a number of explicit warnings then about the possibility of a 'military dictatorship', including warnings from the Irish Farmers' Union and from members of the Irish Clerical and Allied Workers' Union.[15]

By now the danger was such that Griffith carried in his pocket 'a last message' in case he was killed on the journey to Sligo. It would be opened after his death in August 1922 and it read: 'Let the people stand firm for the Free State. It is their national need and economic salvation. Love to the Irish people, to all my colleagues and friends.'[16]

The Free State government waited as attempts were made to persuade anti-treaty forces to accept the wishes of voters and of all major interest groups to let the treaty stand. The thesis that the Civil War started with the attempt to dislodge anti-treaty forces from the Four Courts and Public Records Office is attractive, not least because images of a massive explosion there are part of the sexy representation of the war of the 'Irish revolution' that reduces it to the level of an action movie. Had there not been such an explosion the encounter would now seem much less dramatic as a moment in history. Throw in references to the British putting pressure on the government in Dublin to sort things out by getting on with implementing the treaty, and to the British lending the new Free State Army a couple of artillery pieces, and you have a recipe for a perspective that is intended to shame the democratically elected government in the face of a series of provocations from early in 1922. Yet deaths and serious injuries were few in the clash by the River Liffey, and the defeated occupants of the Four Courts were permitted to assemble calmly together afterwards on the quays before being marched off to jail. While the use of artillery by the Provisional Government has itself been weaponised to suggest that indecent force was used against the insurgents, it may be noted that during that week in June when anti-treaty forces were cleared out of the buildings that they had occupied in central Dublin at least twenty-five National Army soldiers were killed in comparison to only fourteen anti-treaty IRA deaths. The ratio was to be similar elsewhere, as the UCC Irish Civil War Fatalities Project notes:

> 'In most civil wars, the losing side takes far more casualties than the winners. Their memory is often also stricken from the historical record. In the case of the Irish Civil War neither of these things were true.
>
> The striking thing about anti-treaty fatalities is that they were far fewer than pro-treaty ones ... At least 402 pro-treaty personnel were killed in action or died of wounds, whereas only 185 among the IRA and its auxiliaries fell in combat. Or, to put it bluntly, National Army and other Free State personnel were more than twice as likely as republicans to die in, or as a result of, armed engagements ... there were far more casualties and fatalities among

> the pro-treaty forces, who were attacking fortified positions held by the anti-treatyites.'[17]

Meanwhile, hundreds of non-combatants also died in the crossfire, and damage was inflicted on the infrastructure and reputation of the emerging state. It is a small mercy that the Irish Civil War was not nearly as deadly, relative to the total population, as those in some other countries. Since it ended, 'the losing side' has very actively memorialised its own casualties in stone and story so that, as the UCC Project above notes, their existence is certainly not 'stricken from the historical record'.

One could say that the Civil War started on 2 March 1922 with the shooting in Limerick, and the persistent defiance thereafter of the democratically elected Dáil Éireann by anti-treaty forces. Clearly, the choice of date for the 'start' of the Civil War is a politically loaded judgement and that of 28 June 1922 should not be parroted by academics and journalists as if it were not problematic and propagandist. Given the way in which events on that date are weaponised, it is naïve for serious writers to repeat it without great caution as to the implications of their choice of date.

22

MICHAEL DAVITT WAS A PHILO-SEMITE?

Words like 'philo-Semite' should not be used lightly. The Greek *philos* means 'friend' or 'beloved'. The *Oxford English Dictionary* defines 'philo-Semite' simply as 'a person who supports or is favourably disposed towards Jews'. It does not ask why one might support or be more or less favourably disposed towards Jews than towards any other nation or people.

Late in 2024 Israel closed its embassy in Ireland, complaining of the Irish government's 'extreme anti-Israel policy' and 'the actions and anti-Semitic rhetoric used by Ireland against Israel'. Its foreign minister described Ireland's prime minister, Taoiseach Simon Harris, as 'anti-Semitic'. The Israeli government was particularly annoyed by the decision of the Republic of Ireland to recognise a Palestinian state and to support proceedings against Israel at the International Criminal Court relating to Gaza. The Irish government rejected the accusation that it was in any way anti-Semitic.

There are undoubtedly many Irish people who, not least because of Ireland's own experience of dispossession and imperialism, sympathise with Palestinians and abhor the collective punishment and ostensible 'ethnic cleansing' of Gaza by the Israeli Defence Forces.

Some may be anti-Semitic. Most recoil from such a suggestion and reject it vehemently.

Had Ireland really fallen to the depths of anti-Semitism since 1829, when its leading politician made a renowned declaration? In that year the foremost Irish nationalist leader, Daniel O'Connell MP, known in Ireland as 'the Liberator' because of his successful campaign for Catholic rights and emancipation from legislative discrimination by the British masters of Ireland, expressed support for Jews who were campaigning for civil liberties within the United Kingdom of Great Britain and Ireland. He famously told the English campaigner Isaac Goldsmid:

> 'Ireland has claims on your ancient race as it is the only Christian community that I know of unsullied by any one act of persecution of the Jews … you will find me the constant and active friend to every measure which tends to give the Jews an equality of civil rights with all other the King's subjects, a perfect unconditional equality …'[1]

That having been said, O'Connell also clashed publicly in 1835 with the Jewish-born future British prime minister Benjamin Disraeli, who accused him of 'scurrilous allusions to my origins'.

> 'It is quite clear that the "hereditary bondsman" [O'Connell] has already forgotten the clank of his fetter. I know the tactics of your church; it clamours for toleration, and it labours for supremacy. I see that you are quite prepared to persecute.'[2]

When referring to Jews in Ireland, Irish writers have tended to overlook Disraeli's barb and to take pride in the fact that, when consecrating a new synagogue in Dublin in 1892, the chief rabbi of the United Kingdom (of which Ireland was then a part) specifically recalled O'Connell's words of 1829 concerning the absence of past persecution in Ireland, which never had many Jewish residents. Chief Rabbi Hermann Adler told the congregation: 'You have come here from a country like unto Egypt of old to a land which offers you hospitable shelter'.[3]

Copper-fastening the favourable view of Ireland's record on the treatment of Jews at that time, Michael Davitt (1846–1906), who became a hero of the movement for land reform in nineteenth-century Ireland, has been described as 'one of Ireland's relatively few philo-Semites',[4] and he is quite frequently contrasted favourably with Arthur Griffith, who published a small number of anti-Semitic references in his weekly newspapers. On 8 July this year an *Irish Times* columnist held Davitt up as an exemplar of Ireland's history of solidarity with Jewish people.

Davitt's reputation rests on two pillars, one being a single letter that he wrote at the time of a boycott of some Jews in Limerick in 1904 and the other his work as a journalist reporting for the US newspapers of William Randolph Hearst on pogroms in Kishineff, in what today is the state of Moldova and was then part of the Russian empire. Hearst at the time was eager to increase the circulation of his *New York American* and other newspapers in Irish and Jewish immigrant communities in the United States. Irish historians have taken pride in the notion of a leading radical such as Davitt standing against the tide of prejudice in Ireland and beyond.

I have written elsewhere on anti-Semitism in Ireland in the early twentieth century. Griffith, founder of Sinn Féin, was far from exceptional in Irish or British society in holding certain unfavourable opinions about Jews.[5] However, Michael Laffan, one of his biographers, has pointed out that while he attacked Jewish 'cosmopolitans' such as the 'Jew-Jingo brigands' of Johannesburg in the context of the Boer wars (*United Irishman*, 21 October 1899), in general his few harsh articles were 'prejudices of his youth and, with occasional lapses, he outgrew them'.[6]

In fact, Griffith and Davitt both distinguished between criticism of Jews as a race or religion and criticism of Jews who did bad things. Such distinctions are not always convincing but may be valid, and the Irish government today defends its position on Palestine and Gaza in the same way. Some Israelis have weaponised the accusation of anti-Semitism for political purposes.

Both Griffith and Davitt expressly supported Zionism, reflecting in Griffith's case his admiration of militant nationalism and in Davitt's to some extent his view that Jews would be better off out of Europe and that Europe might also benefit from their going.[7] Some of Davitt's views on Jews were ambivalent, to say the least, and in one remarkable instance he explicitly justified anti-Semitism where he felt that it was merited against those whom he regarded as unsavoury. As his papers in Trinity College Dublin reveal, Hearst's editors spiked one of his articles that included criticism of Russian Jews.[8] In the case of the Limerick Jews, Davitt's letter was unexceptional. Other Irish politicians, including John Redmond, had previously penned similar ones in defence of the Jews of the Irish province of Munster.[9]

It has to be asked why such facts are ignored or missed, as they make it very difficult to understand how anyone could describe Davitt simply as a 'philo-Semite'. Likewise, in the case of James Larkin, trade union hero of the 1913 Lockout in Dublin, we have not heard as much about his anti-Semitic lapses as we have about Griffith's handful.[10] There is also the later resistance by Éamon de Valera's government to Jewish immigration at the time of World War II. Why has Griffith borne the brunt of criticism? Might it be, perhaps, that if one acknowledges a wider Irish phenomenon, in the case of idealised individuals such as Davitt and Larkin or, more broadly, in the case of some small newspaper advertisements in the *Irish Times* and elsewhere, this takes some of the shine off heroes of 'the Irish revolution'?

On 25 December 1915 an editorial in Griffith's *Nationality* paper declared: 'We do not know of one Nationalist Irishman ... who holds the creed that an Irish Jew should be ineligible for any office he was competent to fill in an Irish government'. This was a sentiment worthy of the precedent set by Daniel O'Connell, so perhaps it is not surprising to find that on 18 August 1922 the *Irish Times* reported that the Dublin Jewish Students' Union had learned with 'dismay' of Griffith's death. Its members sent a message to his widow expressing 'its sincere and respectful sympathy'. Griffith may not have been a 'philo-Semite' but there were very few Irish Catholics or Protestants who were, and in that respect 'the Irish revolution' made little difference. Griffith used to play chess in the DBC café on Dublin's Sackville Street with Abraham Briscoe, father of Robert, Dublin's first Jewish lord mayor. Robert became a Fianna Fáil member of Dáil Éireann and was said to be a close friend of de Valera, but de Valera never made him a government minister or even a parliamentary secretary and tightly restricted access for Jewish refugees to 'neutral' Ireland during World War II.[11]

Questions of racial tolerance and prejudice have arisen again in Ireland in recent years, not least in respect of Moslems and Jews. Immigration has seen the number of Moslems in Ireland surpass the number of Methodists, causing a certain level of disquiet to those who feel threatened by their lifestyle and beliefs. Meanwhile, the number of Jews in the Republic of Ireland has fallen very substantially from the time of Davitt and Griffith and Larkin, but—as recent tensions between the Irish and Israeli governments demonstrate—the question of anti-Semitism has not disappeared.

NEW YORK AMERICAN AND JOURNAL, SUNDAY, JUNE 14, 1903.

HERE IS PHOTOGRAPHIC EVIDENCE OF RUSSIAN MOB OUTRAGES ON THE JEWS

MICHAEL DAVITT IN THE JEWISH CEMETERY —THE 44 MOUNDS ARE THE NEWLY MADE GRAVES OF THE MASSACRED.

Proofs of Massacres More Eloquent Than Words

$14,529.07 MORE IS CABLED TO KISHINEFF.

HOW 3 WOMEN PLAN TO SPEND PART OF $1,000,000.

Michael Davitt Explains the Causes of Anti-Jewish Outrages at Kishineff.

BY MICHAEL DAVITT,
The "AMERICAN" Special Commissioner to Investigate the Kishineff Massacre.

Michael Davitt at the graves of Jewish victims of a pogrom in Kinshineff in the Russian Empire, now in Moldova (*New York American*, 14 June 1903).

23

GRIFFITH KEPT DEV IN THE DARK?

The remarkable rise to power of Éamon de Valera's Fianna Fáil so soon after the Civil War, and the publication in 1935 of Frank Pakenham's highly influential *Peace by Ordeal* that was favourable to de Valera, made it easier for those who wished to represent Griffith's efforts in London as somehow a betrayal. Pakenham's loose references to 'secrecy' on the part of Griffith were invidious and served to absolve de Valera and his supporters from responsibility for the outcome of talks in London.

There was in fact a steady flow of documents and information on all substantial points between the Irish delegation in London and de Valera and the cabinet in Dublin. Griffith pointed out in the Dáil on 27 April 1922 that a special courier had been sent to Dublin every night during the talks. Griffith personally wrote a series of confidential letters to de Valera to keep him abreast of what was happening, some of which have been published. Childers and others also kept the president of the Dáil directly informed. Delegates even made the long journey back and forth by train and boat to Dublin a number of times, and most notably twice in the final fortnight, including for a chaotic cabinet meeting on the Saturday before they signed the agreement for a treaty in the early hours of Tuesday 6 December 1922.[1]

Two assertions by Pakenham reinforced one another: that there were 'secret' or unreported meetings and that there was a secret deal. The more serious assertion, that Griffith somehow made a secret deal with Lloyd George that prejudiced the outcome of negotiations (the 'damnable lie', as Griffith called it), is addressed below in a different section. The assertions provided de Valera with a means to distance himself from his own strategy of staying in Dublin despite pleas by the plenipotentiaries and others to get directly involved in the negotiations, but they also allowed the pro-treaty side to put some distance between themselves and what had transpired, to lay any blame for falling short of aspirations at the feet of the two senior negotiators, who were conveniently dead after 1922. Neither Fianna Fáil nor Fine Gael would benefit by suggesting that the delegates did exactly what they were sent to do, or by insisting that the team won as good a deal as was possible in circumstances where the British and Irish had fought the War of Independence to a standstill and the British were once more threatening outright hostilities.

Any references to 'secret' meetings in London should be examined to see what exactly is meant. 'Secret' and 'private' are not necessarily the same thing and neither is necessarily surreptitious in a malign way. When de Valera went over to London almost immediately after the truce was called in July 1921 to set up substantive peace talks, he alone of the Irish cabinet entered the meeting room each time he met Lloyd George. The ministers who went to London with him were left outside. Not even his most senior minister, Griffith, was allowed in. Yet the word 'secret' is seldom if ever used of the sessions in July 1921 when de Valera was left under no illusion as to Lloyd George's red lines in any future negotiations about a treaty. Lloyd George subsequently made it clear in a letter to de Valera that Ireland was being offered dominion status within the British Empire, a status equivalent to that of Canada, and that remained the British position to the end of negotiations in

December 1921. As de Valera told Dáil Éireann in September that year, 'He knew fairly well from his experience over in London how far it was possible to get the British government to go' and anticipated a breakdown.[2] It is usual during serious negotiations such as peace talks to have various kinds of session, from plenary sessions involving everybody to subcommittees involving a few and one-to-one meetings involving senior players. Some talks may take place at official locations and others in more informal environments, over dinner or in a corridor. In the end, all five Irish plenipotentiaries had to sign the agreement in 1922, and they all did so knowing what they were signing. Even had there been 'secret' meetings, what they were asked to sign ultimately was laid out in writing for all five to see and either agree to or reject.

The plenipotentiaries had never expected to get at a table everything that the Volunteers/IRA had been unable to get by armed insurrection. As Griffith told the Dáil in April 1922,

> 'We were sent there to arrange how best the aspirations of Ireland could be reconciled with the community of nations known as the British Commonwealth; not an Irish Republic. That is what we were sent there for.
>
> Mr de Valera has pretended to the Irish people that somehow he didn't know what was going on or what happened in London. Every night from Hans Place a special courier was sent to Mr de Valera and everything that happened was conveyed to Mr de Valera.
>
> Now Mr de Valera is suggesting to the Irish people that somehow he was kept in the dark. I say at once, and now—because events may happen to us through Mr de Valera's friends—that I brand that as a falsehood. He knew everything that was going on. That is all I want to say on this subject. Those people have got up here and professed themselves die-hard Republicans. Why didn't he send Lloyd

> George in July 1921 a simple statement that we would negotiate on no other basis but the recognition of the Republic? Why did he withdraw that basis and send us there? We went there, and fought there, and we won there.'[3]

Language is very important in this context, and even recently historians are found using terms such as 'secret' and 'private' interchangeably as if there is no difference. For example, in his useful account of 'the Irish revolution', *A Nation and Not a Rabble*, Diarmaid Ferriter writes that

> 'Griffith and Collins kept de Valera and the cabinet in Dublin in the dark about their secret dealings with Lloyd George and Tom Jones, who referred in his diaries to the "private discussions and bargaining" that went on'.

In his footnote reference with this damning statement, Professor Ferriter cites as his only source page 174 of the first volume of the published version of diaries kept by the UK cabinet secretary Tom Jones, which had remained confidential and unpublished for decades after the events of 1921.[4] This is problematic for a number of reasons.

1. The word 'secret' does not appear anywhere on page 174 of the published diary (the word 'private' does). Jones does refer earlier, on page 148, to the Irish wanting 'the agreement as to secrecy to be maintained by both sides' but this was in the context of a request from Duggan, 'Chief Liaison Officer of the Irish delegation', conveying on 28 October the concern of his fellow plenipotentiaries that the British would not leak the ongoing confidential conversations between both

sides. Such 'secrecy' is a *sine qua non* of negotiations, where nothing is agreed until everything is agreed and each side explores the boundaries of the other's flexibility in respect to possible modifications of their initial bargaining positions. Both sides in London were worried about selective leaks, fearing that the other was spinning developments. That the talks were at a sensitive stage on 28 October when Duggan expressed concern to Jones is evident from the letter Griffith had sent to de Valera on the previous evening, concerning a 90-minute meeting on 27 October between Griffith and Collins on one side and Lloyd George and Birkenhead on the other. He told de Valera: 'The conversation was general. The gist of it was that if we would accept the Crown they would send for Craig, i.e.—force "Ulster" in [to some form of united Ireland], as I understood. We told them we had no power to do so [accept a role for the Crown/King in the constitution of a new Irish state]. We might recommend some form of association [with the Crown] if all other matters were satisfactory—above all Ireland unified. We are to send them [Lloyd George and Birkenhead] a reply to-morrow. I am writing in great haste. I deeply appreciate your letter.'[5] Thus, far from keeping de Valera in the dark, Griffith was working hand in glove with him. To the same end de Valera himself was supportive of offering 'some kind of association' with the Crown—in his case 'external association' with the British Empire/Commonwealth. This ultimately proved insufficient for the British, despite Griffith's efforts.

2. There were various 'private' discussions between persons involved in the negotiations as negotiators or secretaries, including between Childers and Jones from time to time, for example. Griffith and/or Collins also met Lloyd George on a number of occasions, with both sides thus being represented

in ongoing discussions by just one or two of their number. For example, Griffith and Collins met Lloyd George in private on 15 November to advance the drafting of a treaty, but that very evening Griffith reported in writing on the same meeting to de Valera and promised to have the new draft sent on to him when received from the British. This was subsequently done.[6] This is an example of how 'private' does not mean 'secret', even if the secretary Childers or other members of the delegation might have liked to be more centrally or completely involved in discussions with its senior members. Frequently at least two Irish delegates were involved in any 'private' discussions, but the team's official chairman Arthur Griffith sometimes met Lloyd George alone, as de Valera had in London in July 1921. Ultimately, nothing could be agreed until everything was agreed, in a situation where each plenipotentiary's vote had equal weight.

3. The words 'private discussions and bargaining' quoted by Professor Ferriter do indeed appear on page 174 of the published *Whitehall Diary*. However, they are the words not of Jones but of the diary's editor, Keith Middlemas, whose textual interpositions here and elsewhere indicate that he was guided closely by Pakenham's version of events. This is especially evident on pages 179 and 180, where a long editorial interposition is explicitly based on *Peace by Ordeal* as 'the best account' without any other supporting references and without any evident support from the very diary of Thomas Jones that Middlemas is editing. Middlemas even appears here to cross-reference another of his own interpositions based on Pakenham. We find him talking of a 'pledge' by Arthur Griffith on 12 November and an 'approval' by Arthur Griffith on 13 November when no such pledge or assurance of the type Middlemas means is men-

tioned by Jones in his diary entries on those dates. In his recent book on the boundary commission, Cormac Moore has cited another interposition by Middlemas on p. 164 of the published version of the Jones diary which is likewise misleading because it is in fact based not on anything in the diary itself but on Pakenham's version of events in *Peace by Ordeal*.[7]

4. There is published evidence in the first volume of the Royal Irish Academy's *Documents on Irish Foreign Policy* series and elsewhere of a series of letters from Griffith to de Valera during the talks keeping him abreast of significant developments (the texts of eighteen letters have been published and other letters are mentioned). Delegates also returned personally to Dublin a number of times for talks with the four senior members of the cabinet who were not plenipotentiaries.
5. Those who refer to 'secret' or 'private' meetings that they believe were somehow crucial should give details of each meeting's location and identify anything that they think was agreed there that was not previously or subsequently discussed either with any of the five delegates who did not attend such meetings or with the cabinet in Dublin. The plenipotentiaries were at times quite careful to avoid creating a bad impression by accepting hospitality from the English, although their resolve perhaps waned as weeks went by. However, speculation is no substitute for facts in this context.
6. Critics need to clarify whether they believe that all political negotiations should take place in public and plenary sessions to avoid the allegation of bad faith against those who participate in other forms of meeting. From Jones's diaries and Griffith's letters and elsewhere, it is clear that there were sub-sessions and one-to-one conversations of various kinds during the two

> months that the Irish were in London, but there is no reason to assume that these were detrimental to the Irish side.

De Valera had agreed that the negotiations would take place in London, on British home turf. He also allowed them to continue on a rolling basis. These facts alone increased the likelihood of many informal encounters between the two sides.

There can be no doubt from reading Jones's diary that the British did not like Erskine Childers and felt that he was difficult and obstructive. He was *not* one of the plenipotentiaries, as is sometimes thought, but a secretary to the Irish delegation. An Englishman who had converted to Irish republicanism, Childers was close to de Valera and in touch with de Valera throughout. On 26 October Thomas Jones noted in his diary: 'I thought it important that the next British document which Grigg was drafting should be shewn in advance to Griffith and Collins so as to secure as much agreement as possible before it got into the hands of Childers'.[8]

We know from de Valera that he picked Childers to retard the negotiations, so it is not surprising that those who wished to make a deal found him obstructive. In a confidential letter that de Valera sent to his republican backer Joe McGarrity in New York in December 1921, de Valera was eager to represent the treaty delegates as having strayed off message. Apologising to McGarrity that 'there is so much of the ego in this', de Valera contemptuously described Griffith and Collins as 'bait' intended by him to lure Lloyd George into concessions rather than to conclude a deal, and he referred to the two delegates Gavan Duffy and Éamonn Duggan as 'mere legal padding'. Childers, however, was 'an intellectual republican' sent to give Robert Barton (the fifth of five delegates, and a near cousin and close friend of Childers) 'added strength' as 'a retarding force'.[9]

In the end Childers seems to have gone too far and unintentionally drove Barton to sign the agreement.

Paradoxically, one of just two references by Jones in this period to something being kept 'secret' is to a promise made privately on a phone call to Childers himself to 'keep as secret as possible' a memorandum of 29 October by the Irish delegation in reply to a British memorandum of 27 October 1921.[10] Griffith and Collins had made it clear that they did not trust putting things down in black and white in advance, lest, as the UK cabinet secretary noted,

> 'it would be tantamount to giving the P.M. [prime minister] a blank cheque … The P.M. would then go to Craig, tell Craig all that Sinn Féin was prepared to do, Craig would say nothing, yield nothing, but go back to Ulster and announce to all Ireland that the Sinn Féin leaders had sold their followers. Over and over in the past Irish negotiators had been let down in this way by British statesmen. I admitted the force of this but urged that the P.M. wanted to be secure in his own mind as to how far Sinn Féin would go when he entered into negotiations with Craig.'[11]

The British prime minister was also ready to exclude his own people from meetings at sensitive points. On 7 November, for example, he turned down a suggestion by Chamberlain to have the lord chancellor at a meeting with Craig 'because that would mean bringing in Winston [Churchill]' and 'I cannot rely on Winston in a crisis. I never could.'[12]

Griffith believed that he had done the best he could for Ireland at the talks in London, and the evidence in both his published correspondence with de Valera during the talks and in the cabinet diaries of Thomas Jones indicates that he declined to agree to anything until everything was settled, and that he also made it clear that he could not bind the other four delegates. The diaries should be compulsory reading for Irish historians because they provide many profound insights into the various strains on both sides and into the interaction of British and Irish delegates. Griffith, incidentally, comes out of them not as a patsy but as someone trying to get the job of peace done with Lloyd George, while each was suspected by some on his own side of selling out their principles. In April 1922 Griffith told the Dáil:

> 'And when I was going to London Mr de Valera said to me "There may have to be scapegoats." There is a member here on the Opposition side who heard that remark [in an interesting exchange in the Dáil on 17 December Kathleen Clarke had confirmed that the remark was made in her presence and de Valera replied 'I forget what particular idea was in my mind at the time']. I said I was willing to be a scapegoat to save him from some of his present supporters' criticism; and Mr Collins and myself were willing to be scapegoats so long as Mr de Valera got what he wanted and so long as Mr de Valera's face was saved. That is the inner history of what happened. And the reason I am referring to it is this because of something that has happened and is happening within the last two weeks. In the last two weeks an attempt was made on the life of my colleague Michael Collins. ('Shame' and laughter from some Deputies). Yes; there is laughter there; you are going to hear something more of it.'[13]

Already the side that had lost the Dáil vote on the agreement was weaponising the manner in which difficult negotiations had been conducted. Such bitter critics would neither give Griffith any credit nor ask hard questions of de Valera as to why he had not plunged into negotiations sooner when he had the chance to begin them on the more neutral territory of Scotland and why he himself did not lead them in London despite his reservations.[14] Why, even then, had he chosen to 'retard' them as he explained to McGarrity?

Suggestions that Griffith held improper secret meetings of some sort were hurtful, but the suggestion that he made some kind of secret and deadly deal with Lloyd George that determined the outcome of talks was savage, being based on a misunderstanding or being simply a vicious lie that poisoned Irish politics at the very foundation of the independent state. In Dáil Éireann on 10 January 1922 Griffith called it 'a damnable lie'.

It is noteworthy that all five delegates in London signed and voted for the final agreement. They thought that signing the agreement was the least worst option in such circumstances. Each of them commended the terms of the agreement to Dáil Éireann and each voted for it there, on the basis that the alternative was the immediate resumption of warfare again by the British. A number objected to the pressure that they had been put under, and on 19 December 1922 in Dáil Éireann Barton highlighted Griffith's efforts to resist the British ultimatum that they sign or face immediate war:

> 'On Sunday, December 4th, the Conference [negotiations] had precipitately and definitely broken down. An intermediary effected contact next day, and on Monday at 3 p.m., Arthur Griffith, Michael Collins, and myself met the English representatives. In the struggle that ensued Arthur Griffith sought repeatedly to have the decision between war and peace on the terms of the treaty referred back to this assembly [Dáil Éireann]. This proposal Mr Lloyd George directly negatived. He claimed that we were plenipotentiaries and that we must either accept or reject. Speaking for himself and his colleagues, the English Prime Minister with all the solemnity and

> the power of conviction that he alone, of all men I met, can impart by word and gesture—the vehicles by which the mind of one man oppresses and impresses the mind of another—declared that the signature and recommendation of every member of our delegation was necessary or war would follow immediately.'

More than three decades later—almost two decades after Pakenham's *Peace by Ordeal* had been published and after giving years of support to de Valera's Fianna Fáil party—Barton's version of events as given to the Bureau of Military History included complaints about how Griffith and Collins conducted some negotiations by way of 'private meetings' that Barton claimed 'took the place of Delegation Conferences'. Griffith and Collins, by 1954 long dead, could not then respond. Remarkably, Barton's account to the Bureau explicitly relies on Pakenham's 1935 book. He claims that, 'soon after the private meetings' became a problem, Gavan Duffy crossed to Dublin to express concern to other members of the cabinet ('The date can be found in *Peace By Ordeal*', writes Barton in 1954). They wished to 'acquaint the Cabinet and de Valera that we were not at all sure that the reports given us of what transpired at private conferences were comprehensive and feared that the general position was being undermined'. Yet Barton indicates that they only raised the matter a fortnight before the final and decisive session of the talks began on 3 December, during which fortnight final drafts of the entire proposed agreement for a treaty were circulated to the whole cabinet and Griffith demanded and attended a cabinet meeting in Dublin to discuss them. It was the text of the final document that would matter at the end of the day. For that or other reasons Gavan Duffy's concerns were given little weight in Dublin. Barton admitted to the Bureau of Military History that

> 'He [Gavan Duffy] put our case [to de Valera], I suppose, as well as he could, and he got little or no satisfaction. I don't remember how it was expressed but, at any rate, Gavan Duffy came back from Ireland with the information that he had got very little support for our contention.'

In reality, a bigger concern for the two men appears to have been that de Valera would not go to London himself to attend meetings. Barton continued:

> 'There was a suggestion that de Valera should go over to London, but that was later than Gavan Duffy's visit. De Valera can give you his account of that better than I can, but my memory of it is that I pressed de Valera to return with us to London on the score that it would be impossible for us to get the maximum terms without his being present and that it was unfair to expect us to get the best terms without his assistance. He was, however, unwilling to move from the decision which he had made earlier that he would stay here as being the last defence.'

The 'last defence' was perhaps a sporting metaphor inspired by his decade of playing rugby at Blackrock and Rockwell colleges. On 14 September 1921, when the plenipotentiaries were named, his minister for local government W.T. Cosgrave had complained 'that this was a team they were sending over and they were leaving their ablest player in reserve. Now it was not usual to leave the ablest players in reserve.' That day de Valera had defended his decision:

> 'As he told them at the last meeting he thought it wisest he should not be a member of the delegation the reason being … that they wanted to emphasise in these negotiations they were not entering as a political

> party but as a nation .... To be in the very best position for the possibilities of a break down and to be in the best position to deal with those questions as they would arise and not to be involved in anything that might take place in those negotiations—to be perfectly free —he asked the Cabinet not to insist on his going as one of the deputation.'

According to his letter to Joseph McGarrity in December 1921 he had conceived of the plenipotentiaries luring the British into making concessions before the talks reached an impasse, at which point he would ride in like a knight in shining armour and somehow score the final goal that the War of Independence had not. This would have required Prime Minister Lloyd George, who had devoted considerable time and effort to the negotiations in London and who had described de Valera to his cabinet as a poor negotiator after meeting him in July 1921, submitting to de Valera. Yet de Valera would soon boast to Dáil Éireann that he was no politician, and his claim that he was better placed in Dublin than in London to win concessions in the negotiations seems naïve, and surely rash. The tactic achieved nothing in the end.

Given his exclusion of his own cabinet colleagues when he met Lloyd George in London on four occasions a few months earlier, de Valera could scarcely fault Griffith and Collins together agreeing to some small meetings. Yet Barton in 1954 thought that 'it was a specious argument of Lloyd George's that he was leader of a coalition Government and that many of his colleagues—some of them, at any rate—were difficult to deal with, that they held different political views from his and that a smaller delegation on his side would be likely to make better progress and, therefore, there should be a smaller delegation on our side'.

In 1964 Barton fell back on Pakenham to support his suppositions, referring vaguely to 'documents' that could confirm what Pakenham wrote. This is a graphic example of the continuing influence of Pakenham's version of events that undermined Griffith's reputation. Barton told the Bureau: '*Possibly* Lloyd George also felt that he could make more progress with Griffith and Collins than he had made with a full delegation. That is *supposition* on my part. There is little in that book of Pakenham's which you cannot confirm from the documents. I am merely *speculating* as to why Lloyd George made this proposal of small meetings ...' [emphasis added]. As demonstrated within the covers of the present book there are actually significant claims in Pakenham's *Peace by Ordeal* that are not confirmed from and are even contradicted by identifiable 'documents'.

However, having expressed himself more than three decades after the event with those vague words 'possibly', 'supposition' and 'speculation', Barton actually admitted that he himself at first had 'thought' more progress might be made by smaller meetings. In his helping of hindsight for the Bureau of Military History, he wrote that 'It was not until later that Gavan Duffy, Childers and I realised that Griffith and Collins were prepared to settle for less than we thought it possible to obtain':

> 'Obviously you can get a better idea of what is in another person's mind when talking privately than when talking to five. People might be more nervous of stating precise views if they were more or less publicly expressed before four or five than would be the case when two talk confidentially. I think we all thought more progress might be made in this way, and Gavan Duffy and I had not at that stage lost confidence in our colleagues!'[15]

It is easy to forget when reading Barton's views that he and Gavan Duffy voted with Griffith and Collins and Duggan for the agreement made in Downing Street in December 1921 and voted for it again in Dáil Éireann two months later. They were two of five adults in London for Sinn Féin; if they felt that the mode of meetings was fatally compromised or that the draft agreement itself was fatally compromised and/or that it should not be signed even under a British threat of immediate war, they could have resigned or refused to sign. They did neither. In this, as in other instances, one should pay close attention to the timing and sequencing of particular statements that are later relied on by historians or others.

24

FRANK PAKENHAM: AUTHOR OF QUALITY?

One of the most influential accounts of modern Irish history was not written by a historian and includes few precise references to sources. Despite those striking facts, as a contemporary reviewer has correctly observed, '*Peace by Ordeal: An Account from First-Hand Sources of the Negotiation and Signature of the Anglo-Irish Treaty of 1921*, by Frank Pakenham, is considered a definitive account of the Anglo-Irish treaty negotiations of 1921'.[1] It ought not to be.

In 1994 Pakenham boasted in his autobiographical *Avowed Intent* that *Peace by Ordeal* 'stood the test of time'. The current professor of modern Irish history at University College Dublin has also noted:

> 'Writer and politician Frank Pakenham produced a quality account of the treaty negotiations, *Peace by Ordeal*, which has retained its status. He had the advantage of being able to talk to key participants on both sides and managed with verve to produce a balanced assessment, at a time when the issues were still raw and emotive.'[2]

By no means all readers have found it balanced. Pakenham's prose is fluid, but its 'verve' does not stand up to close scrutiny when it comes to his representation of key aspects of the treaty negotiations. Indeed, he could not and did not speak to *the* key participants on the Irish side of the treaty talks, because both Griffith and Collins had been dead for more than a decade by the time he was writing. He relied heavily for his version of events on the memories and accounts of one senior Tory minister and of de Valera, whose official biographer he became in due course. Robert Barton also stated in 1954—by which time this signatory of the treaty agreement in London was a staunch Fianna Fáil supporter—that he had given any information he possessed to the writer of *Peace by Ordeal*, 'Lord Pakenham'.[3] Pakenham also boasted of access through a 'private source' to many documents (which he did not identify clearly). He also purported to quote from but did not clearly identify a key document on which he hung his book's plot. Asked later by Brian Maye, one of Griffith's biographers, to identify precisely the document and its location, Pakenham failed to do so.[4]

Pakenham's *Peace by Ordeal* enmeshes within persuasive prose a theory that Griffith was somehow duped into giving prior and even 'secret' prejudicial assent to the treaty deal in London in 1921. There are strong grounds for treating Pakenham's book with great caution, as demonstrated in detail in the next section below. Later in the same decade in which *Peace by Ordeal* appeared, the first issue of *Irish Historical Studies* was published. This journal was part of a push by a new generation of Irish historians, spearheaded by Robert Dudley Edwards and T.W. Moody, to put the study of Irish history on a more objective or professional footing. Nevertheless, despite developments in Irish historiography since 1935, the old-school *Peace by Ordeal* has retained a charm for many writers, who choose to reference rather than interrogate it. Pakenham's weakly referenced version of events has been integrated into the fabric of later accounts—without that source of those accounts even being identified in some cases. Such secondary accounts are themselves cited in turn as if original research.

If Robert Harris is usually deemed a novelist and journalist rather than a historian when dealing with historical themes, his attention to sources in some of his books such as *Precipice*—about certain events in the life of Prime Minister H.H. Asquith—is not inferior to that of Pakenham in his 'history' of the treaty negotiations. Given the status of *Peace by Ordeal*, it is remarkable that its author's background, motives and methodology have received so little attention. It is also regrettable that no senior academic in a history department has lately attempted a comprehensive, discrete and fully referenced study of the treaty negotiations that would include a close examination of the undoubted influence of Pakenham's far from carefully 'balanced assessment' of events on both the scholarly and popular mind.

Pakenham underpins an anti-treaty narrative of avoidable failure in London. Instead of applauding Griffith and his team for achieving as much as or more than might realistically have been expected, he ultimately damns them for purportedly being seduced by Tory cunning. Griffith is said by him to have secretly approved a key document in November 1921. Lloyd George dramatically flourished this on the last night of talks in December. Yet the fact that Pakenham avoided a question from Brian Maye, who, when writing his biography of Griffith in the 1990s, enquired where one might find that document is telling.[5] There is no evidence that Griffith signed or approved it, and there *is* evidence to the contrary, as will be demonstrated later below.

SO WHO WAS PAKENHAM?

Born in England in 1905, in the year that Arthur Griffith was first articulating his Sinn Féin policy, Frank Pakenham was to become the seventh Lord Longford in 1961. He grew up between his Anglo-Irish family's mansion in Oxfordshire, its house in London and its castle in County Westmeath. He inherited great wealth from relatives, including town houses in England. He lived a long life, dying in 2001. He said that he wrote *Peace by Ordeal* deliberately to redress British antipathy to de Valera: 'I had heard of him before I met him as "a Portuguese Jew" or worse', he wrote later.[6] Nicholas Mansergh has described Pakenham as 'sympathetic to de Valera's position'.[7] But if Pakenham wished to redeem Dev, he damned Griffith.

In 1932 de Valera became the new Irish state's prime minister ('taoiseach' today). A decade earlier he had reportedly warned of people having to wade through Irish blood and 'perhaps through that of some of the members of the Irish Government' to overthrow the Anglo-Irish treaty of 1921–2. In 1935 the *Irish Press*, which had been set up by de Valera, shamelessly recommended *Peace by Ordeal* because it 'justifies for all time those who refused to compromise on a question of vital national principle' (the anti-treaty fighters) and its importance 'is impossible to exaggerate'. The *Irish Independent* serialised it, reflecting its widespread impact.

Pakenham's objective was not simply to write history. Indeed, he had dropped history after his first term at the University of Oxford and switched to modern philosophy, politics and economics. Schooled at Eton, Pakenham at Oxford was a member of the élite Bullingdon Club. He was a close friend of Freddie, only son of F.E. Smith (first earl of Birkenhead) who had actively supported Carson at Ulster loyalist rallies. Birkenhead, as England's lord chancellor, was one of the two top treaty negotiators for the Tories. His wife Margaret and Pakenham's mother had also been 'close friends in childhood'. Pakenham, in other words, was part of the British élite.[8] Regarded by the historian Hugh Trevor-Roper and 'most of his Oxford colleagues' as 'a little "touched in the brain"',[9]

Pakenham was to enjoy a privileged life free of financial worries and prominently dedicated to worthy causes such as Ireland, prison reform and the control of pornography.

Lord Birkenhead welcomed his son Freddie's friend Pakenham into his home, Charlton. Pakenham wrote that between 1928 and 1932 'much of my social life centred upon the Birkenhead family'.[10] He described himself as 'a fully fledged member of the Charlton circle' and came under what he called 'the magic of Lord Birkenhead's personality'. They played golf and tennis and went riding together, and Birkenhead encouraged his speech-making. Pakenham added that 'Freddie and his family soon came to occupy a place apart in my eyes'.[11] Freddie was a godson of Birkenhead's closest friend, Winston Churchill,[12] who had also been on the British treaty team in 1921.

In 1929 Pakenham took a job in the Conservative Research Department, which was chaired by Neville Chamberlain, a future prime minister and a half-brother of Austen. Pakenham's maternal grandmother was a first cousin of Neville and Austen. In 1931 two Chamberlain girls were bridesmaids at Pakenham's wedding, and Birkenhead's son was his best man. During the 1930s Lady Birkenhead was a guest of Pakenham and his wife.[13]

It is said that Austen Chamberlain offered to show Pakenham official British documents relating to the treaty talks when Pakenham was preparing to write *Peace by Ordeal*, but changed his mind after Frank admitted to 'increasingly pro-Irish sympathies'.[14] Nevertheless, he spoke to Pakenham, who chose to believe him on Griffith. Austen Chamberlain, as Tory leader, had been that party's other top negotiator on the treaty alongside Birkenhead. They were the senior members of a coalition government led by Prime Minister Lloyd George, a Liberal, but in which their Tory party had a majority.

Did Austen Chamberlain not tell Pakenham that in 1924, as a letter in the Churchill Archives reveals, Birkenhead had admitted to him that the Irish arguably had reason to think what Griffith and Collins believed was the case—that the English accepted that the boundary commission would assign significant portions of Northern Ireland to the Irish Free State?[15]

While 'working officially for the Conservative Party' in its research department, Pakenham suggested an investigation of 'the Irish Question'.[16] He then made contact with de Valera for the first time and, according to his biographer Mary Craig, 'fell instant victim to Dev's charm'. He converted to the Labour Party and Catholicism later, decisions that were likely to boost his reputation in Ireland.

It was 'through a happy accident, and the crucial intervention of my friend Eleanor Smith [Birkenhead's daughter]', noted Frank, that 'I was invited to write a book on the Anglo-Irish treaty'. His wife went further and attributed to Lady Eleanor—a popular novelist—not just the securing of a publisher but 'the actual idea of the book'.[17]

While Pakenham's chief sources were Éamon de Valera and Austen Chamberlain, and also Robert Barton, Lloyd George brushed off an attempted interview. In 1994 Pakenham claimed that Thomas Jones, the former prime minister's cabinet secretary, 'talked to me generously'.[18] By 1994, however, Jones's diary of 1921 had been published and supported Griffith's version of events in that it showed that the Irish leader resisted attempts to seduce him personally into premature agreement with British proposals, so Pakenham may have felt a defensive need to identify Jones belatedly as a verbal authority for his own 1935 version of events.

In his introduction to *Peace by Ordeal*, on which de Valera co-operated, Pakenham boasts that he has been granted sight of certain records that were not then publicly available for inspection:

> 'I have been exceptionally fortunate in my material, having had access through a private source to a large mass of documents never before published or made the basis of published work. They include copies of the correspondence that passed between President de Valera and Arthur Griffith, Chairman of the Irish Delegation, during the treaty negotiations of October to December 1921. Also copies of the official Irish records of all the Downing Street Plenary Sessions, and a great deal of other matter indicative of the proposals put forward by both sides and of the discussions concerning them.'

Likewise, later in the 1960s de Valera took steps to arrange access to relevant but restricted government files for 'bona-fide historians', particularly in the context of his 1970 'authorised biography' by Frank Pakenham (by then Lord Longford) and Thomas P. O'Neill.[19] One cannot say whether access in any case was entirely unrestricted or whether it was filtered by de Valera, who, as noted earlier, long maintained an active interest in the cultivation of his reputation.[20] Pakenham does not explain what exactly constituted this 'large mass of documents' that he claims to have seen, or what exactly were 'the official Irish records' of the plenary sessions (no minutes were made of sessions). He omits from *Peace by Ordeal* precise referencing to what documents he does quote. Selectively determining who might be a 'bona-fide historian' and what papers that person might be allowed to see is not the best way to ensure that history is as objective as possible.

Decades after *Peace by Ordeal* appeared, and while co-authoring with T.P. O'Neill their favourable biography of de Valera, published in 1970, Pakenham expressed regret that de Valera was not the leader of a great power 'where his abilities would have had more scope'.[21] De Valera, then Ireland's president, was again co-operating closely with Pakenham.

Although Barton had signed and voted for the treaty agreement, he later supported de Valera. In 1933, while Pakenham wrote *Peace by Ordeal*, de Valera's Fianna Fáil government made Barton chairman of the Agricultural Credit Corporation. While conceiving *Peace by Ordeal*, Pakenham and his wife spent weekends at Barton's Anglo-Irish family home—Glendalough House, Co. Wicklow—where Barton's cousin Erskine Childers (a bitter critic of Griffith during the treaty talks) had also grown up. The Pakenhams were shown where Erskine was arrested there during the Civil War, before his execution by the Free State for possession of a firearm. Barton had given Erskine's widow Molly a home there. When the Pakenhams were guests, Molly and her mother were sometimes present: 'I must have heard the story of his death twenty times if I heard it once', wrote Pakenham's wife.[22] In the 1930s, Glendalough was a febrile haunt for the young Oxford graduate honing his career.

In 1954 Barton told the Bureau of Military History that 'the most terrific things' were said privately by Griffith and Collins to get him to sign the agreement in London. However, the diary of Erskine Childers—now among the archives of Trinity College Dublin—reveals that on 6 December 1921 Barton told Childers that 'my [Childers's] allusion to Molly's support for refusal to sign last night made him [Barton] sign—*deciding element*—because her name reminded him of thousands of homes to be ransacked'.[23] This is a frank private admission that he signed ultimately for much the same reason as Griffith and Collins did, to avoid further suffering in the circumstances.

Quite what Pakenham's career might become when he wrote *Peace by Ordeal* was uncertain. He was one of a number of persons of Anglo-Irish background who were embedded in the British establishment when they appeared to embrace Irish republican ideals in some form. It may be that they simply recognised the need for change within and beyond the British Empire, as did others who went much further and worked to support the Soviet Union. There is no reason to assume a darker motive, even if some of these persons of Anglo-Irish background are known to have worked for the British intelligence services. Many subjects served their king in that way.

The two leading secretaries on the Irish team negotiating the Anglo-Irish treaty in late 1921 were the Anglo-Irish Erskine Childers and John Smith Chartres. Both Chartres and Childers were employed in gathering intelligence for British government departments immediately before their respective conversions to Irish republicanism. Each helped to run guns to the Irish Volunteers (the emerging 'IRA'). From 1917 Chartres also contributed articles to Arthur Griffith's latest weekly paper, *Nationality*, under the pen-name *Haud Immemor* ('not forgotten').[24] Chartres, born in England to Irish parents, had been employed by the London *Times* before World War I. He became its 'head of intelligence' (news research, indexing and reference) at a time when Edward Grigg worked for *The Times* as head of its colonial department. Grigg later became Lloyd George's private secretary and in 1921 helped his fellow official Lionel Curtis to draft the boundary commission proposal. Childers and Curtis had both attended Haileybury College in Hertfordshire.[25]

During World War II, the historian Nicholas Mansergh became a director of the Empire Division of the Ministry of Information, being its expert on Irish affairs.[26] Early during that war Pakenham himself came to Dublin on a mission from the Ministry of Information. He had been released from entering active military service after he suffered a mental and physical breakdown and was twice admitted to hospital. Officials then approached him and asked him to go to Ireland 'to help secure the Irish involvement in the war and the use of Irish ports'. Pakenham's biographer, Peter Stanford, writes that Pakenham felt uneasy in a role that he himself described as that of 'double agent', given his advocacy for de Valera and the Irish state in England.[27] He cannot have been comfortable on any mission to entice people into a war in which he himself could not or would not fight.

The British historian Hugh Trevor-Roper has written of meeting Frank Pakenham at the Unicorn Restarant in Dublin during World War II when the latter was dining with Frank Gallagher, editor of the *Irish Press* and confidant of de Valera. Trevor-Roper was eating there with John Betjeman, a press attaché at the British Embassy in Dublin, who also acted for the British Ministry of Information (besides being a poet). Pakenham and Betjeman were already close friends. Later that night gardaí raided Trevor-Roper's room in a Dublin hotel. Although they found nothing to suggest that he was active as a British agent in Dublin, he was an officer in MI8, the Radio Security Service, and was permitted to publish results of his investigation for Britain's secret service into Adolf Hitler's last days as a book that was well received. The IRA at one point considered shooting him as a spy. Trevor-Roper's reputation was undone years later when he wrongly identified forged diaries as authentically those of Hitler. His biographer Sisman's curious account of the meeting at the Unicorn Restaurant is open to speculative interpretation.[28]

Peter Stanford has referred to Pakenham's 'long-standing role as unofficial emissary between the British government and the Irish leader' and to the 'many occasions on which he had stayed at the president's residence in Dublin's Phoenix Park'. Stanford regards Pakenham's relationship with de Valera as just 'another case of hero-worship, another larger-than-life man of independent spirit in the mould of F.E. Smith [Lord Birkenhead]'.[29]

Among those whom Pakenham consulted when writing *Peace by Ordeal* was Moya Llewelyn Davies, who had been a friend to Michael Collins in London. Six years after Pakenham's book appeared, she told P.S. O'Hegarty that 'De Valera and Bob Barton superintended every line he wrote. I saw their pencilled comments down every margin of the typescript.' She added that, when she saw this, she ceased co-operating with Pakenham.[30]

The marriage of Frank Pakenham and Elizabeth Harman at St Margaret's Church, Westminster, on 3 November 1931: 'twelve tall bridesmaids' followed the bride, including Miss Dorothy Chamberlain and Miss Christina Chamberlain. Their best man was the son of Lord Chancellor Birkenhead (*Irish Times*, 4 Nov. 1931; *Cork Examiner*, 6 Nov. 1931).

25

SECRET ASSENT?— 'DAMNABLE LIE!'

In 1935 Frank Pakenham alleged that Arthur Griffith was duped into making 'startling and secret concessions' to Lloyd George.[1] Pakenham's book (*Peace by Ordeal*) enshrined assertions that were being circulated almost as soon as the ink was dry on the agreement signed in London in 1921. As the debate over the proposed treaty grew increasingly bitter, Griffith had responded angrily in Dáil Éireann on 10 January 1922:

> 'I protest against the misrepresentation that I was a man who pledged his word to something. The Deputy for Wexford [Seán Etchingham] also charged me with something—he intended to convey to the Irish people that I, in some way, connived with Lloyd George. That is a damnable lie and he knows it.'

Pakenham's account of the Anglo-Irish treaty talks in London has continued to dominate the narrative of what happened in 1921 and subsequently. Frequently praised by historians, not least for its fluidity, it has lost its charm for the present author, who was once amongst those impressed by its confidence and style. It is challenged robustly and at length below, where the author greatly elaborates the argument found more briefly in his short book *Midnight in London: The Anglo-Irish Treaty Crisis 1921* (Eastwood,

2021). Here full academic referencing and new sources are now added, and the specific matter is teased out in detail because so much of how we understand the fundamental nature of the Irish state depends on understanding Griffith's leadership of the treaty delegates.

The damning of Griffith has helped to frame the treaty as a disappointment instead of understanding the agreement as the fruit of years of struggle and a considerable achievement on the back of a stalled and weakening War of Independence. Negative framing of the negotiations in London was to give retrospective cover to those who defied the acceptance of the treaty by the majority of TDs and citizens and who took up arms against Dáil Éireann. It also helped to distance the Free State government and later Fine Gael from aspects of the treaty, as the dead Collins and Griffith could be held responsible for not having done better than de Valera claimed that he would have done had they not signed in 1921. Failure to distinguish carefully between different 'assurances' to which records refer, to attend to the exact sequencing of meetings and correspondence and to identify clearly what Griffith told de Valera promptly about discussions with Lloyd George and other British negotiators have all contributed to the lasting impact of Pakenham's 1935 version of what happened.

The interpretation of events in London on the weekend of 12–13 November 1921 is crucial to any understanding of the continuing negotiations that resulted the following month in an agreement for a treaty leading to the foundation of the Irish Free State. It is thus also central to the negative narrative about Griffith.

The idea that something significantly better might have been wrung from the British in respect of the status of Ireland as either a dominion or a republic—the key issue for de Valera at the time, along with the oath required of members of Dáil Éireann—not only fuelled a destructive civil war that helped to render the boundary commission ineffective but also still underpins the notion that there was some kind of moral equivalence between a government approved by both Dáil Éireann and its voters on one side and an insurrectionist rump on the other that rejected the majority opinion and tried to seize power at gunpoint. De Valera's rhetoric, as a kind of high priest of republicanism, was a rationale for further rebellion. As a youth he had told the Blackrock College debating society that 'constant elections disturb a nation and are thus not conducive to the prosperity of the people'. He thought then that 'there is no rule so tyrannical as that of them all', and his view seems not to have changed much even when he later professed republicanism, for he famously asserted in 1922 that 'The people had never a right to do wrong'.[2] This sentiment was philosophically sound but democratically suspect.

In such a polarised historical context especially it is crucial to examine a certain key memorandum referencing the proposed boundary commission that was enshrined in the treaty. Prime Minister Lloyd George dramatically flourished the text of part of this memorandum during final negotiations on the night of 5–6 December in what Erskine Childers called 'a strange episode'. Lloyd George reportedly claimed that Arthur Griffith had agreed to its contents. Griffith had not.

The present author strongly refutes suggestions that Arthur Griffith signed or agreed unconditionally to the boundary commission proposal when it was shown to him in November 1921, and that he thus weakened the Irish negotiating position. There is no evidence that the document flourished by Lloyd George supported such suggestions. There is a document, found by the present author among Lloyd George's papers—and quite possibly the very one flourished by the prime minister because it includes text that the

Irish plenipotentiary Robert Barton quoted from the latter—that in fact supports a more sanguine interpretation of what occurred, especially when one pays close attention to the details of other contemporary sources.

The substance of the detailed and referenced argument below was first submitted to a leading Irish history journal for publication. That journal's reader's report on the submission found it 'interesting, persuasive and well-researched', but the proposed article was rejected for publication. The reason given was that the key argument was said to have been 'strongly stated' and already 'out there' in the author's *Midnight in London*. However, the entire footnote apparatus below is not found in that short book, and further relevant information has also been discovered. The referenced elaboration that appears here challenges historians to stop relying on Pakenham and on other writers who rely only on Pakenham as their source.

The author is grateful to John Dorney for having published a version of this argument on his website *The Irish Story*, a lively and worthwhile forum for ideas.

THAT KEY DOCUMENT

A key document in the historiography and mythology of the Anglo-Irish treaty and its associated troubles was laid on the table at Downing Street on the last night of negotiations for a treaty agreement, 5–6 December 1921. In what Erskine Childers next day called a 'strange episode',[3] Prime Minister Lloyd George placed it there. In doing so, Lloyd George appears to have confused the Irish delegates. So far as the present author is aware, the nature of that document and its subsequent location had not been identified until the author's

Midnight in London was published in 2021. The text of all or some of the document—as transcribed and included later that day in the typed notes of the Irish delegate Robert Barton TD—has been identified by the present author as being verbatim that on the last page of an extant memorandum found by the author among the Lloyd George papers in the Parliamentary Archives at Westminster. A photograph of that important last page is reproduced later below.[4] The significance of that text and its use in 1921 are examined below, and the conclusion that is reached challenges what the author believes is a dominant but deeply flawed historical narrative of the Anglo-Irish treaty talks. The examination and conclusion will make crucial distinctions between references to that memorandum and to another document which was purported to be a 'letter', and between related or relevant 'assurances' that have frequently been conflated or misunderstood.

According to the dominant narrative of the Anglo-Irish treaty, the British seduced Griffith into betraying Irish republican ambitions by assenting to a scheme that copper-fastened partition and somehow bound or bamboozled his colleagues. As a man of honour—so this version goes—Griffith was unable to undo a broad assurance allegedly given by him on 12–13 November when he was later confronted with it on the last night of treaty talks.

Pakenham embedded a noxious version of events within a broader credible framework, juggling his personal interpretation of documents and actions in order to claim that Griffith fell victim to '*tricks*', that he somehow 'made *startling and secret concessions*' and that he '*indicated his assent*' to 'proposals' in a certain '*paper*' later flourished at the final round of negotiations by Lloyd George (present author's emphasis).[5] These are in fact startling and damning assertions by Pakenham, and I believe that not one of them is well founded. Pakenham based them on what he asserted to have seemed 'a fair reconstruction of Griffith's mental attitude' at the time. It 'seems' that Pakenham satisfied himself that he had guessed correctly what Griffith was thinking.

While one may certainly identify fairly what were from an Irish perspective weaknesses in the agreement for a treaty as signed in 1921, particularly in respect to the possible enforceability of aspects of the boundary commission as understood by Collins and Griffith, the whole cabinet—its members in London and its members who stayed in Dublin—share the blame or responsibility for not identifying and more firmly addressing those weaknesses at the time. They all knew days in advance precisely what that proposal was, as it was included in the draft treaty circulated to the Irish cabinet. The negotiations themselves were conducted in a proper manner until the British threatened war and—as will be demonstrated here—any possible concession that Griffith offered was conditional and strategic and expressly did not bind the other plenipotentiaries, and related to matters that were openly discussed by the Irish cabinet. He successfully resisted pressure from the British to endorse 'proposals' in a paper said to have been shown to him by Jones on 13 November 1921. For Pakenham to claim in 1935, when working closely with de Valera on an account of the treaty, that Griffith had made 'startling and secret concessions' and had assented secretly to proposals ought to have required exact, reliable and incontrovertible sources at the very least. It was effectively to treat Griffith as a traitor or a fool and to blame him for causing a very bitter civil war that was still playing out its effects politically and personally when Pakenham wrote in the 1930s.

So pervasive is the Pakenham narrative that it is easy to forget that Pakenham himself conceded that his account of the vital events of that weekend was speculative and was centrally informed verbally by the former Tory leader Austen Chamberlain, with whom Pakenham's family had personal connections. As seen earlier, Pakenham was working for the Conservative Party when he undertook to write his book and had family ties with both Austen Chamberlain and Lord Birkenhead, who had been senior Tory ministers and two of the British team negotiating the treaty.[6]

The present author here proposes an alternative and less conspiratorial narrative, one that is supported by precise referencing and analysis. Before considering it, the fact that Griffith was reserved, at times to the point of muteness, is worth observing. He was not the type of person who rushed into an affirmation of any proposal. Griffith was quiet and considered—taking Lloyd George by surprise at the opening session by the brevity and restraint of his contribution, for example.[7] Likewise, Thomas Jones, the UK cabinet secretary in 1921, wrote in his diary of the strains emerging during the treaty talks and noted that on 8 November he saw Griffith and Collins at the Grosvenor Hotel in London, where 'Collins was obviously very much upset' but 'it is much harder to tell what Griffith feels about anything as he keeps himself well in hand'. At another point Jones noted privately that Griffith 'is a man of very few words and said very little, and most of the little he did say I had to extract from him'.[8]

Certain 'assurances' that Griffith is known to have given in the course of negotiations, and that were recorded in internal Irish communications as assurances, were carefully qualified and should be clearly distinguished from whatever actual or alleged 'assurance' he gave on 12–13 November. Circumspect then too, as will be demonstrated, he appears to have rebuffed that week a number of efforts by the British to get him to approve in some binding way the substance or text of a proposal for a boundary commission that the British said they were about to put to the government of Northern Ireland.

From an Irish nationalist perspective, that British proposal of early November for a boundary commission remained for Griffith tentative and conditional until the very end, when all five plenipotentiaries felt obliged to sign the agreement under the threat of immediate British war in Ireland. The British soon after 13 November had formally enshrined the proposal in a draft or suggested treaty that was then forwarded to Dublin.[9] The idea or proposal was not a secret that Griffith kept from other delegates in London, or from de Valera or the rest of the Irish inner cabinet. The fact that Erskine Childers—a secretary to the negotiators in London and someone critical of their chairman, Griffith—complained in his private diary at this time that Griffith was not reporting in sufficient detail conversations that Griffith and Collins were having with British negotiators does not alter the fact that the proposal shown to Griffith on 12–13 November was immediately repeated in a letter from Griffith to de Valera and was formally circulated to de Valera and the Irish cabinet in the form of a draft treaty soon afterwards, well before the final session of talks.[10]

Collins and Griffith believed that a boundary commission could deliver counties Fermanagh and Tyrone and other areas of Northern Ireland into the Irish Free State, and from the outset wanted an indication of how the government of Northern Ireland regarded the proposal before the Sinn Féin team in London responded to it as a possible part of a peace settlement. In that respect John Chartres, who had been one of the two principal secretaries to the Irish treaty team, stated in 1924 that he thought that their expectation of progress had been reasonably founded on statements by Lloyd George, at the conference session 'in which the Boundary question in this particular aspect was discussed':[11]

> 'The English delegates were present in full force. The whole of the argument of the Irish delegation, illustrated by a series of careful maps, went to show that there was no question of slight rectification and that the transfer of substantial areas was involved. This position was fully accepted by the English representatives, as indeed appears from one of Mr. Lloyd George's subsequent public speeches. It was only to meet the difficulty of isolated 'islands' as indicated by Mr. Lloyd George himself – e.g. the Nationalist district in the Glens of Antrim – that the limiting words as to economic and geographical considerations were introduced.'

Indeed, at this point in 1924 the Irish Free State supported the construction that Chartres then put on the boundary commission provision by having the Free State's Governor General Tim Healy write to the Colonial Secretary Winston Churchill to press for changes to the border for those persons in Northern Ireland 'whose interests Clause 12, without which the Treaty would never have been accepted was especially designed to protect.' The Irish case in 1924 was gravely weakened by the silencing of Collins and Griffith though death.

The recent Brexit negotiations, with all of their carping and assertions of bad faith, have been an instructive reminder of the difficulties of completing an international deal and of the frequent need to fudge issues to achieve a result—notwithstanding that such fudges leave some problems to fester. The leadership of Griffith and Collins—the two most senior of the five Irish plenipotentiaries in London—in discussing the idea of a boundary commission allowed negotiations to proceed towards a possible agreement, and de Valera did not object to this when informed of it at the time. Griffith and Collins made no secret arrangements and gave no essential or irrevocable assurances in respect of such a boundary commission for Ulster. In the event, as many historians have pointed out, Ulster itself was not a matter of the greatest—or even great—concern to critics of the agreement and was not to feature prominently in the Dáil's treaty debates, where the principal bones of contention were Ireland's membership of the empire or commonwealth and the oath of fidelity to the king.[12]

Arthur Griffith and Lloyd George sat down in London with one overarching purpose, which was to reach agreement. Each had spent his life immersed in politics, and each believed strongly that his respective national electorate wanted a result other than further warfare. Each was assailed by demands for irreconcilable objectives. Breathing down the necks of Chamberlain and his fellow Tory negotiator F.E. Smith (Lord Birkenhead) was the former Tory leader Bonar Law, poised to return to active politics after a period of recuperation and threatening to play 'the Orange card'. While many Sinn Féin TDs in Ireland feared that Lloyd George, who was already nicknamed in Britain 'the Welsh wizard', might outsmart the Irish delegates, Conservative MPs in England had a corresponding concern about Lloyd George. Might he yield too much and so imperil the British Empire?

It is too easily forgotten in Ireland that Lloyd George headed a fragile coalition, in which his Liberal Party was the minority partner with the Conservative and Unionist Party—and in relation to which Tory 'die-hards' were crying betrayal. Unionists on both sides of the Irish Sea were up in arms, some literally so.[13] On another front, the government in London was under immense pressure from organised labour too. Insights into the depths of Lloyd George's political insecurity have been cited earlier, from the UK cabinet secretary's diary for 14, 17 and 21 October. His partners in coalition were distrustful. Many Tories in particular felt that the Irish were taking the British for a ride. Chamberlain himself told Jones on 29 October that, as regards the Irish, 'in my opinion they are just playing with us, just fooling us' and 'he bade me tell the Irish that we were being fooled'. Some Tories saw the discussions as a chance to do down the coalition government in which they participated but which they also resented. As noted earlier, at Waterloo Station on 17 November Lloyd George complained to Jones privately about 'the unfriendly part' that Bonar Law, who would eventually supplant Chamberlain, had played: 'He felt that Bonar had meant to make a bid for the leadership of the Conservatives and a break up of the Coalition'.[14]

Distrust within the British cabinet between Conservatives and Liberals may have been subconsciously exacerbated by English prejudices. There was a whiff of the exotic about Lloyd George's nickname, 'the Welsh Wizard', with its overtones of Celtic twilight. Although born in Manchester, his parents were Welsh and he was brought up in Wales and was regarded as a Welsh nationalist. As an aspiring politician and fiery orator, he is said by Kenneth O. Morgan to have 'made a particular impact in a brilliant performance on a platform in Blaenau Ffestiniog in January 1886 when the main speaker was the Irish nationalist and land leaguer Michael Davitt'.[15] This was not a man with a strong motive to do down Irish constitutional ambitions. He is the only Welsh person or person whose first language was not English to have become prime minister of the United Kingdom. He used to speak Welsh with the cabinet secretary Tom Jones, and his personal secretary claimed that he displayed some knowledge of the Irish language when he met de Valera in London in July 1921.[16] What was Chamberlain thinking, and what might Lloyd George have thought, when at a private meeting of the British negotiators the former supported an instruction to Jones to 'de-floridise' (make less flowery) a particular draft document for the unionists by 'reminding the P.M. that we were now not writing to Celts but to Anglo-Saxons'?[17]

Lloyd George used his 'wizardry' to concede to the Irish the mechanism of a treaty, usually confined to agreements between existing states. Sinn Féin wanted this as a symbolical recognition of Ireland's independence, and it meant that the United Kingdom parliament did not get to debate, amend or stall Irish ambitions in the way that previous efforts to pass a satisfactory Home Rule Act for limited independence had been frustrated. A treaty would be negotiated at cabinet level and presented to parliament for approval, if not quite as a done deal then as something close to one. In her recent examination of Lloyd George's strategy, the senior counsel Bláthna Ruane has described it as 'maverick, opportunistic, legally inconsistent and unprincipled in many respects, but it proved to be a very important element in allowing negotiations to take place and reaching a settlement.'[18]

Considerable internal political strains in the British coalition were caused not least by back-benchers known as 'die-hards', and these strains are very evident from even a cursory reading of British political correspondence and newspapers of the time. Close to midnight on 13 November, Tory leader Austen Chamberlain wrote to his wife that

> 'Over all hangs the cloud of Thursday's speech—in Liverpool, the stronghold of English Orange feeling—and of the afternoon Conference which the Die-hards are working tooth and nail to capture. It will be a very critical meeting and how it will go I cannot foresee. Much depends on how much we can say by that time and one of the horrors of the moment is that I cannot really prepare my speech because the position changes from day to day and almost from hour to hour. Things are moving and I am hopeful. The

> country wants peace. They are tired of Ireland and more tired of Ulster ... I think that the next few days will see the crisis and I hope an accepted peace ... I have staked my political life for what I believe to be right. If we succeed, all men will bless us sooner or later. If we fail, my career will be at an end and many hard things will be said which you will not find easy to hear.'[19]

Chamberlain was told in early November that Bonar Law wanted him to know that 'if you found that the P.M. was tricking and broke away he [Bonar Law] would serve under you'.[20] Whatever about the likelihood or sincerity of that promise of service being fulfilled, the former part of that destabilising message reflects the febrile atmosphere at that time. Unionist and right-wing criticism on a number of fronts would soon undo Lloyd George's coalition, which was to fall during 1922. The Conservative and Unionist Party's withdrawal from government at that point obliged Lloyd George to resign, and the king invited Bonar Law to form a new administration.

OPENING GAMBITS FOR A TREATY

Sinn Féin had comfortably secured a majority of parliamentary seats in Ireland in the United Kingdom general election of December 1918. Its MPs thereupon declined to sit at Westminster and established instead in Ireland the representative assembly known as Dáil Éireann. A guerrilla war of independence ensued until 1921. During 1920, the UK Government of Ireland Act was passed in London. This partitioned Ireland by creating a new border between six northern counties ('Northern Ireland' in which a majority of voters favoured remaining in the United Kingdom) and the remaining twenty-six counties on the island. The majority of voters on the island of Ireland regarded the partition of 1920 as an imposition.[21] Northern Ireland now had its own government. Its new local parliament met for the first time on 7 June 1921, with a cabinet appointed under Sir James Craig. The British were still trying to suppress Sinn Féin and Dáil Éireann south of the border.

In July 1921 a truce was agreed between the British government and Sinn Féin. During the following months the parties to the truce agreed that a peace conference would be held in London with a view to ascertaining 'how the association of Ireland with the community of Nations known as the British Empire may best be reconciled with Irish national aspirations'. This was what Lloyd George dubbed 'the Inverness formula'.[22] It took its name from the Scottish town where in September 1921 the first UK cabinet meeting ever held outside London took place, at a time when peace talks with de Valera might have begun in Scotland but were delayed by convoluted correspondence between de Valera and Lloyd George.[23]

The peace conference that began in London on 11 October was to end in the early hours of 6 December 1921. Dáil Éireann had approved five of its members as plenipotentiaries to negotiate for it, these being, as noted above, Arthur Griffith TD (chairman and minister for foreign affairs), Michael Collins TD (minister for finance), Robert Barton TD (minister for economic affairs), Éamonn Duggan TD and George Gavan Duffy TD. Griffith and Collins were by far the most senior members of the group politically. Griffith had founded the Sinn Féin movement and was not only foreign minister but by this point had served longer than de Valera as president of Dáil Éireann, acting officially in that capacity during de Valera's eighteen months' absence in America for most of the War of Independence. Collins was a national hero who was not only minister for finance but who had a great command of armed republicans in the field and knew their current strengths and weaknesses at least as well as anyone else.

For reasons that are still debated and disputed, the Dáil's president, Éamon de Valera, decided not to be one of the negotiators in London. In the present context, why he did not go is less important than the fact that the Irish head of government was absent while the British prime minister was present.

Negotiations having commenced in London on 11 October, Ulster unionist intransigence loomed large by the first week of November. The Northern Ireland government was not party to the bilateral talks but was never far off-stage. From time to time Lloyd George consulted Sir James Craig, the premier of Northern Ireland, and was now facing a difficult meeting with conservatives and unionists in Liverpool on Thursday 17 November 1921.

Arthur Griffith, under pressure from militant republicans, had yielded the presidency of Sinn Féin to de Valera in 1917 but now found himself despatched by Dáil Éireann to lead its team in London. De Valera insisted from a distance that the British permit part of Ireland to become a republic (or to have 'external association' with the empire, as he put it). Both Griffith and Lloyd George needed to be somewhat flexible, otherwise no deal would be possible and the manifest purpose of the peace conference would be vitiated. Flexibility ought not to be confused with weakness.

When it became clear that Northern Ireland could not be forced into a united Ireland, the two leaders developed an alternative strategy that included the proposed provision of a boundary commission to delimit the existing border in an already divided Ireland—an idea that was familiar at the time within the context of the Treaty of Versailles, which had established commissions to delimit national boundaries after World War I in ways that were still being given effect.[24] The term 'delimit' does not mean simply 'limit' or 'reduce' but rather, as the *Oxford English Dictionary* indicates, the marking or determination of a boundary. Griffith was a keen chess player and in his dealings with the British he moved deliberately, with an eye to the end-game. Whatever the ultimate shortcomings of the boundary commission enshrined in the treaty, his decision not to reject it out of hand in November 1921 made possible a deal on other matters and saved Ireland from a continuation and escalation of the War of Independence. Townshend's reference to the boundary commission proposal as a 'ploy' seems to pass negative judgment on what may also be seen as a useful strategic idea that did not have to end as the actual boundary commission did in practice.[25]

At the request of Arthur Griffith, on 6–7 December 1921 his fellow plenipotentiary Robert Barton made notes of the proceedings of the last sessions of the peace conference on 5–6 December. In his notes Barton included what purported to be a transcription of the key document under consideration here, described by him then as a 'memorandum'.[26] Barton's transcription corresponds verbatim or exactly to the text on a sheet of paper that is among the surviving papers of Lloyd George. The Parliamentary Archives today identify that sheet of paper in their care as the last page of a typed memorandum prepared by Lionel Curtis in early November 1921. A handwritten note at the foot of that last page, signed by the then acting UK cabinet secretary, Thomas Jones, and not by Griffith, states: 'Retyped. Copy shown A.G. Sunday 13.xi.21 [i.e. 13 Nov. 1921]'. The initials 'A.G.' ostensibly signify Arthur Griffith, chairman of the Irish plenipotentiaries.[27] It is not known whether the document that Lloyd George laid on the table in Downing Street was the very sheet in the Parliamentary Archives today or a different sheet with the same words typed on it.

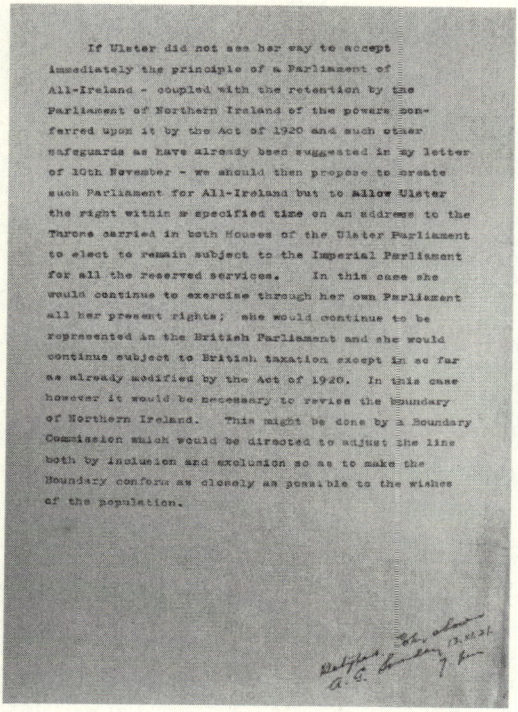

If Ulster did not see her way to accept immediately the principle of a Parliament of All-Ireland - coupled with the retention by the Parliament of Northern Ireland of the powers conferred upon it by the Act of 1920 and such other safeguards as have already been suggested in my letter of 10th November - we should then propose to create such Parliament for All-Ireland but to allow Ulster the right within a specified time on an address to the Throne carried in both Houses of the Ulster Parliament to elect to remain subject to the Imperial Parliament for all the reserved services. In this case she would continue to exercise through her own Parliament all her present rights; she would continue to be represented in the British Parliament and she would continue subject to British taxation except in so far as already modified by the Act of 1920. In this case however it would be necessary to revise the boundary of Northern Ireland. This might be done by a Boundary Commission which would be directed to adjust the line both by inclusion and exclusion so as to make the Boundary conform as closely as possible to the wishes of the population.

From Lionel Curtis, UK secretary to Peace Conference, to Prime Minister Lloyd George, 'Proposals to Ulster', memorandum dated 8 November 1921, p. 14 (courtesy of the Parliamentary Archives, Houses of Parliament, London LG/F/181/4/1). The note at the bottom of the page, handwritten by the UK cabinet secretary Thomas Jones, reads 'Retyped. Copy Shown A.G. Sunday 13.xi.21'. The present author discovered this document among Lloyd George's papers.

In a misleading footnote on page 164 of the published version of Thomas Jones's diary, its editor in 1971 insisted boldly (without there being any support for his contention within the contents of the diary itself and without him giving any source other than Pakenham's unreliable *Peace by Ordeal*) that 'there is no doubt that Griffith approved' this document, which Griffith was ostensibly shown by Jones on Sunday 13 November. The editorial footnote actually refers to and concerns in practice only the content of one of the passages of his commentary that the editor there interposed in italics in Jones's diary. That interposition itself entirely depends or relies on Pakenham for its content, is not supported by any entry in the diary and is—as will be seen—quite confused in a number of ways. The editor also does not distinguish between the full Curtis memorandum and the last retyped page of it, stating that 'the memorandum is printed in Pakenham', when in fact Pakenham merely quotes Barton's transcription of the last page of the memorandum and does not identify the original document.[28] Here and elsewhere the editor of the cabinet diary appears to have relied unduly on Pakenham's book and gone beyond the bounds or contents of the diaries that he was employed to edit.

The present author rejects that editor's assertion that 'there is no doubt that Griffith approved' the document. On the contrary, the present author finds no evidence that he approved it and does find evidence that he did *not* do so. The editor in his footnote and elsewhere has explicitly, like many other writers, relied solely on Pakenham's version of the treaty negotiations, published in London in 1935. It is one of the more egregious examples of how Pakenham's version has fuelled a narrative by a succession of writers who represent Griffith as 'approving' or even 'signing' the document or 'proposition', or 'secretly' assenting to it, or even writing a 'letter' of assent or assurance to Lloyd George concerning the specific proposal in the text reportedly shown to Griffith by Jones.

Such versions lend themselves to the polemics of those who opposed the Anglo-Irish treaty or disliked Griffith and are liable to distort public understanding of what occurred and of what the plenipotentiaries achieved. In attempting to identify exactly what is known about the document and its content, and in distinguishing this from potent interpretations of it, it will be necessary to quote at some length from some relevant contemporary sources that are glossed over at the historian's peril.

The typed wording on the sheet that is the final page of the Curtis memo in the Parliamentary Archives corresponds exactly to the text of the transcription by Robert Barton in his notes of the document waved by Lloyd George at the final talks in London. It is typed out line by line on that sheet in the archives as follows:

> 'If Ulster did not see her way to accept immediately the principle of a Parliament of All-Ireland—coupled with the retention by the Parliament of Northern Ireland of the powers conferred upon it by the Act of 1920 and such other safeguards as have already been suggested in my letter of 10th November—we should then propose to create such Parliament for All-Ireland but to allow Ulster the right within a specified time on an address to the Throne carried in both houses of the Ulster Parliament to elect to remain subject to the Imperial Parliament for all the reserved services. In this case she would continue to exercise through her own Parliament all her present rights; she would continue to be represented in the British Parliament and she would continue subject to British taxation except in so far as already modified by the Act of 1920. In this case however it would be necessary to revise the boundary of Northern Ireland. This might be done by a Boundary Commission which would be directed to adjust the line both by inclusion and exclusion so as to make the Boundary conform as closely as possible to the wishes of the population.'[29]

This wording set the scene for how the existing Irish border 'might' (last sentence) be altered by a boundary commission. The Anglo-Irish treaty was to include provision for such a commission.

A LITTLE BACKGROUND

The British were insisting that all of Ireland must remain in the British Empire (an association of countries dominated by Britain but gradually becoming known as the commonwealth). The Irish negotiators were seeking not only an independent state but also both an adjustment of the Irish border that had been created by the UK Government of Ireland Act 1920 and recognition of the 'essential unity' of Ireland by way of some form of all-Ireland arrangement in which a reduced Northern Ireland would participate. The British were contemplating a scenario in which the unionists could retain, within a unified but independent constitutional arrangement or dominion consisting of the entire island of Ireland, considerable powers of devolved government similar to those they already now had in Northern Ireland from the British under the existing provisions of the Government of Ireland Act 1920. For his part, the president of Sinn Féin and of Dáil Éireann, Éamon de Valera, had already made a remarkable and seldom-noted concession at a private session of Dáil Éireann, giving counties the right to vote themselves out of an Irish republic.[30] His words did not mean that Sinn Féin accepted the existing border as a basis for any final settlement, for it was clear from the general election of 1918 that both Tyrone and Fermanagh had nationalist majorities. The plenipotentiaries in London wanted these two counties and other areas of Northern Ireland to be included ultimately in any independent Irish state.

Lloyd George was surprised that de Valera had not pressed the issue of Ulster when the two men had met alone in London in July 1921 for talks about possible peace negotiations. Lloyd George told his cabinet: 'I was greatly relieved to go through the conversations with him without Tyrone and Fermanagh being raised. He was an unskilful negotiator but you cannot always count on his being maladroit.' The prime minister added that, if Britain were to give in and yield too much, 'It will give the impression that we have lost our grip, that the Empire has no further force and will have an effect in India and throughout Europe'. He thought that 'without acceptance of Throne and Empire you march into the bog'. He predicted how a conversation might go at future peace talks (assuming then that de Valera personally would attend them):

> 'He says—"What about Tyrone and Fermanagh?"
>
> Shall I say—"Tyrone and Fermanagh are already in the Northern area?"
>
> De Valera says—"What about your representative principle?"
>
> De Valera will talk about Tyrone and Fermanagh and the break will come on forcing these two counties against their will. Men will die for the Throne and Empire. I do not know who will die for Tyrone and Fermanagh. The feeling for Ulster is not as strong as in 1913/14. Lots feel a bit annoyed about Ulster, think them unreasonable, narrow. You will divide the nation [...] you may get a majority against you.'[31]

In saying that 'lots' of people 'feel a bit annoyed about Ulster, think them unreasonable and narrow', Lloyd George was expressing a frustration that—according to Jones—was soon to be echoed within the cabinet itself by the Tory leader Austen Chamberlain, as Ulster unionists made further demands.[32]

THE CURTIS MEMO

On 8 November 1921 Lionel Curtis, a United Kingdom secretary to the Anglo-Irish Peace Conference and a key figure in the treaty's development, sent Lloyd George a draft of 'proposals to Ulster'. In a cover note, Curtis told Lloyd George that the draft 'has been hastily written as a basis for further instructions'. It had been discussed with Thomas Jones and Sir Edward Grigg, 'and the result of these discussions is shewn in the written corrections and marginal notes'.[33]

The first thirteen pages of the Curtis memorandum in the parliamentary archives are numbered, with handwritten corrections or observations on most of those pages. The last page of the memorandum is unnumbered and includes the note signed by Jones stating that he showed it to Griffith on 13 November.[34] This page contained the proposal that included the possibility of a boundary commission, the very text that was to be waved by Lloyd George at the final talks in 5–6 December 1921. It is not clear when this page was 'retyped' (as Jones noted on it that it had been), or to what extent it may differ from an earlier version—a version that may have been marked with similar 'written corrections and marginal notes' similar to those on the other pages of the Curtis memorandum. Nor is it known when the 'retyped' final page was added to the original memo. Jones's note on it may or may not refer only to the page of the memo on which it is written.

On the day that Curtis sent his memorandum to Lloyd George, and again later that week, the prospects of a boundary commission were discussed in some depth with three members of the Irish negotiating team. The idea of a commission had only been mentioned in broad terms earlier in the negotiations.[35]

It is important to note in the present context that Arthur Griffith now responded to this idea by repeatedly putting it on record that he had said to the British that the proposal in the memorandum was a British one and that he would not be a party to it. He so recorded this in letters to de Valera that survive.[36] That it was actually his attitude is corroborated by the UK cabinet secretary Thomas Jones in contemporary entries in his diary that remained unpublished for fifty years.[37]

Moreover, the note by Jones on the last page of the memo does not assert that Griffith had agreed or assented to anything, and the page is neither signed nor initialled by Griffith. It seems very likely that Jones would have noted on the page or in his diary any assent by Griffith to the proposal in the memo. The fact that Griffith did not write to tell de Valera of being (reportedly) shown the text of this part of the memo does not indicate that he 'unwittingly assented' to it.[38] Griffith certainly communicated promptly to de Valera the British ideas contained within it, for on 8 November he reported to de Valera that the British were proposing a boundary commission 'to delimit "Ulster", confining this Ulster to its existing powers. This would give us most of Tyrone, Fermanagh, and part of Armagh, Down, etc.' Griffith added: 'We did not give any definite opinion on the matter. It is their look-out for the moment.' That remained his position on subsequent days that week.

On 9 November, accompanied by Éamonn Duggan TD, Griffith again told Jones (as quoted by Jones privately in his cabinet diary): 'It is not our proposal, but if the Prime Minister cares to make it we would not make his position impossible. We cannot give him a pledge but we will not turn him down on it. We are not going to queer his pitch. We would prefer a plebiscite [where people could simply vote by district or county to join the Free State], but in essentials a Boundary Commission is very much the same. It would have to be not for Tyrone and Fermanagh only but for the six counties.'[39] There is corroboration of this in a letter that Griffith wrote to de Valera that evening to brief him once more: 'Lloyd George proposes … that a Boundary Commission to delimit the six-county area be established so as to give us the districts in which we are a majority'. Jones 'asked us did we think the "Ulstermen" would accept this proposal. We said we were quite sure they would not. He said that was his own opinion. The move was a tactical one to deprive "Ulster" of support in England by showing it was utterly unreasonable in insisting to coerce areas that wished to get out. He asked us would we stand behind such a proposal. We said that it would be their proposal—not ours, and we would not, therefore, be bound by it but we realised the value as a tactical manoeuvre and if Lloyd George made it we would not queer his position. He was satisfied with this.'[40]

Griffith and Collins hoped that the proposal would induce Northern Ireland to negotiate a united Ireland. They thought that, if it did not, then at least Northern Ireland would be reduced in size and might before long prove to be unviable outside a united Ireland.[41] They were mistaken in believing that a boundary commission would necessarily be 'very much the same' as a plebiscite of all voters in an area. De Valera displayed no interest in such details.

On the evening of 9 November, according to Jones himself, Lloyd George surprised his cabinet secretary by telling Jones that a boundary commission would be in fact for the nine counties of Ulster. This meant that it could also permit some unionist districts of the proposed Irish Free State to opt into Northern Ireland. Jones added: 'I told him that I certainly had not made that clear. That I had spoken of six counties.' It was an important distinction.[42]

De Valera had been slow to respond to recent developments as reported to him by Griffith and now bundled his reaction to some of Griffith's letters into one very short memo of 9 November, in which he acknowledged receipt of the last six of Griffith's letters (dated 27 and 31 October, 1, 3, 5 and 8 November). He went on in the same memo to compliment the delegation on 'admirably' managing to focus attention on Ulster intransigence rather than on the questions of Ireland's continuing relationship to Empire and Crown. However, he cautioned somewhat ambiguously that 'The danger now is that we should be tempted, in order to put them more hopelessly in the wrong, to make further advances on our side. I think, as far as the "Crown and Empire connection" is concerned, we should not budge a single inch from the point where the negotiations have now led us.'[43] This indicates that de Valera at this point was more concerned about the status of an independent state than about the Irish border.

It is difficult to discern de Valera's precise meaning, but this could be read as his being willing to 'budge an inch' as far as Ulster was concerned, in respect of which it should be remembered that he had in Dáil Éireann on 22 August 1921 eschewed violence and stated that he favoured 'giving each county power to vote itself out of Republic if it so wishes'. So why did he make no explicit reference to the boundary commission idea when he replied to Griffith on 9 November? Pakenham holds Griffith responsible, because (writes Pakenham) Griffith 'made this issue seem secondary', and also—'the slowest of us can see it now' —Lloyd George 'rammed home a tiny advantage' for which Jones opened the door during the previous week.[44] Not only was Griffith duped but also he had in turn failed de Valera. It's obvious to Pakenham, but he fails to explain how so, or why de Valera was not replying promptly to every letter from Griffith or why he left Dublin for the west of Ireland as the talks reached their climax

On 10 November, about noon, Jones told Éamonn Duggan to tell Griffith that in the prime minister's mind 'a Boundary

Commission should apply not to the 6 Counties only but to the 9 Counties of Ulster'.[45] It is not known whether Duggan did so.[46] It was also on 10 November that Lloyd George wrote formally and significantly to James Craig, setting out the nature of 'the settlement towards which His Majesty's Ministers have been working' and which he said was 'closely based' on the proposals made to de Valera on 20 July 1921, comprising the following main principles: Ireland would give her allegiance to the Crown and be a member of the Empire; provision would be made for UK naval security; Northern Ireland would retain all of its devolved powers (and its parliament) under the Government of Ireland Act 1920—but 'the unity of Ireland would be recognised by the establishment of an all-Ireland Parliament' and it would be under that parliament rather than Westminster that Northern Ireland would henceforth enjoy its devolved powers.[47] It is important to recognise that this is the context within which the discussion about the boundary commission that Griffith reported to de Valera had taken place on 9 November, with it being seen within an all-Ireland framework at this point.

On the afternoon of Friday 11 November Griffith met Jones, at the latter's request, at the Grosvenor Hotel. Jones showed him a brief reply from Craig that had just been received. It ruled out discussing the British proposals so long as the suggestion of an all-Ireland parliament remained on the table. A more detailed response was expected. Griffith now wrote a report for de Valera stating that Lloyd George evidently believed that 'the Ulsterites are being gingered up' so that at the meeting of the National Conservative Association scheduled to take place in Liverpool on the following Thursday (17 November) the government's strategy would be rejected. Griffith concluded: 'The "Ulster" crowd are in the pit they digged for us, and if we keep them there, we'll have England and the Dominions out against them in the next week or two'.[48]

Later on that same day, 11 November, Craig wrote a longer reply to Lloyd George.[49] It was a comprehensive rebuff and added to Lloyd George's difficulties—not least in respect of the upcoming meeting in Liverpool. Craig expressed 'considerable concern' that the area of Northern Ireland was being treated as open to possible revision. He rejected, out of hand 'under existing circumstances', participation in an all-Ireland parliament and demanded that the proposal be withdrawn. And, in a suggestion that irritated many British ministers, he proposed that Northern Ireland itself could become a Dominion, even if that meant losing representation in the UK parliament. Such a change might also reduce the burden of taxation in Northern Ireland, at a cost to the UK exchequer and at no benefit to Lloyd George's efforts to reach an Irish settlement.

At 9.45 a.m. on Saturday 12 November Thomas Jones sent Craig's full reply out by taxi to British negotiators. Far from feeling that he had Griffith in the bag, Jones was worried. Less than an hour later, Jones took a taxi to 22 Hans Place, headquarters of the Irish delegation,

> 'where I saw Arthur Griffith alone, showed him a copy of Craig's reply, drawing his special attention to the closing pages. He was pleased to see that the cloven hoof of Ulster's sordidness had shown itself in their willingness to forego representation at Westminster for the sake of lower income tax. I said that if Sinn Féin cooperated with the P.M. we might have Ulster in before many months had passed.'

Jones then proceeded to a meeting of British ministers at 10 Downing Street, where even the Tory leader Chamberlain (according to Jones) was now impatient with the Ulster unionists. The latter reportedly said, as Jones noted in his diary,

> 'If the correspondence were published … there would be a great revulsion of feeling against Ulster. Hitherto they had always wanted to be full members of the U.K. They now actually ask for Dominion status. This will come as a shock to those accustomed to receive their passionate assurances of union. They have put themselves very much in the wrong. The P.M. agreed that the Reply was a fatal document for Ulster …'[50]

The reply from Craig was not, in fact, to prove at all 'fatal' for the Ulster unionists.

The entry in Jones's published diary for this particular date ends with Churchill standing by a fireplace in Downing Street, where 'he soliloquized aloud about mediaeval hatreds and barbarous passions which brought men to the stake, still rampant in Ulster'.

The next diary entry by Jones will be dated Monday 14 November. However, the editor of the cabinet diary indicates that after the cabinet meeting ended on 12 November Lloyd George went to meet Arthur Griffith for a late lunch at the fine London house of Sir Philip Sassoon, member of parliament for Hythe in Kent and a parliamentary private secretary to the prime minister. Precisely how that day and the next unfolded is unclear, but it is at the nub of the dominant narrative of events.

AN ASSURANCE

According to Griffith himself, he now gave Lloyd George an assurance. It is very important, however, to be clear that Griffith said that this assurance on 12 November was simply that he would not repudiate publicly the outline proposal on a boundary commission that Lloyd George was about to put to the unionists of Northern Ireland when responding to Craig's rebuff. Griffith thus acknowledged the existing fact of partition but not its principle, which was no more than de Valera himself had already done in the Dáil. There is no evidence that Griffith gave any other assurance to Lloyd George that day, and in a vital letter immediately after the meeting with the British prime minister Griffith himself informed de Valera that he had scrupulously avoided doing so. Griffith wrote as follows, in a letter marked 'very secret' that deserves careful attention:

> 'He showed me the letter the British Cabinet sent to the "Ulster" Ministers [see 10 November above] and their reply [see 11 November above].
>
> The British letter was to the effect that as they considered they could arrange with us on the points of difference (this is not the phrasing; I had only a hurried reading of it, but the effect) Ulster should come in under an All-Ireland Parliament, their present powers as a subordinate legislature being retained—(the area[51] was left open for a possible reconsideration). In the alternative the Ulstermen were told that if they refused this and insisted on being represented in the British Parliament, their area would be delimited[52] and the part that desired to remain in the British Parliament would have to bear the same taxation as England.
>
> The "Ulster" reply was a voluminous one—4 pages about Loyalty, the Crown, the Empire and representation in the British Parliament—things they would never give up, and never under any consideration come under an All-Ireland Parliament. Then—the climax. They proposed "Ulster" should be formed into a Dominion and pay none except a voluntary contribution to England.

This reply has simply astounded all the principal members of the Cabinet, except Lloyd George. Even Bonar Law, they say, is a bit knocked out by it. Lord Derby on the ground of this reply offers to go to Liverpool to the Unionist Conference to speak against the Ulster crowd if they don't retract.

This meeting on Thursday is a critical one for the Unionist leaders—as it will be a fight between the Die-hards and themselves, who are mustering all their forces for the occasion.

Lloyd George and his colleagues are sending a further reply to the Ulstermen—refusing their Dominion proposal, but offering to create an All-Ireland Parliament, Ulster to have the right to vote itself out within 12 months, but if it does a Boundary Commission to be set up to delimit the area, and the part that remains after the Commission has acted to be subject to equal financial burdens with England.

Lloyd George intimated this would be their last word to Ulster. If they refused, as he believed they would, he would fight, summon Parliament, appeal to it against Ulster, dissolve, or pass an Act establishing the All-Ireland Parliament.

I told him it was his proposal, not ours. He agreed, but he said that when they were fighting next Thursday with the Die-hards and "Ulster" in front, they were lost if we cut the ground away behind them by repudiating the proposal.

I said we would not do that, if he meant that he thought we would come out in public decrying it. It was his own proposal. If the Ulstermen accepted it, we would have to discuss it with him in the privacy of the Conference. I could not guarantee its acceptance, as, of course, my colleagues knew nothing of it yet. *But I would guarantee that while he was fighting the "Ulster" crowd we would not help them by repudiating him* [emphasis added].

> This satisfied him. They are to send this letter on Monday [14 November]. Birkenhead, Chamberlain, and Derby will go to the Liverpool Unionist Convention, and if the "Ulstermen" refuse, start in on "Ulster". Until after that there is not likely to be much development.
>
> Before I left I told him that as I was helping him over the "Ulster" difficulty, he should help us over "the Crown and Empire", when it came up.
>
> He is most anxious it should not be known that we met, for the reason that the "Ulster" crowd and the *Morning Post* would, before the Thursday meeting, raise the cry that he was "conspiring" with me against "Ulster". So please confine this strictly to the Inner Cabinet.'[53]

Thus it is evident from this letter of 12 November 1922 that Griffith told de Valera that he had assured Lloyd George only of silence and inaction in respect of Lloyd George's proposal to the unionists, pending the meeting in Liverpool. In confining the information to de Valera and the inner cabinet, he may have kept it back from the two plenipotentiaries who were not government ministers, and from Childers, whom he found unhelpful, but in any event he clearly was not keeping it 'secret' from de Valera.

It appears that while Griffith was meeting David Lloyd George that day Frances Stevenson was waiting upstairs. She was Lloyd George's secretary and lover. She wrote in her diary:

> 'D. [David] & I went down to Trent for the weekend. But D. first of all went to Philip Sassoon's house in Park Lane for lunch, & got Arthur Griffith along to have a serious talk with him so that he might know exactly where he was. The Ulster people had definitely refused the terms in the morning—refusing even to come into a dis-

> cussion so long as it involved a question of an All I. P. [All-Ireland Parliament]. D therefore wanted to decide on his next move, for he is determined to pull this thing through. I do not think I have ever seen D so excited about anything before. He talked to A.G. [Griffith] for a long time, & D came up from below very jubilant—but very excited & said that A.G. would agree to his new scheme, & that the Ulster people would be "done in". Then F.E. [F.E. Smith, Lord Birkenhead] & Chamberlain came along & they talked over the form in which it was to be drafted, and eventually we went off to Trent, arriving in time for dinner ... D says that if the Ulster men accept they will do so in the hope that the S.F.s [Sinn Féiners] would refuse it. They (the Ulstermen) are quite ignorant of the fact that the S.F.s have already agreed. It is a very subtle plan & I hope it will not have any hitch.'[54]

What exactly happened after Griffith left Lloyd George that weekend is unclear, but Frank Pakenham was to suggest in 1935 that it involved a successful conspiracy to entrap Griffith into a concession. However, a letter that Chamberlain sent to his wife in Madrid that same day is more ambiguous than what he ostensibly gave Pakenham to understand more than a decade later, for Chamberlain wrote on that weekend in 1921 that

> 'Ulster has point blank refused even to meet us in conference on any plans for definitely and finally including her in an all-Ireland Parliament. We have an alternative which fulfils our pledges, which Ulster must I believe accept and—most important of all—which we have reason to know S.F. [Sinn Féin] will accept. But this last fact is at this moment known only to the P.M. [Prime Minister], F.E. and me ... And so we move forward secretly whilst the storm rages all around us and F.E. [Smith, Lord Birkenhead] and I are

> denounced as traitors and called all the hard names in the language ... I think that the next few days will see the crisis and I hope an accepted peace ... Griffith realises that we are staking everything on our attempt to make peace and I have by now an assured confidence that he will do his part and not let us down on that side.'[55]

Thus Stevenson writes that Lloyd George came upstairs from the meeting and 'said that A.G. *would* agree to his new scheme', while Chamberlain writes that he and Birkenhead 'have reason to know S.F. *will* accept' the alternative proposal, presumably that of a boundary commission (emphasis on 'would' and 'will' added here). Neither indicates that Griffith had actually agreed to the scheme, still less agreed unconditionally without reference to what the Irish demanded on Crown and Empire and expected concerning a boundary commission. There is ample evidence that the British were subsequently frustrated a number of times in pinning down any of the Irish delegates, a clear indication that no final deal had been done. For example, Chamberlain wrote to his wife on 23 November 1921: 'we have been on the verge of a break with S.F. [Sinn Féin]. They are not very clever and some of them are very stupid. I think we shall yet pull it off, but heaven save me from such another negotiation.'[56] He later wrote that even on the last day of negotiations 'we seemed as far from agreement as ever; indeed the prospect of an agreement seemed to have receded since we last met. All the old questions were reopened; the Irish delegates appeared to have gone back on the decisions already reached.'[57] A strong indication that nothing had been firmly agreed or sewn up in advance is that Chamberlain and his cabinet colleagues then found it advisable on 5–6 December to issue their infamous ultimatum to the plenipotentiaries.

GRIFFITH SEES BUT DOES NOT SIGN

Thomas Jones wrote that on 13 November (the day *after* Lloyd George had met Griffith on his own in Philip Sassoon's house) he himself met Griffith and showed him the text of what is found on the fourteenth page of the Curtis memo dated 8 November 1921. Some historians suggest that Griffith merely glanced at the document (implying carelessness), but there is no evidence of how much attention he paid to its contents. Jones nowhere suggests that Griffith assented to any proposal in the memo or initialled or signed it. The simplest explanation for why Jones let Griffith see it was that he wished to avoid any misunderstanding about what Lloyd George was proposing to Craig.

At some point on 12–14 November officials prepared two drafts of Lloyd George's planned next letter to Craig. Each version included the text concerning a boundary commission that Jones said that he showed Griffith on 13 November,[58] but the actual letter sent to Craig on 14 November did *not* in the end include this. In a letter to de Valera on 15 November, Griffith wrote about this change that

> 'M [Michael Collins] and myself met Lloyd George this evening.
>
> The answer he sent Craig was not as he first arranged. It was that the British Government would not consent to setting up "Ulster" as a Dominion, but that it was willing to meet the Ulstermen in Conference. The second part of their reply [re a boundary commission] they are keeping until after Thursday's meeting. To put it up then as an ultimatum to "Ulster".'[59]

Gallagher later represented Lloyd George as having thus omitted the text concerning a boundary commission because it 'might stiffen that meeting [in Liverpool] against a settlement'. It is a fair supposition, although it is not one explicitly supported by Griffith's letter.[60]

Nevertheless, the general proposal in the text that Jones showed Griffith on 13 November, namely that for a boundary commission, was thereafter firmed up as part of the British draft for a treaty and was delivered on 30 November to the Irish plenipotentiaries in London, whence it also went to members of the Irish cabinet in Dublin. That draft was to be debated by the Irish cabinet in Dublin on 3 December and by the two sides in London on 5–6 December. The Irish were not bound to accept it. In fact, with de Valera pressing Griffith to reiterate in various forms the absolute Sinn Féin desire for a republic, for a state only 'externally' connected to the commonwealth and having no direct link to the Crown, the British felt blocked. On 22 November Jones attended a UK cabinet meeting and listened 'in complete silence' as various ministers expressed their frustrations 'with great vehemence'. Chamberlain said that he would not have gone to Liverpool and made the speech he did about the peace negotiations had he known the sort of position that the Sinn Féiners were to continue taking.[61] Leaving this agitated meeting, Jones went to Hans Place, where he met Griffith and Collins and told them that Lloyd George was 'in despair' about Sinn Féin's attitude. Griffith reported to de Valera:

> 'In the course of the conversation I suggested the British Government was trying to get a blank cheque from us—a thing that would play Craig's game. Jones was taken aback at this view which he denied. It is really not my view, however, that they are doing so. They hoped to meet Craig on Thursday under an agreement with us that would enable them to defy him and his backers.

> Owing to the crux over the Crown and Empire, they feel their position weakened if not gone.'

Here Griffith is explicitly pointing to the conditionality of any arrangement concerning Ulster, which for the Irish was dependent on a deal over Crown and Empire. He continued:

> 'Mr Collins, Mr Barton, and myself have arranged to meet Lloyd George and Birkenhead and possibly Chamberlain at 10, Downing Street to-morrow [23 November]. We shall argue the acceptability of the arrangement re Association we have proposed [i.e. that Ireland not be in the Empire/Commonwealth but still somehow externally associated with it], but I have little hope of any good result. If the conversation fails, I presume Lloyd George will send a letter terminating the negotiations, and to this we shall reply, and then leave London for home, unless you think the time has come for you to cross over here.'[62]

Having met with Griffith and Collins on 22 November, Jones remarked on 'their fear that if they put down all they were prepared to do in black and white in advance, it would be tantamount to giving the P.M. a blank cheque. The P.M. would then go to Craig, tell Craig all that Sinn Féin was prepared to do, Craig would say nothing, yield nothing, but go back to Ulster and announce to all Ireland that the Sinn Féin leaders had sold their followers. Over and over again in the past Irish negotiators had been let down in this way by British statesmen.'[63]

A SIGNIFICANT LETTER

On 23 November Griffith, Collins and Barton met Lloyd George with Chamberlain and Birkenhead at Downing Street as planned. It is important to note that Lloyd George still had not put the boundary commission proposal to Craig (in the form discussed with Arthur Griffith by the prime minister on 12 November). Later that day Griffith reported to de Valera by means of a significant communication that refers precisely to the assurance that Griffith believed he had given to Lloyd George on 12 November ('I would not let him down'), and to the conditional nature of that assurance. He told de Valera:

> 'On Ulster, Lloyd George declared that I had assured him I would not let him down, if he put up the proposals subsequently embodied in their memorandum to Craig, and we had not embodied them in our memorandum [dated London, 22 Nov. 1921 (NAI DE 2/304/1)]. I said I had given him that assurance and I now repeated it, but I told him at the time it was his proposal—not ours. Therefore, it did not appear in our document. Our proposal was, in our opinion, better but it was different. He was satisfied. He had misunderstood us in this instance and said as much. He would put his proposal to Craig from himself only. He would like to consult privately with his colleagues for a few minutes.
>
> They then retired and consulted for a time. On their return Lloyd George said that before he met Craig, he must know where he stood on the fundamentals. If he had to fight on fundamentals, there was no help for it, but it would be a tragedy if we broke up on any verbal or technical misunderstandings. He suggested, therefore, that as myself and Mr Collins had seen Lord Birkenhead before I

> wrote the letter [of 2–3 November, below] on which they had been acting, we should do so again, and go over the document with him.
>
> Lord Birkenhead suggested that we should bring a constitutional lawyer with us. We have arranged to meet him to-morrow at 10.30 and bring Mr Chartres with us. Lloyd George has postponed his interview with Craig until 5 in the evening to await the result, if any, of the meeting.'[64]

That 'letter' on which Lloyd George on 23 November said the British 'had been acting' earlier was one that had been sent by Griffith to the prime minister after careful drafting on 2–3 November 1921. Dated 2 November 1921, it included certain assurances to which all the Irish plenipotentiaries had eventually consented before it was sent, following debate amongst themselves. Griffith had drafted it in consultation with the British, who wanted such a letter, but carefully hedged his assurances by conditions and sent it only in the form of a 'personal assurance', albeit on official notepaper.[65] Griffith and Collins had met Birkenhead alone at the House of Lords on the morning of 2 November to discuss the draft of that letter, and later that same day had met Chamberlain with Birkenhead. The final draft was discussed on the following day (3 November) by Griffith and Collins with Lloyd George, Chamberlain and Birkenhead at Downing Street, and thereafter formally agreed by all five Irish plenipotentiaries and sent.[66] That the letter upon which Lloyd George said the British 'had been acting' was this one dated 2 November 1921 and not the document that Jones is said to have shown Griffith at the Grosvenor Hotel on 13 November is confirmed by Jones himself.[67]

It is necessary for clarity to distinguish Griffith's formal assurances in the official letter that he sent the British on 3 November from the different 'assurance' and 'personal assurances' that he was to mention in letters of 23 November and 4 December to de Valera. On the latter two dates he was referring back to (and only to) the particular promise he had made on 12 November to Lloyd George, which was that he would not oppose publicly for the time being the British government's idea of a boundary commission.

A DRAMATIC FLOURISH

The text that Jones said that he showed to Arthur Griffith on 13 November was flourished unexpectedly by Lloyd George at Downing Street on the last day of negotiations in December 1921. This made a dramatic impact, according to his fellow delegate Robert Barton. Barton wrote next day that Lloyd George claimed that he had shown the piece of paper to Griffith at Philip Sassoon's house (where they had met on 12 November) and that Griffith had 'agreed to its contents'.[68] Yet Chamberlain's version to Pakenham has the Tory leader composing that text only *after* Lloyd George and Griffith left. One must be circumspect in reading Barton's official notes of the final talks on 5–6 December, notes that Pakenham also used to bolster his theory. They are far from entirely lucid and certainly not comprehensive, and Barton was labouring under great personal stress. On 15 December 1921 he told the Dáil of the 'pretty severe' strain and struggle that night and was unable to answer a direct question about it from Kevin O'Higgins, adding that he could not 'swear an oath' that Lloyd George directly addressed him and saying he had given his 'impressions' of the meeting in the short official notes of it that he compiled. He was to claim in 1954 that Griffith and Collins and Duggan said 'the most terrific things' to get him to sign the agreement that night.[69] He did not reveal in that 1954 statement that his close cousin Erskine Childers, who had grown up with him and who was a secretary to the delegation, had also applied pressure on him by invoking his own wife's sentiments to stiffen Barton *against* signing the agreement. Paradoxically, as already observed elsewhere above, this was counterproductive, as Childers admitted in his diary on the day the agreement was signed: 'Privately today R.C.B. [Robert Childers Barton] said that my allusion to Molly's support for refusal to sign last night made him sign—*deciding element*—because her name reminded him of thousands of homes to be ransacked'.[70]

Griffith himself also wrote a report on the final negotiating sessions of 5–6 December, earlier and shorter than Barton's. This has received little attention and, quite remarkably, considering that the chairman of the plenipotentiaries himself wrote it, is not included in the first volume of *Documents on Irish Foreign Policy*. It is now reproduced below in this book. Childers at the time dismissed Griffith's account as 'brief and jejune [i.e. superficial]'[71] but it is not devoid of significance, especially given Barton's confession a few days later that he could not confidently answer a simple question about events such as 'Was it or was it not?'

There are no formal minutes, agreed or otherwise, of the peace negotiations in London, including of the crucial final sessions on 5–6 December. The Irish had decided at the outset in October to dispense with an exact record of proceedings. The penultimate session lasted from approximately 3.00 p.m. until 8.00 p.m. on Monday 5 December and, after a break, the final session ran from 11.15 p.m. on that Monday until 2.20 a.m. on Tuesday 6 December—a combined duration, excluding breaks, of about eight hours. Griffith's official notes are just 450 words long, and those that Barton wrote at Griffith's request are only 2,500 words (taking less than five minutes and twenty minutes respectively to read). Both sides were tired and strained, and the final sessions were fraught. Griffith's note of the sessions begins:

> 'Things were so strenuous and exhausting that the sequence of conversation is not in many cases clear in my mind today [...] The Conference opened with the British Delegates in a bad mood. They had a full Cabinet meeting previously and apparently had had a rough time.' [See appendix for Griffith's full notes as typed up]

Barton's notes state that Lloyd George soon got excited: 'He shook his papers in the air, declared that we were trying deliberately to bring about a break on Ulster because our people in Ireland had refused to come within the Empire and that Arthur Griffith was letting him down where he had promised not to do so.' Notably, Griffith's own notes state:

> 'Lloyd George began by suggesting we had let him down over the Ulster proposals.
>
> *We denied this* [emphasis added here] and argued we must have a reply from Craig refusing or accepting these proposals before we proceeded.
>
> The others [i.e. the British] pointed out that as they were prepared to go ahead with their proposals irrespective of Craig there was no ground for our contention. We went on this line of argument for a while when Lloyd George declared we were trying to bring about a break on Ulster.'

Barton wrote that Lloyd George began by declaring that he must know once and for all exactly where the Irish stood as regards the Ulster proposals, and that Lloyd George claimed that the Ulster proposals that the British had sent to the Irish in a draft agreement the previous week, and that had been discussed on Saturday in Dublin, 'were exactly those to which Arthur Griffith had agreed and on which he had undertaken not to let him down'. According to Barton, Griffith replied 'that he had not let him down and did not intend to do so, but that before he gave a decision on the earlier articles in the document he must have a reply from Craig either accepting or refusing the unity of Ireland'. Collins backed him on this.

Griffith had sought such a clarification of Ulster's response to the boundary commission idea from the outset, as well as repeating the basic Sinn Féin call for unionists to recognise the 'essential' unity of Ireland in some form. Yet both Chamberlain and Lloyd George, wrote Barton, now argued strongly that the demand for a unionist commitment at this stage was 'inadmissible, unreasonable and contrary to the undertaking not to let Lloyd George down'. Barton wrote that Chamberlain claimed that 'it was due to the confidence they had in our undertaking that they would not be let down by us that his colleagues and he had adopted the attitude they did [...] and staked thereon their political future'.

Had Lloyd George actually convinced the Tory negotiators that Griffith gave a more definite or definitive response on the weekend of 12–13 November than is evidently the case from reading both the UK cabinet secretary's diary and Griffith's private correspondence with de Valera? This had been Bonar Law's fear, as was seen above, that Lloyd George was playing Tory ministers along. Or were the British infuriated by Griffith perhaps because they were persuaded by Lord Birkenhead that the boundary commission as formulated would have legal powers far more limited than the Irish understood, and the British had convinced themselves that the Irish were so attracted to it that they would simply accept it without a commitment by Craig and without firming up a good deal in return?[72]

However, the official 'personal assurances' that Griffith had sent to Lloyd George with the knowledge of other delegates and de Valera, on 3 November, and his undertaking of 12 November not to dismiss the boundary commission idea before Craig replied had all been (as seen earlier above) conditional and not absolute. Lloyd George never did secure the response from Craig that Griffith sought, and the failure to make Northern Ireland party to the boundary commission proposal was ultimately one of the reasons why that body failed, becoming mired in privy council litigation among other set-backs.[73]

In his own official notes Griffith made no reference to Lloyd George placing the text of the Curtis memo on the table, but Barton, in the account that he wrote at Griffith's request, noted that Lloyd George

> 'produced a paper from an envelope, stated that he had shown it to Arthur Griffith at —'s [Philip Sassoon's] house and that Arthur Griffith had agreed to its contents. Lloyd George referred to this document as a letter and thereby mystified me and appeared to mystify Michael Collins. I could not recollect the existence of any letter on this subject other than the one Arthur Griffith wrote to Lloyd George on November 2nd after consultation with the other members of the Delegation. The paper was then passed across the table. It proved to be a memorandum, not a letter [Barton quotes it, *verbatim* as given above].'

Did Barton not identify the memo's date or nature precisely because he was only seeing one page of it, the last page as retyped before being shown to Griffith on 13 November? As the session unfolded on 5 December, the British were assailing the Irish with references to Griffith's having given an assurance, without Barton recording—or perhaps knowing—what exactly were the specific assurances, if any, that they had in mind. In the absence of clarity and given what was about to happen at the meeting, the British delegates may ultimately have been intent on overwhelming the Irish. That they then proceeded to issue their military ultimatum suggests that this was so.

This was the moment in the talks to which the priest and professor of history F.X. Martin referred in 1965 when he asked Griffith's biographer Seán Ó Lúing whether Griffith was not 'either vain or rigid so as to be caught by Lloyd George on the point of "honour" in the treaty negotiations—any typical Irishman would have dismissed Lloyd George's objection'.[74] The general influence of Pakenham's work is evident in the fact that F.X. Martin, professor of medieval history at UCD, not only uses but places in inverted commas the word 'honour' that Pakenham earlier deployed in print in this context in order to bolster the theory that Griffith was somehow 'caught' by Lloyd George at this point. That Pakenham purports to recognise Griffith's honour more than once is partly why *Peace by Ordeal* is regarded as balanced, but it is a 'balance' that is outweighed by his suggestion of a secret and done deal. Did de Valera not tell Pakenham that Griffith, on the very day that he met Jones and was shown the document later waved by Lloyd George, sent de Valera an account of the meeting? Did de Valera advise Pakenham of Griffith's statement to Jones concerning certain British proposals on Ulster that (as Griffith had informed de Valera) 'I could not guarantee its acceptance, as, of course, my colleagues knew nothing of it yet. But I would guarantee that while he was fighting the "Ulster" crowd we would not help them by repudiating him'?[75]

Whatever one thinks of a Catholic priest suggesting—even in the role of an intellectual 'devil's advocate'—that a 'typical Irishman' might not be so 'vain or rigid' as to keep his word of honour, Griffith's immediate response to Lloyd George on that last night of talks was in fact ambiguous, as recorded in both Barton's and

Griffith's notes made within hours of the final session, and it was not submissive. Griffith declared his adhesion to an understanding between himself and Lloyd George (no such 'understanding' is contained in the waived memo as quoted by Barton or as found in the House of Lords archive), but at the same time Griffith reasserted the conditional nature of that 'understanding' which had been procedural rather than substantive. Indeed, Pakenham himself actually admits that 'there was no definite promise here [i.e. in this context] that Griffith would assent to the terms mentioned [i.e. proposed in the 'paper' or November 'memorandum'] *before* [Pakenham's italics] Craig had consented or even replied'. This is a concession by Pakenham that deserves greater attention than it has received.

Thus even Pakenham casually admits that Griffith had yet to 'assent' to something to which Pakenham also claimed that Griffith had somehow earlier 'indicated his assent'. That does sound rather like contingent or conditional assent, if it is anything. But the author gets over this difficulty by turning a compliment on its head and writing that Lloyd George knew 'Griffith's passionate self-respect, and his abnormal sensitiveness to any charge that involved his own or his country's honour'.[76] Pakenham might have gone further and pointed out that not only had Griffith been let down by Lloyd George in respect to an answer from Craig, but that Lloyd George turned down repeated requests by Griffith that night to be allowed to refer matters back to the whole cabinet in Dublin while at the same time threatening the Irish with renewed warfare.

Pakenham might also have stressed clearly that if there were any declaration by Griffith of his own personal willingness to accept in good faith the proposed deal on Ulster (provided that it include a boundary commission of the kind he believed would see Tyrone and Fermanagh join the independent Irish state) it was made on the understanding that Lloyd George would have an acceptable response for him from Craig and also on the explicit basis in this particular context of Griffith indicating that all other members of the delegation were free to vote on the proposed agreement as they saw fit. Moreover, it was still necessary for the Irish cabinet and Dáil Éireann to accept any agreement signed in London and to finalise a treaty.

This was the context in which Griffith responded to Lloyd George's histrionics by saying now that he personally would dispense with a reply from Craig but that his colleagues were in a different position and had not been involved in the November discussion with Lloyd George about the proposal, and that 'it was not fair to demand acceptance or refusal from them before Craig replied'. It is a common negotiating ploy that the chairman of one side appears flexible while regretting that the other side must still convince the chair's colleagues who need more concessions in order to be persuaded. Given the level of negative speculation about Griffith in this context, one might allow for once that he was consciously playing a smart game of negotiation.

Lloyd George did not react kindly to Griffith's response. According to Barton, the prime minister said that 'he had always taken it that Arthur Griffith spoke for the Delegation'. If so, there was no basis for such an assumption in respect to a boundary commission, for Griffith had explicitly told Jones that this was not the case. The prime minister also delivered his infamous ultimatum. He argued that 'we were all plenipotentiaries and that it was now a matter of peace or war and we must each of us make up our minds'. Gallagher appears to regret this rather mild and factual version by Barton of Lloyd George's words, for he claims that Barton, in what was his almost contemporary account typed up at Griffith's request, does not quote the prime minister's words 'so exactly as he, Barton, did in his speech in the Dáil before the vote on the treaty' a fortnight later![77] On 19 December 1921 Barton told Dáil Éireann that during final negotiations, 'Speaking for himself and his colleagues, the English Prime Minister with all the solemnity and the power of conviction that he alone, of all men I met, can impart by word and gesture—the vehicles by which the mind of one man oppresses and impresses the mind of another—declared that the signature and recommendation of every member of our delegation was necessary or war would follow immediately. He gave us until 10 o'clock to make up our minds, and it was then about 8.30.'

Chamberlain subsequently wrote in a memoir that in December 1921 Lloyd George threatened war within three days if the Irish did not sign.[78] Both the anti-treaty Gallagher and the Tory Chamberlain had their own reasons for favouring versions that had the British government strongly facing down the Irish who signed the agreement. The former made the negotiators look weak, while the latter made Tory ministers look strong.

SCOTT'S UNRELIABLE VERSION

According to C.P. Scott, newspaperman and confidant of Lloyd George, the prime minister was soon claiming credit for outsmarting Griffith. Lloyd George had asked to see Scott on the morning of Monday 5 December 1921. Lloyd George was 'excited and angry' at the Irish. However, when Scott saw the prime minister again on the next day—about ten hours after the agreement for a treaty had been signed—Lloyd George 'was of course in great spirits'. Scott wrote in his diary that Lloyd George had told him of putting it to Griffith 'whether he could sign on behalf of all the Sinn Féin plenipotentiaries. Griffith said he could not. "Then", said Lloyd George, "I must put it to you individually". He put it to Collins. Collins hesitated and declined. The others declined. There was a moment when Griffith stood alone.' Scott continues:

> 'It was then that Lloyd George played his last card. Some days before (before the debate in the House [of Commons or Lords] on the previous Monday, Lloyd George told me) he had seen Griffith alone—"not here" said Lloyd George with a twinkle, "some way from here"—and had come to a general, informal agreement with him as to the terms on which Griffith would be prepared to settle, and it was only after he had made sure of his ground in this way that George challenged a division in the House. Before they parted George said to Griffith for clearness' sake this had better be put into writing and that was done. George now at the critical moment produced the document. "You signed this", George said, "and, knowing you to be the man you are, I am sure you communicated it afterwards to Mr Collins. He therefore is also a party to it. I have fulfilled my part of the bargain. I took the risk of breaking my party. You in Ireland often bring against us in England the charge of breach of faith." (Griffith, said Lloyd George, seemed a little surprised when the terms were read. So evidently he had not kept a copy himself.) That settled it. An extraordinary example of skill and foresight in negotiation. The words I have quoted stuck in my mind. I think they are almost exact. All signed [the agreement for a treaty].'[79]

There are a number of problems with Scott's version. For one thing, the UK parliament did not sit between 10 November 1921 (when the king's speech was delivered) and 14 December 1921.

Thus this reference by Scott in his published diary entry for Monday 5 December cannot be to the 'previous Monday' or any other Monday that month later than 7 November. The meeting between Lloyd George and Griffith to which it refers may well have been that which took place on Sunday 30 October at Winston Churchill's (not Philip Sassoon's) house and which Lloyd George is said to have described as 'much the most satisfactory' meeting. The prime minster spoke on the next day (Monday 31 October) in a major debate in parliament that the government won by 439 votes to 43, that victory being due in part to a sense that satisfactory progress on Ireland was then being made.[80] Moreover, there is no evidence that Griffith had signed the document produced by Lloyd George, and he certainly did not sign the extant copy of the document shown him by Jones on 13 November 1921 that is among Lloyd George's papers. Furthermore, even had Griffith 'communicated' to Collins the important document, of which—from Scott's account—he 'evidently' had not kept a copy himself, such a communication to any person would not bind or make that other person a party to its terms. Also, Lloyd George had not included the text shown to Griffith by Jones on 13 November in the prime minister's subsequent letter to Craig of 14 November—nor otherwise published that proposal—and so did not risk a 'break' on it.

It is unclear how soon after his reported conversation with Lloyd George Scott wrote his entries for 5–6 December. The editor of Scott's diary notes a lack of clarity elsewhere in Scott's account of his two discussions with Lloyd George on those days and remarks that Scott was apparently 'carried away by the drama of the events into unwonted obscurity'.[81] Scott's version has recently been relied on in a dramatic reconstruction of the 1921 negotiations, which includes a fictional scene in which Griffith signs the memorandum brought to him by Jones.[82]

Griffith may well have been 'a little surprised' that night in Downing Street when the 'terms' of the memorandum were read and represented as they were by Lloyd George, but why would Lloyd George have wanted to say this to Scott? Would Scott not have asked and noted why Griffith was so surprised? Or wanted to know what precisely was this 'general, informal agreement with him [Lloyd George] as to the terms on which Griffith would be prepared to settle'? Indeed, what would it mean to sign a 'general, informal agreement'?

If Griffith was indeed 'surprised' by what appears to have been a farrago of inaccurate assertions by Lloyd George, the prime minister was eager to keep his government together by representing himself as having cleverly achieved the best deal for Britain.

'IN SOME SENSE'?

Having observed solemnly that without the meeting of 12 November there might have been no treaty, Pakenham bluntly confesses: 'This makes it the more unfortunate that for once our material is not quite satisfying, so that we are forced to introduce into our narrative an element of speculative reconstruction'.[83] The 'speculative reconstruction' in which he engaged has been highly influential. There is no reason to believe that he saw the cabinet diaries of Thomas Jones and no way to know how much of Griffith's correspondence to de Valera he was shown. These sources do not support Pakenham's account, as can be seen above.

Pakenham's narrative is one of a hapless Griffith outmanoeuvred by the smart British, with some of whom Pakenham was personally associated through family and work. He purports to reconcile Griffith's contemporary account of the meeting with an account given orally to Pakenham by Chamberlain, and to do so in a manner that 'renders intelligible the consequences of what happened that day [12 November 1921]'. Acknowledging that Griffith had made contemporary reports of developments to de Valera and accepting that people might conclude from these that Griffith had made no great concession that day, Pakenham nevertheless asserts that when we turn to Chamberlain's version 'we shall suspect at once that the break on Ulster was from November 12th onwards closed to Sinn Féin'. Note the word 'suspect'. Pakenham appears to accept uncritically Chamberlain's 'understanding' that 'Griffith's promise [which was simply not to decry publicly Lloyd George's proposal to the unionists, while reserving the Sinn Féin position on it subject to the outcome of the talks generally] excluded any further possibility of a break coming on the Ulster head'.[84]

Pakenham conveys Chamberlain's version of what happened after Griffith left Philip Sassoon's house. He writes that 'Lloyd George had given instructions to Tom Jones to draw up a rough summary of the agreement reached', but

> 'Lloyd George himself was in a hurry to leave for the week-end. Would Chamberlain mind checking the document when Tom Jones had drawn it up? The precaution was wise, for Jones, sharpest of secretaries to trap and render into formal draft exact shades of loosely expressed compromise, this once had missed perfection. However, with Chamberlain's help, the plan to which Griffith had become committed passed into memorandum form. Sometime about 7 p.m. the next day, Sunday, November 13th, Jones showed Griffith the paper. Griffith briefly indicated his assent to its proposals.'[85]

There is no evidence to support Pakenham's assertion that Griffith, on the weekend of 12–13 November, made 'a solemn promise' that 'precluded' him from bringing about a break in the negotiations based on Ulster. Griffith had assiduously insisted that he personally could not bind other members of the delegation and that his own willingness to consider a boundary commission, known to and not criticised by de Valera from the outset, was conditional on the nature of Craig's response to the whole idea, a response that the British had promised to secure but never delivered. Griffith could quite rightly deny at the final sessions on 5–6 December that the Irish had let Lloyd George down over 'the Ulster proposals', a denial recorded in Griffith's own report on those sessions and quoted above but ignored by Pakenham.

It was not the only denial by Griffith that Pakenham ignored. Doing down Griffith's reputation, Pakenham claims at the same time that Griffith's error was simply being duped into something that he judged to be of no material importance and asserts implausibly that not even Griffith's most bitter critics ever suggested that he 'had acted unwisely—much less improperly'.[86] Critics of Griffith have certainly claimed such things, and Pakenham gave them comfort. Griffith's rejection of such accusations as 'a damnable lie' was on the record of Dáil Éireann but Pakenham does not include it in his book. For such a powerful statement to be ignored by him is remarkable.

In reality, the only certain 'agreement reached', or commitment or concession made on 12 November, consisted of Griffith's undertaking not to decry publicly the proposal that Lloyd George had indicated privately to him that British ministers intended to put to Ulster unionists before the meeting of conservatives and unionists in Liverpool actually took place on the following Thursday.

There is no evidence that Griffith 'indicated his assent'—'briefly' or otherwise—to any such options or proposals advanced on the Sunday. Jones's note on the document that he stated that he showed Griffith (reproduced in this chapter) does not suggest this, as it surely would have had Griffith agreed to its content. The fact that Griffith did not report to de Valera that he was shown the text on 13 November (if he was indeed shown the text and read it) does not support Pakenham's assertion of his giving 'secret assent' to it, for Griffith had already briefed de Valera on the actual substance of the proposal and on what he told the British he thought of it. Griffith likewise, soon afterwards, highlighted to de Valera Lloyd George's failure to include the proposal explicitly in the prime minister's subsequent letter to Craig.

Pakenham does not state, as Frances Stevenson does, that Birkenhead also arrived after Griffith left Lloyd George and was part of the discussion about what would happen next. But, having given Chamberlain's self-aggrandising account wihtout question, Pakenham weaves a theory based on it. He claims, for example, that 'Griffith gave some kind of assent to the British Ulster proposals in language, or in a manner, that could afterwards be used to imply a much more far-reaching undertaking than Griffith conceived of at the time' and 'There is no conflict therefore over the *nature* [Pakenham's emphasis] of the terms in which Griffith in some sense acquiesced'.[87]

Really? Had Pakenham not heard of Griffith's categorical description of 'the misrepresentation that I was a man who pledged his word to something … that I in some way connived with Lloyd George' as 'a damnable lie'?[88] If Pakenham in 1935 somehow missed that strong statement, did Barton or de Valera who worked closely with him on his book not put him right?

And what exactly does Pakenham mean by woolly phrases such as 'In some sense' and 'some kind of assent'? Assent that Griffith gave but did not mean or understand? What were those 'terms' exactly? Until the very last session, Griffith was demanding and failing to get Craig's response before committing himself to any final agreement—a final agreement that he insisted had to be satisfactory to Sinn Féin on Crown and Empire and that he explicitly advised the British that he personally could not bind the other plenipotentiaries to accept. If the British thought or wished that Griffith used language 'that could afterwards be used to imply a much more far-reaching undertaking', where was the record of that 'language'?

Pakenham also writes, in a paragraph that hints at one thing but says another, that

> 'It seems certain (from what happened on the last day of the Conference [5–6 December]) that on November 12th Griffith did in fact acquiesce in some sense in *written* proposals [Pakenham's emphasis]. But that he should not have mentioned this fact to de Valera, or apparently to any of his colleagues, need cause no surprise, and is certainly no evidence whatever of any intentional concealment. For as explained above, the British terms were the same as those he had already described in the Dublin Cabinet, and it would seem to him quite unimportant that he had seen them written down.'[89]

There's that same vague qualifier again: 'in some sense'. Pakenham indicates that Griffith bound himself informally and unintentionally in advance of the final night of talks to a proposition of which the Irish cabinet was 'already' fully aware, notwithstanding that Jones wrote in his cabinet diary that Griffith explicitly did not do so and notwithstanding that Griffith told de Valera the same thing and clearly explained to him in November what the British were up to. Griffith's categorical denial of having bound himself as Pakenham claims, made during the treaty debates in Dáil Éireann, counts for nothing.

Regarding what happened on the last day of the conference (5–6 December), Pakenham appears to have relied on Chamberlain and on Barton's notes. Barton's notes are far from entirely clear, and he was—by the time Pakenham wrote—firmly in de Valera's political camp. In fairness to Pakenham, he does admit that other explanations of what happened are possible, giving two in a rare footnote—in which he immediately also affirms his own theory as seeming 'far more likely to be true'.[90] The author is relentless, going on to claim that 'the plan of accepting the Boundary Commission as a tactical manoeuvre only ... was finally stultified by Griffith's acceptance of the document of November 12th'.[91] Griffith actually 'accepted' neither the plan nor the document. Whether Griffith did not condemn the idea out of hand because he thought that Ulster unionists would reject it (which they eventually did, in practice) and that this would make them look bad, or simply because he did not want to cut the ground from under Lloyd George by a public utterance or leak prior to the meeting in Liverpool a few days later, or because he thought that it might actually be worth teasing out the idea given de Valera's acceptance in Dáil Éireann in August 1921 of the principle that some counties of Northern Ireland could choose to remain in the United Kingdom, or a bit of all three of the above, his response cannot be reasonably construed as some kind of 'assent' to the proposal itself. To construe it so, in fact, would require rejecting the contemporary statements of both Griffith himself and the British cabinet secretary Thomas Jones that Griffith explicitly and repeatedly refused to accept or agree to it. Pakenham overcomes this problem by suggesting that Griffith somehow gave binding assent implicitly or logically without wishing to do so, or without realising that he had done so. Clearly, then, for those such as Pakenham, Griffith was responsible for frustrating the claim to a united Ireland, rather than the claim being defeated by the weight of circumstances that de Valera had recognised when he told the Dáil that the counties of Northern Ireland could or would not be compelled to be part of an Irish republic. Nowhere does Pakenham query or criticise the decision by de Valera not to answer each individual letter from Griffith in the week leading up to 12 November, or to be more involved in developments when, as far as de Valera knew from Griffith, Lloyd George might be about to depart as prime minister and be replaced by someone more supportive of the Ulster unionists. While he asserts Griffith's good faith, Pakenham is widely regarded as having become close to de Valera and one is reminded of what in 1922 Griffith told the Dáil: 'When I was going to London Mr de Valera said to me, "There may have to be scapegoats [...] [Michael] Collins and myself were willing to be scapegoats."'[92]

Pakenham concludes with a hammer blow what he admits is his 'speculative reconstruction', one based on broad assumptions. He strikes an ominous note when he suggests that Griffith was ultimately responsible for a situation in which, 'pulled down from their seats into the arena, the signatories would find themselves "struggling for life"'. Griffith's supposed 'acceptance' of the document of 12 November—and it alone, when the crisis came—let Lloyd George off the hook, according to Pakenham, and it prevented the Irish delegates from 'justifiably' denying that they were committed to a boundary commission, regardless of whether or not Craig's consent to it had been secured. 'Responsibility, greater or less, for his escape rests with all those on the Irish side who were privy to the gradual emergence, though it were for tactical purposes only, between the 8th and the 12th [of November] of the Boundary Commission as an alternative to the all-Ireland parliament. Most of all, however, with Griffith ...'[93] But not with de Valera as president of Dáil Éireann, the leader who failed to go to London in the first place, who avoided answering Griffith's letters individually that crucial week in November and who was not there when the British prime minister threatened immediate war? Pakenham does not explain how Craig's outright rejection of an all-Ireland parliament might have been countered without the talks entirely breaking down.

Here it should again be repeated—given the remarkable influence of Pakenham's book—that Griffith had explicitly distanced himself personally from the proposal in the document that he reportedly saw on 12–13 November; he had explicitly stated that he would not commit himself and could not bind the others in advance, and had asked to be informed of Craig's reaction to the idea.

The boundary commission proposal never in fact became a major bone of contention for Sinn Féin at that time, neither at the last full cabinet meeting in Dublin days before the agreement for a treaty was signed, nor at the last session of the negotiations on 5–6 December (where Empire and Crown dominated). Moreover, had it been the crucial issue, nothing precluded any delegate from rejecting it—not least because Lloyd George never did get Craig to respond formally to it. It was clear that the unionists did not accept the idea. Pakenham asks his readers 'not to entertain for an instant an idea ... that the story told here in any way reflects discredit on the memory of two Irishmen now dead, Arthur Griffith and Michael Collins', but his version of the events of 12–13 November does just that.[94]

Pakenham's book in general is very thin on explicit sources, although he has clearly drawn on some official records. Sources that he identified in the present context, besides Chamberlain, were some of Griffith's correspondence with de Valera (which correspondence as now published works against his theory) and Barton's notes of the last night (which were written at Griffith's request and are far from being a transcript of proceedings, as they survive in typed-up form).

So where did Pakenham find the 'personal recollection' or 'account' of events by Sir Austen Chamberlain that he mentions on pages 214 and 216 respectively? It seems that one must turn back to the second page of Pakenham's introduction, where one reads this: 'I have discussed the events of this period in some detail with Sir Austen Chamberlain. Sir Austen Chamberlain, though feeling unable to give me the use of his papers, has read me his contemporary notes of the crucial meetings. On this material I have formed my own judgement …'

More than a decade after the event, Chamberlain, who already by mid-December 1921 had delivered in parliament a contentious account of the boundary commission provision in the agreement for a treaty,[95] gave Pakenham an interview during which he purportedly relied on papers that he refused to show the interviewer.[96] It is remarkable that so many historians, including the editor of the diary of Thomas Jones, have relied heavily on Pakenham's book as if it were the definitive authority on the treaty. The present author admits to having on one occasion, under the influence of Pakenham, referred to Griffith's 'assenting' in some way to a substantive proposal on the weekend of 12–13 November. It was a mistake to do so.

THE BOUNDARY COMMISSION

In hindsight we know that the boundary commission that was actually established did not achieve what Griffith and Collins, before their early deaths in 1922, had hoped it might. For one thing, the Irish Civil War intervened. One may take the view that the Irish were naïve, and that such a commission was never likely to yield as much as the result of county or local plebiscites in Northern Ireland would have. Collins and Griffith also appear to have assumed throughout that a delimiting boundary commission would in practice only limit Northern Ireland to a smaller portion of its six counties—consistent with the wishes of people living there—and never fully acknowledged even to themselves the possibility that unionist districts in Cavan, Monaghan and Donegal might successfully opt into Northern Ireland, as Lloyd George allowed. Yet adjustments to the border envisaged in a British draft memo for presentation to the Northern Ireland parliament as early as 10 November 1921 clearly referenced nine counties.[97] And Collins revealed his political inexperience when he reported on a vital personal meeting with Lloyd George on the morning before the agreement was signed in December. He noted then that Lloyd George 'remarked that I myself pointed out on a previous occasion that the North would be forced economically to come in. I assented ...' This was a reference to the Irish belief that if the voters of Tyrone and Fermanagh were allowed to choose they would join the Irish Free State, and that the remaining four counties of Northern Ireland would then not be a viable unit. However, Lloyd George had not endorsed that view but merely quoted Collins. Thus Collins had in effect 'assented' only to having said it himself and was not assenting to a proposition made by Lloyd George.[98] On the other hand, in the House of Commons on 14 December 1921—just a few days after the agreement was signed—Prime Minister Lloyd George did say quite clearly:

> 'There is no doubt—certainly since the [Government of Ireland] Act of 1920—that the majority of the people of two counties prefer being with their Southern neighbours to being in the Northern Parliament. Take it either by constituency or by Poor Law unions, or, if you like, by counting heads, and you will find that the majority in these two counties prefer to be with their Southern neighbours. What does that mean? If Ulster is to remain a separate community, you can only by means of coercion keep them there, and although I am against the coercion of Ulster, I do not believe in Ulster coercing other units. Apart from that, would it be an advantage to Ulster? There is no doubt it would give her trouble.'

From this and from other statements he made that were very critical of the line of the Irish border, there is reason to believe that Lloyd George would have supported with Griffith and Collins a significant redrawing of it. But within a year Griffith and Collins were dead and Lloyd George was no longer in government.

The Irish plenipotentiaries were working under very stressful circumstances against highly skilled adversaries, and at times may have let their guard down or engaged in wishful thinking. Yet there is no evidence that their cabinet colleagues in Dublin proposed a better wording for the boundary commission article than that eventually enshrined in the treaty. Bitter disagreement then or later about other aspects of the agreement should not be allowed to colour our understanding of what happened in London on the weekend of 12–13 November 1921, a weekend when Griffith and Lloyd George mutually found a pragmatic way to avoid the imminent breakdown of negotiations without either of them committing himself to a final outcome.

26

MICHAEL PORTILLO'S POISONED GAS?

On Wednesday 10 May 2023 RTÉ gave a platform to Michael Portillo to advance in prime time an overblown theory about the alleged relationship between Michael Collins and Winston Churchill. In doing so it gave a new lease of life to the dominant anti-treaty narrative that Collins and Griffith were patsies of the Brits, and further suggested that the Irishmen were willing to release a poison gas in their capital city of Dublin similar to that used in the trenches during World War I. It is remarkable that two men who became government ministers in Britain have in turn had a go at Griffith's reputation since his death, first in 1935 Pakenham (as Lord Longford, secretary of state for the colonies 1965–6) and eighty-eight years later Portillo (secretary of state for defence 1995–7).

Portillo's programme appears to have confused lethal poison gas with what is more usually described as 'tear gas' in a colourful account of the Irish government's being allegedly prepared to obtain such gas from the British and to deploy it against their own people on the streets of Ireland's capital city. Portillo relied heavily on a selected section of the minutes of a British cabinet meeting held on 4 July 1922.

His theory matters because the version of history of the losing, anti-treaty side in the Civil War became, paradoxically, the domi-

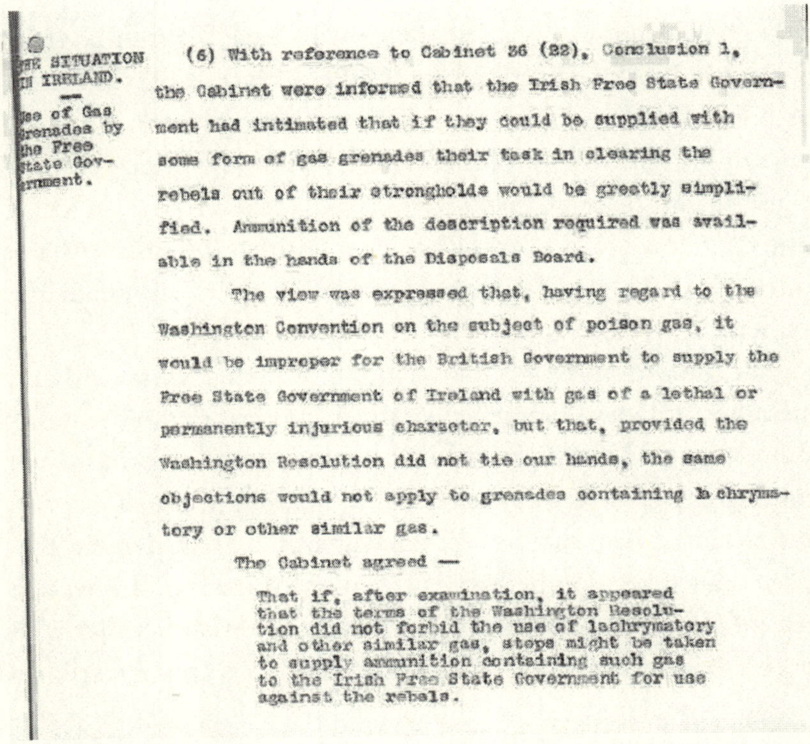

HE SITUATION
N IRELAND.
—
se of Gas
renades by
he Free
tate Gov-
rnment.

(6) With reference to Cabinet 36 (22), Conclusion 1, the Cabinet were informed that the Irish Free State Government had intimated that if they could be supplied with some form of gas grenades their task in clearing the rebels out of their strongholds would be greatly simplified. Ammunition of the description required was available in the hands of the Disposals Board.

The view was expressed that, having regard to the Washington Convention on the subject of poison gas, it would be improper for the British Government to supply the Free State Government of Ireland with gas of a lethal or permanently injurious character, but that, provided the Washington Resolution did not tie our hands, the same objections would not apply to grenades containing lachrymatory or other similar gas.

The Cabinet agreed —

That if, after examination, it appeared that the terms of the Washington Resolution did not forbid the use of lachrymatory and other similar gas, steps might be taken to supply ammunition containing such gas to the Irish Free State Government for use against the rebels.

The entire minute of the discussion about gas grenades and Ireland, from Cabinet 37 (22), Conclusions of a meeting of the cabinet, 4 July 1922 (courtesy of the UK National Archives, CAB-23-30-15, p. 263).

nant narrative of the Irish state's foundational story once de Valera came to power. Little credit has been given to those who in 1921 negotiated the agreement for a treaty, while de Valera's role immediately before and during the Civil War is justified, played down or explained away.

The main plank of Portillo's programme was an alleged message from Collins to Churchill shortly before Collins died. The message was a version of the old Gaelic 'A woman told me that a woman told her …', except that in this case Churchill wrote (seven years later) that a friend had told him that Collins had said, shortly before dying, 'Tell Winston we could never have done anything without him'.[1] Not only is the quotation unverified hearsay but also it cannot be taken to have reflected the mind of Michael Collins. Collins was not beholden to the British for an Irish state, and the Civil War was far from over when he allegedly made the statement.

What the programme showed in fact was that Churchill and some other British militants held dangerous ideas that wiser heads in London and Dublin rejected. Lloyd George long disdained Churchill as a loose cannon, literally comparing him to a torpedo and describing him during World War I as 'a great danger' following a failed mission by British troops at Antwerp.[2] This was an aspect of Churchill's character of which many Irish families who later lost relatives in the Dardanelles/Gallipoli campaign still do not need to be reminded. In June 1922 Lloyd George told his cabinet secretary that 'No Churchill was ever loyal' and compared him to 'a chauffeur who apparently is perfectly sane and drives with great skill for months, then suddenly he takes you over a precipice'. He thought that 'there was a strain of lunacy' there.[3] While Portillo quoted the cabinet secretary's diaries elsewhere, he did not mention this entry.

Portillo also ignored the fate of the boundary commission after Griffith and Collins died, a commission that the latter pair believed—and had been given grounds by the British to believe—could change the Irish border significantly.

Within the first few minutes of the television programme Portillo had set the tone, saying that 'Michael Collins signed a treaty with the British' and that 'the British intervened decisively to ensure that their side won' (where 'their side' here meant those who had fought the British for independence and who supported the treaty). Portillo threw in gossip about Hazel Lavery and an anecdote. This is pernicious. Collins was just one of five delegates who *all* signed the agreement in London on 6 December 1921. Collins was not even the leader there; Griffith—whom Portillo barely mentioned—was. What Portillo also neglected to stress was that Churchill and the other British held a gun to Irish heads that night in London by threatening an immediate renewal of outright war unless the Irish signed.

And the description of the elected government of Dáil Éireann as a 'side' in the Civil War is quite disingenuous in this context. The Irish government drew its authority from the Irish people and was supported by a majority in Dáil Éireann. The fact that it took delivery of a couple of artillery pieces from the British Army was not necessarily crucial. The state's new army had to get weapons somewhere, and both 'sides' indeed had already received former British weapons.

Portillo included from British cabinet papers a British note stating that the Irish officially sought gas from the British to use in Sackville (now O'Connell) Street and elsewhere in the summer of 1922. Like British contingency plans to bomb Dublin about then this idea also came to nothing in the end.

Portillo claimed: 'The Irish who signed it [the treaty] and the British ministers were agreed that they should smash republican dissenters. The willingness of the British to supply artillery and ammunition was matched by the zeal of the Irish Provisional government to accept British ordnance to pulverize the foe.' There is no evidence that in the first six months of 1922 the provisional government was zealous to 'pulverize' erstwhile colleagues.

There was no 'Faustian pact', as claimed by Portillo. The Irish cabinet and members of Dáil Éireann consisted of republicans on both 'sides' but were split on whether or not to accept the treaty as a means to an eventual end. The Irish cabinet tried to reconcile republican 'dissenters', overlooking armed attacks for months, but they could not indefinitely let the emerging state be held to ransom violently by a minority of its citizens.

It was not just Collins but the whole Irish government that finally decided to act against the insurrection. Even then in June 1922 it did not wish 'to pulverize the foe'. It thought and hoped that, by recapturing the Four Courts, violence would quickly cease. Liam Lynch, an anti-treaty IRA leader, was detained on his way to catch a train but was soon released from captivity as an act of good will. Suggestions that this was because Lynch gave assurances that he would express disapproval of the policy of further armed action against the government were denied.[4]

Portillo's account was sensational and misleading. Thus the *Irish Times* TV critic Ed Power formed his opinion from the programme that, during the Civil War in 1922, 'the Dublin government canvassed Britain for poison gas. The request was received with horror by the British' (*Irish Times*, 13 May). I had feared when watching the programme—which Ed Power regarded as 'a fun dash through the archives'—that it would create precisely the impression that Power took from it, for Portillo had stated baldly that the Irish government 'asked the British for gas'. The authority cited was a UK cabinet minute of 4 July 1922, freely available online from the UK National Archives. Unfortunately, only part of the minute was shown on the TV programme, but it is now reproduced here in its entirety.

The British minute stated that 'the cabinet was informed that the Irish Free State Government had intimated that if they could be provided with some form of gas grenades their task of clearing the rebels out of their strongholds would be greatly simplified'. This use of the ambiguous word 'intimated' in respect to 'some form of gas' was followed in the minute by *British* ministers referring to 'poison gas'.

Even if accurate, that minute did not say who 'informed' ministers, or what exactly 'intimated' meant in this context, or who had been in contact allegedly on behalf of the Free State government. The whole exercise may have been a ready-up by British intelligence eager to propose gas to Dublin. The minute certainly does not state that the Irish sought 'poison' gas nor that the British government reacted with 'horror'. *British* ministers merely noted that under an international convention it would be 'improper to supply poison gas' but, in a portion of the minute not quoted by Portillo on the programme, they agreed that they might supply *tear gas*.

There is no reasonable possibility that the Irish government would have used *poison* gas in central Dublin, heavily populated by civilians and where it was then in the process of clearing anti-treaty forces from occupied buildings. That very morning of 4 July 1922 the *Irish Times* was already reporting 'The Revolt Broken' and 'Mutineers' Last Stand'. The Irish government might have used *tear* gas, for it had tried patiently for months to end with minimum force the insurrection by those determined to overthrow the government in the face of overwhelming public support for the Anglo-Irish treaty as the least bad option. This matters precisely because events then are still weaponised today for various purposes. Collins and Griffith were neither British stooges nor uncivilised.

I explained in a national newspaper article and in a letter to the editor of the *Irish Times* at that time what I saw as major flaws in the Portillo programme.[5] However, that did not prevent the matter from being aired again a few months later, this time in a national newspaper and with additional information that seemed to me to be also misleading. A report in the *Irish Times* on 8 August 2023

('Britain sent "banned" grenades to counter anti-treaty rebels') amplified the claim first made by Portillo in the RTÉ documentary that the Free State government 'canvassed the British for poison gas' to use against anti-treaty forces in Dublin in June 1922. The *Irish Times* now reported that the programme's researchers had found evidence that the British later sent to Dublin 'poison' grenades containing 'liquid ethyl iodoacetate, a lachrymatory (tear) gas first used by the British at the Battle of Loos [in late 1915]'. There were still some British forces in Dublin throughout 1922 and, if such gas was ever sent, it may have been sent to them.

But the key document underlying the *Irish Times* report of August 2023 was still that brief UK cabinet minute of 4 July 1922 partly cited by Portillo. The full minute is freely available online and is fully reproduced above. This does not refer to any (as claimed) 'missive from Dublin'. Nor does it state that the UK cabinet was 'stunned' or reacted with 'horror' to the idea of using 'some form of gas', although this was now asserted to have been the case. In fact, part of the cabinet minute (for some reason not reproduced in full in the Portillo programme on RTÉ) records that the UK cabinet promptly decided to supply 'lachrymatory' grenades. These were explicitly to be not 'of a lethal or other injurious character' or of a kind that was 'banned'.

The word 'lachrymatory' comes from the Latin *lacrima*, meaning 'tears'. At the time tear gas was being widely demonstrated in the USA for use in civil disturbances. Its use to clear Dublin city centre of anti-treaty forces that week might have saved lives and avoided the destruction of buildings again in an area devastated just six years earlier during the Easter Rising of 1916. This was not a sinister option for the elected Irish government.

The gas grenades now said to have been sent subsequently to those British Army forces still in Dublin (but not to the Irish Free

State army) resembled more closely the tear gas used by American police forces than what most people understand by 'poison gas' in the lethal context of World War I from the year 1916. According to a classic text by Lieutenant Colonel Augustin Prentiss of the US Chemical Warfare Service, ethyl iodoacetate (used at the Battle of Loos in 1915) was on its own generally *not* lethal in the field and was superseded during World War I by much more deadly concoctions, including those containing phosgene.[6]

It is possible that the entire 'intimation' to cabinet and delivery to Dublin was engineered for British purposes by Mr Portillo's predecessor in the UK cabinet, for the cabinet minute explicitly refers back to a recent meeting at which UK ministers ostensibly decided to offer arms to the Irish government and to apply great pressure on Dublin to quash anti-treaty forces more vigorously. The information in the *Irish Times* report that non-lethal gas was later brought to Dublin by British forces but that the Free State government apparently did not take delivery of even this gas tends to undermine any allegation that Irish ministers had ever agreed to request or wished to use more lethal 'poison' grenades.

27

ONLY PLAY-ACTING?

'In the play, I have Griffith sign the memo,' admits Colin Murphy. A playwright may tell an untruth for dramatic effect. It doesn't make it right and, as will be seen below, the present writer has disagreed with Colin Murphy about his recent perpetuation on the stage of what, in my opinion, existing evidence indicates is a damning falsehood—one that has skewed the entire narrative of Ireland's 'Troubles' in the twentieth century. According to this narrative, Arthur Griffith is to blame for a supposed surrender of principle during the treaty talks in London. As early as 1935 Frank Pakenham, the future Lord Longford and admirer of Éamon de Valera, had enshrined this version of events in a purportedly balanced account of the treaty negotiations. The full details of how he did this have been given earlier, but are recapped in summary in the following paragraph before questioning the practice of taking 'poetic licence' with history as Murphy has done.

In a coy sentence in 1935, unsupported by documentary evidence as demonstrated above, Pakenham claimed that on 13 November 1921 'Griffith briefly indicated his assent' to certain 'proposals' on a document shown to him by the UK cabinet secretary Thomas Jones.[1] Pakenham does not say how Griffith supposedly 'indicated' this; he does not identify the nature of the document or its precise contents. It is clear from what Pakenham does write that he supposes this to be the same 'paper' that Lloyd George flourished dramatically at the last session of negotiations in 1921, when the prime minister said that Griffith had given an 'undertaking'. The text of that 'paper' was copied by the Irish delegate Robert Barton into a record of the last session that he made within twenty-four hours, at Griffith's request. It consisted of a proposal that the UK government was planning to make in whole or in part to Ulster unionists in November 1921. But Barton did not identify clearly in his note the nature of the 'paper'. Nor did Pakenham in his book, and he also did not do so for one of Griffith's biographers (Brian Maye) when asked years later to identify its nature and location. It appears, however, that what Lloyd George waved was the text on a page of a typed memorandum drafted for sending to Ulster unionist leaders that I lately discovered among the Lloyd George papers in the parliamentary archives of the House of Lords when writing *Midnight in London* and that is reproduced herein. The page is signed by Jones, who notes that he showed it to Griffith but does *not* record on it or elsewhere that Griffith in any way indicated his assent to what was written on the page, as one would have expected Jones to do on the page itself or in his cabinet diary if Griffith had agreed to the text. It is not evidence of an undertaking by Griffith in any sense. Lloyd George's use of the note caused confusion.[2] Historians who later wrote that Griffith assented to or even signed the paper waved by Lloyd George have simply relied on Pakenham's account. As indicated earlier, sources that were only made public on both sides of the Irish Sea decades after the treaty negotiations, including contemporary correspondence between Griffith and de Valera and the diary of the British cabinet secretary himself, vindicate Griffith's conduct in respect to British efforts in November to have him privately endorse the proposal that Lloyd George waved at the final session of talks. He refused to do so.

Yet the version of events peddled by Pakenham did not die and is sometimes enhanced by the suggestion that Griffith even recklessly *signed* a secret undertaking for the British. Collins and Griffith died in 1922 and could thereafter no longer defend themselves from such allegations.

The damning version of Griffith's actions was repeated in Colin Murphy's otherwise worthy dramatisation of the treaty negotiations. I became aware of the script early on and asked Murphy to delete it from his play. He declined to do so, writing publicly as follows:

> 'On Thursday night, after our first preview [at the National Concert Hall], I returned home to an email from Colum Kenny, biographer of Arthur Griffith … Earlier this year, Kenny made a substantial discovery in the archives of the Houses of Parliament, unearthing a memo about the boundary commission long referred to as having been signed by Arthur Griffith: the allegation repeated in many accounts of the treaty negotiations was that, by signing this memo, Griffith had—in naivety or duplicity—given away a crucial Irish position. The memo, Kenny proved, had not been signed by Griffith: the story that it had been signed by the man [Griffith] was, he argued, a calumny.
>
> In the play, I have Griffith sign the memo. Kenny is appalled: this is a "cruel falsification", he writes, and appeals to me to rewrite it, suggesting apposite lines. I argue the moment is crucial to the compressed and heightened telling of the story on stage. My job is not to give the audience a full, accurate account of the negotiations but to help them feel the different burdens carried by the protagonists—and thereby identify whatever trauma they may be carrying with the trauma manifest on stage.
>
> This is the catharsis that Aristotle identified as the purpose of tragedy, more than 2,000 years ago. Ever since, playwrights have

> looked to history for stories. But those history plays are never really about the history: they are always about the present, and the trauma of today.'[3]

Murphy's explanation in this passage seems to be that the truth of a serious allegation, which was part of the rationale for an insurrection by a minority of elected politicians and others, does not matter so long as it serves some other useful purpose. I strongly disagree, for the allegation goes to the very heart of an entire narrative of betrayal that has been fundamental to the attempted justification or 'understanding' of a destructive and futile civil war. It is a narrative that has set a tone for modern Ireland. Understanding accurately why there are 'different burdens carried by the protagonists' is at least as important as helping people today to 'feel' them.

The extent to which an author or playwright engages in licence is relevant to any judgment of the value of their work. The prominent German writer Daniel Kehlmann has recently written *The Director*, a book based on the life of the Austrian filmmaker G.W. Pabst. He has subsequently defended his decision to portray Pabst as having used inmates from Terezín concentration camp as 'extras' while filming during World War II, which Pabst does not appear to have done in fact: 'And I was thinking very hard about, am I allowed to do that morally? The main reason I felt I could do it is because in the Nazi era they did it for other films. He [Pabst] was the co-director of a film where it was actually done, Leni Riefenstahl's *Tiefland* [which we see Pabst co-direct in the novel]. And then there was slave labor everywhere around the German movie industry, so in the films he did make in the Third Reich, they actually used forced labourers from Eastern Europe. And I don't think there's such a big moral difference between using forced labor or using extras from the concentration camp. The one thing is more radical as an artistic choice, but I don't feel it's ontologically on a completely different level.'[4] However, inventing Griffith crucially and secretly signing a key paper he actually refused to sign is on 'a completely different level'.

The fusing of fact and fiction may result in exciting books or films, as readers of Colm Toíbín and Robert Harris, for example, can attest. W.G. Sebald also did it in a fascinating way, for example in his critically acclaimed *Austerlitz*. Yet a historian finds in Sebald's *The Rings of Saturn* certain references to Roger Casement that undermine its publisher's claims for the work. Sebald incorrectly writes that Casement had no legal representation at his trial in London. It is the case that English lawyers refused to represent Casement, a man accused of treason during war, and his solicitor of Irish descent is said to have lost his job in an English legal firm for doing so, but Casement was in fact represented at his trial.[5] And if Casement 'could not rid his thoughts of the fact that almost half the population of Ireland had been murdered by Cromwell's soldiers', Sebald might have checked that quantitative 'fact' with contemporary historians. War in the Cromwellian period had a catastrophic impact on Ireland, but accuracy matters in history, if not in fiction. Similarly, the life of Michael Collins provided ample drama for a gripping and popular film by Neil Jordan about the Irish rebel leader, but factual accuracy was not always achieved in the telling of that story.

Likewise, a recent television documentary seemed to include a re-enactment of an episode of history. It showed Éamon de Valera stepping up to a window, his revolver blazing. Exposed to British fire, he was in the thick of it, shooting down Northumberland Road from Mount Street bridge as the enemy advanced. This was one of the fiercest engagements of the Easter Rising of 1916, an engagement often recalled for its impact, and de Valera seemed reckless in his courageous abandon—except for the fact that he was not actually there. Although the battle certainly took place, de Valera was elsewhere. He was the local senior commandant of the rebels involved, but he himself was some distance away with other Volunteers in Boland's Mills. The scene described was included for dramatic purposes in a two-part 'historical documentary' screened by TG4 in which the ideals and fate of certain revolutionary women who supported de Valera were considered. TG4 had bolstered his reputation by creating a new myth.[6]

Television has a potentially powerful influence on public opinion, so the assertions of its programme-makers should be weighed carefully before being broadcast. Referring to the Irish War of Independence over film footage of armed men on an Irish country road, the narrator of another TG4 documentary, *De Valera i Meiriceá* (2019), states that 'Ireland is going through possibly the worst war in its history'. A greater knowledge of events in the seventeenth-century, for example, might have convinced the narrator that this was far from the case. The statement inflates the scale of 'the Irish revolution' of the early twentieth century.

A frame from a documentary on TG4 about de Valera's visit to America in 1919–20 (De Valera i Meiriceá), including its subtitle.

28

GRIFFITH WAS POISONED?

There is no evidence that Arthur Griffith was poisoned, although he was rumoured to have been and his reputation was certainly contaminated by the malice of some detractors.

On 12 August 1922 Griffith, founder of Sinn Féin and president of Dáil Éireann, collapsed and died while in a nursing home to receive medical attention during the Civil War. Not long after his death, in an Ireland horrified by fratricide and stunned by the killing of Michael Collins later that same month, rumours began to circulate about how Griffith died. It was hardly surprising if some thought that he might have been killed too.

On 7 September 1922 the *Belfast Telegraph* reported that one John Steele, London correspondent of the *Chicago Tribune*, had sent to his newspaper a report that also that day appeared in the *Daily Telegraph* as follows:

> 'I am informed today from two reliable persons who have just returned to London from Dublin that the Free State authorities have exhumed the body of the late President of Dáil Éireann, Mr Arthur Griffith. It is reported that poison has been found in the body. A doctor and two nurses are said to have been arrested. The news, it is understood, has been repressed by the Dublin censors.'

The *Belfast Telegraph* added, however, that the *Irish Independent* was saying that this story 'has been circulating in Dublin for weeks and is totally untrue'. A week later, on 13 September, the *Albany Advertiser* was still telling US readers that 'A great sensation has been caused by the report that evidence is available to prove the late Mr Arthur Griffith was poisoned'. It went on to note an official denial of the rumour.

The story continued to circulate despite the Irish government's denials. On 16 September the *Sligo Champion* claimed that 'the absurd report gained no credence in Dublin, but prominence has been given to the matter by the Americans and some English papers, which has [*sic*] added some picturesque details concerning arrests'. Griffith's close friend Walter Cole described the report as 'absolutely absurd', while an official of the Catholic Cemeteries Committee said that 'Mr Griffith's remains had not been exhumed, nor had any application been made with that end in view'. An inspection of Griffith's grave was said to have shown that it had not been disturbed since being filled in.

A clue as to why such a rumour circulated, either by conscious or subconscious design, was provided by the content and tone of a report in the London *Morning Post* of 8 September. While ostensibly reassuring readers that Griffith's grave had been undisturbed and observing that a medical report on Griffith's death by his doctor and friend Oliver St John Gogarty gave its cause as 'cerebral haemorrhage', the paper observed that 'In normal times, and in civilised countries, when a politician dies it is fairly safe to assume that he dies a natural death. But Ireland at the present time is neither normal nor civilised.' It added in respect to the medical report that

> 'The words remind us painfully of the customary verdict of Irish juries at the inquests on the murdered British officers, who were

> also invariably found to have died from haemorrhage. In this case we must decorously assume in the absence of definite information to the contrary, that the haemorrhage was due to internal and not to external causes.'

The writer went on to use the rumours as a springboard for criticising Lloyd George for having negotiated with 'the agents of a secret society which used murder for political ends', for having 'embarked upon the negotiation with crime' and much more in the same vein. It referred to 'the miserable wreckage of the Irish Free State'. If floated as black propaganda against Sinn Féin, the poison rumours were serving their purpose.

When later graphically describing Griffith's demise, Dr Gogarty brushed aside the rumours of poisoning without actually dispelling them:

> 'It would have been a simple thing for me to order an inquest and to have viscera examined for poison. But the poison that slew Griffith was envy and jealousy and calumny, which can be deadlier than prussic acid, and, what is more mortal to a martyr, ingratitude.'[1]

Griffith was aged only 51 when he died, but he had been worn out by hard work, harassment and imprisonment by the British. The strain of treaty talks and subsequent efforts to reconcile to the new state those fellow countrymen who wished to destroy it even as it came into being further depressed him. The rumour of his poisoning was certainly persistent, not least because one cannot prove a negative, in this case the proposition that Griffith was *not* murdered.

Even when I was writing my recent biography of Griffith, a couple of well-meaning people who are not historians quietly let me know that it was said that Griffith had been poisoned. However, it seems most likely that those who in 1922 claimed poison as the cause of his death had no evidence of this and were peddling fake news.

Large crowds lined Dublin streets for Griffith's funeral to Glasnevin Cemetery. His grave, marked by a broken pillar, is modest and a little out of the way. Those giving patriotic tours of the cemetery do not always stop at it. The founder of Sinn Féin, 'father-of-us-all' as Michael Collins reportedly described him, has never fitted cosily into the narrative of 'the Irish Revolution'.

People lining the route of Griffith's funeral cortege watch Michael Collins and Richard Mulcahy pass. Within weeks Collins was shot dead (photo courtesy of the National Library of Ireland, POLF20).

29

A MAJORITY FAVOURED REVOLUTION?

In 1896 the editors of *Shan Van Vocht* in Belfast published a signal article by the socialist James Connolly, headlined 'Can Irish republicans be politicians?' In it he argued that 'to counsel rebellion without first obtaining the moral sanction of the people would be an act of criminal folly which would only end in disaster'.[1]

One may say of 'the Irish revolution' that it did not, in fact, have the moral sanction of the people in 1916, when Connolly marched out with his Citizen Army and other Volunteers, as many voters still thought that Home Rule alone was possible and adequate. However, the idea of a republic had considerable public support after the United Kingdom general election of 1918, when Sinn Féin candidates won most of the parliamentary seats in Ireland.

Connolly in 1896 was responding to a contribution in the previous issue of the same publication.[2] Early the following year, 'Trade Union Labour' reprinted the text of Connolly's *Shan Van Vocht* article as a penny pamphlet for the Irish Socialist Republican Party. The pamphlet was entitled *Erin's Hope: The End and the Means* and it also included three articles that Connolly had written for the *Labour Leader* in Glasgow at the request of its editor, Keir Hardie.[3]

The title of the Belfast monthly paper *Shan Van Vocht*—echoing that of a popular song from the time of the United Irishmen rebellion of 1798—was an Anglicisation of the Gaelic words *sean bhean bhocht*, meaning 'poor old woman', which signified a personification of Ireland. She was to feature notably at the end of that influential play *Kathleen Ni Houlihan*, written by W.B. Yeats with Lady Gregory, which was first performed in 1902, when it starred Maud Gonne. In it the 'old woman' undergoes a metamorphosis to become young again, in final lines that Arthur Griffith said he gave to Yeats:

> PETER.
> [*To* PATRICK, *laying a hand on his arm.*]
> Did you see an old woman going down the path?
> PATRICK.
> I did not, but I saw a young girl, and she had the walk of a queen.[4]

The editor of the 1909 American edition of *Erin's Hope: The End and the Means* stated that in 1896 'the advanced nationalists of Ireland had at that time only one monthly literary magazine, the *Shan Van Vocht*'.[5] Other contributors to that Belfast paper included Arthur Griffith and Griffith's close friend and collaborator William Rooney, a railway worker and writer who died young of typhoid.[6] In 1899 its editors, Alice Milligan and Anna Johnston, closed down their paper and gave their list of subscribers to Griffith and Rooney to use for the *United Irishman*, a new weekly paper about to be edited and produced by Griffith in Dublin with the financial backing of the Irish Republican Brotherhood.[7] Through this and other papers that he was to edit, Griffith was instrumental in inspiring future revolutionaries.

On 4 March 1899 Griffith made clear his new paper's outlook in the first number of the *United Irishman*:

> 'Lest there be a doubt in any mind, we will say that we accept the [revolutionary] Nationalism of [17]98, [18]48 and [18]67 as the true

Postcard of James Connolly, 'Commandant General Dublin Division' and signatory of the 1916 proclamation of the Irish Republic. In 1909 Connolly described Arthur Griffith as his 'old friend' (courtesy of the National Library of Ireland, NPA POLF53).

> Nationalism; and Grattan's cry "Live Ireland—Perish the Empire!" as the watchword of patriotism'.

By 1909, seven years before the British executed him for his part in the Easter Rising, James Connolly came to refer publicly to Arthur Griffith as 'my old friend'.[8] The acquaintanceship was not only intellectual. In 1899, for example, Griffith and Connolly and Maud Gonne (also Griffith's friend) caused a disturbance that James Joyce was later to feature in his novel *Ulysses*. They did so during a trip to Dublin by Joseph Chamberlain MP, colonial secretary of the United Kingdom, who came to receive an honorary doctorate from Trinity College. Chamberlain had done his utmost to strengthen the imperial power in South Africa. Police chased and captured Connolly, Gonne and Griffith when they attempted to drive a two-horse wagon to Beresford Place in order to proceed with a banned protest against the Boer War. Griffith's evidence in court, displaying a lapse of memory, helped to acquit Connolly of a particular charge that the police had brought against him then.[9]

In his signal *Shan Van Vocht* article of 1896, Connolly addressed the relationship between constitutional and revolutionary strategy in a way that was fresh, if not entirely new. Michael Davitt and John Devoy had in the late 1870s pioneered a policy for the Fenian movement that Moody says called for a departure from high Fenian orthodoxy, which had been committed to armed rebellion as the only means of ultimately achieving national independence. That old way had involved a contemptuous rejection of open and constitutional action. Moody explains that

> 'The Davitt–Devoy "new departure" of 1878 ... was initiated with the backing of American Fenians: it proposed that the I.R.B. as such should cooperate, on specified conditions, with home rulers of

the combative kind typified by Parnell, in a united effort to obtain national self-government and a radical settlement of the land question at an early date. This idea did not become a political reality, but it helped to prepare the minds of nationalists for a different "new departure" (the third in the series) with more limited and practical aims: a popular front for the immediate purpose of protecting Irish tenant farmers against their landlords ... Conducted, under Davitt's inspiration, within the law but in a spirit of "aggressive moral force", the "land war" brought about a revolution in the psychological relations between landlords and tenants, which was quickly followed by a revolution in their legal relations ... in the liquidation of the old landlords as a class and the transformation of their former tenantry into owner-occupiers.'[10]

In his 1896 article Connolly envisaged a freshly focused political and revolutionary plan, with an advanced nationalist platform more 'combative' or radical than that of the Irish Parliamentary Party, which sought merely 'Home Rule'. In his article in *Shan Van Vocht* he framed in a prescient way key questions for the Irish revolutionary movement. Might one succeed without the evident democratic support of the people? Might the actual and developing democratic wishes of the people impinge on the objectives of the revolutionary leadership? If Griffith and other Sinn Féin members of Dáil Éireann who in January 1922 voted for the Anglo-Irish treaty were correct in thinking that most voters approved in practice of the treaty (and that does appear from voting in subsequent elections to have been the case), it left stranded those Sinn Féin deputies who believed that they had been elected in 1918 on a principled pledge not to settle for anything less than the establishment of an Irish republic.

Connolly insisted in 1896 that the people must be won over to radical ideas for a definite end if revolution were to succeed: 'Were a political party formed in Ireland to educate the people in sound national ideas by pledging every candidate to openly repudiate the authority of the Crown, and work for the realization of republican principles, it would achieve a much-needed transformation in Irish politics'.[11]

In 1898 Griffith returned from a short spell working in South Africa to embark on a project that was to see him spearhead broad political radicalisation through his editorship of the *United Irishman* and of successor weekly newspapers. These papers received some of their funding from the Irish Republican Brotherhood. In 1905 Griffith also founded the Sinn Féin movement, proclaiming Ireland to be 'a distinct nation' that should be bound only by laws made by its own parliament, even if sharing a monarch with Britain. While he himself had joined the IRB, Griffith did not believe that many voters at that time were ready for Ireland to break completely with the Crown.[12] Nevertheless, in 1914 he attended a crucial and sometimes overlooked meeting with the future signatories of the revolutionary proclamation of 1916, described earlier, at which those attending plotted to use the opportunity of World War I to break completely with England.

In his 1896 article Connolly developed a theoretical and practical foundation for his 'Science of Revolution' that was both more radical and narrower than Devoy's and Davitt's 'new departure' of 1878 had been:

> 'Hitherto every Irish agitation has sought to make its programme as broad and loosely defined as possible, in order to enrol under its banner every section of Irish national opinion—loyal Home Rulers, Conservative Nationalists, Compromising Whigs, and Nationalist Democrats—all alike were welcome. Such a basis is undoubtedly best for the purposes of an "agitation", but it is worse than use-

less for the purposes of earnest revolutionists seeking a definite end. But such a party as I speak of, with an avowedly republican programme, would, in its very definiteness and coherence, have immense advantage to recommend it to the consideration and support of practical-minded men. It would prevent the emasculation of our young men by the vapourings of 'constitutional' patriots; it would effectually expose the sham Nationalists, and, let us hope, drive them from political life; it would at every election in which it took part afford a plebiscite of the people for or against the republic; it would enlist the sympathy of many earnest patriots whose open natures shrink from secret conspiracy; it would ascertain with mathematical accuracy the moment when the majority of the Irish people were ripe for revolution, and it could not be suppressed while representative government was left in Ireland.'

If Connolly in 1916 tried to 'ascertain with mathematical accuracy' the views of the majority of the Irish people before he and his Irish Citizen Army embarked on the Easter Rising, he can hardly have concluded that most men and women supported the rebellion. Griffith feared as much. Yet just two years later, partly because of public revulsion at the British response to that rebellion and partly in response to a British threat to extend conscription to Ireland, Sinn Féin triumphed in the general election of 1918 and its new MPs withdrew from Westminster to form a new parliament in Dublin, as Griffith had long advocated. This democratic victory provided moral sanction for the War of Independence of 1919–21 in the face of imperial intransigence. As Connolly had written in 1896, when advocating political as well as military action to achieve a republic,

'By adhering steadily to the policy of pledging every candidate to its full programme, whether they stood for Parliament or local governing bodies, it would insure that when a majority of the Irish people had at the ballot boxes declared in favour of the revolutionary party every soldier of the cause would know that in the fight he was waging he was not merely one of a numerically insignificant band of malcontents, but a citizen soldier fighting under orders publicly expressed in face of all the world by a majority of his fellow-countrymen. This I hold to be an eminently practical method of obtaining our end. It would exclude the possibility of our national principles being betrayed in the moment of danger, or compromised in the hour of success to suit the convenience of interested party politicians; it would inspire confidence in the most timid by its recognition of the fact that to counsel rebellion without first obtaining the moral sanction of the people would be an act of criminal folly which would only end in disaster. It would make Irish republicanism no longer the "politics of despair", but the Science of Revolution.[13]

Connolly here wrote of 'national principles' even as he himself was to remain in a small minority by being principally a revolutionary socialist as distinct from an 'advanced nationalist'.

A key insight into the relationship between Connolly and Griffith was provided by Seán T. Ó Ceallaigh (O'Kelly) when president of Ireland. In 1952, as noted earlier, Ó Ceallaigh provided a witness statement to the Bureau of Military History referring to the top-level meeting that he had convened in 1914 at the request of the Irish Republican Brotherhood after the outbreak of World War I. His statement included this information, in addition to what was quoted earlier:

'We discussed there the possibility of doing active propaganda against the war and, of course, spread[ing] pro-independence

> propaganda. Somebody suggested then that any organisation of that kind that we would establish would be suppressed. That was generally accepted and we decided that even if one organisation was suppressed we could immediately try to establish another, and keep the propaganda going. We had agreed that public meetings against the war and against participation by Ireland in the war and against recruiting for the British Army would be necessary. It was also agreed that it would be necessary to keep the weekly *Sinn Féin* newspaper and, if possible, more than one weekly newspaper going to promote our objects. Connolly, I remember, declared that he would see to it that *The Irish Worker* would be kept going as long as he could get the printer to print and publish it for him.
>
> I think it must have been about the 2nd or 3rd December 1914 that *Sinn Féin*, the weekly organ of the Sinn Féin movement, edited by Arthur Griffith and of which I was Manager, ceased publication [having been suppressed]. Therefore it was decided that a weekly newspaper of some kind to be edited by Griffith should be kept going. That decision was come to at that meeting that I have referred to. Actually the *Sinn Féin* paper did continue for perhaps two or three months after this meeting. The money for the new weekly which was called *Nationality* was provided by the I.R.B.'[14]

Connolly's strategy was consistent with the ideas of Marx, who had used the term 'permanent revolution' to encompass a period of necessary reliance on or co-operation with the bourgeoisie. Griffith was sometimes prepared to co-operate with socialists on one side and with Home Rulers on the other if he thought that this advanced his nationalist agenda of Irish independence. Trotsky might point out the pitfalls of such a strategy for socialists, but Connolly and Griffith were impatient to see progress.

One of those who understood and supported Griffith's efforts to bring people along, even if that meant Sinn Féin itself before 1914 recognising and co-operating with the less-radical demands of Home Rulers, was Éamonn Ceannt.[15] In the end, however, or rather in 1916, Ceannt, like Connolly, sided with those who decided not to wait for the Irish public to catch up with them at election time. Griffith understood their action but thought its timing premature and likely to rebound worst against the poorest people. For him, who had seen the damage caused by disunity when Parnell fell and who wished to bring the unionists with him into an independent Ireland that he did not think needed to be socialist, it was important to continue trying to convince the broad public of Sinn Féin's cause, even if the movement he founded in 1905 had made very limited progress at the ballot box. Ultimately, he valued political unity more than Connolly did. Connolly had written in his 1896 article:

> 'It may be urged against such a proposal that the first need of Irish politics is unity, and that such a [revolutionary or advanced nationalist] party would only accentuate the division at present existing. This, however, could only be the case if our present representatives refuse to accept the pledge of loyalty to the free Irish Republic, and to it alone. If they do so refuse, then they are unfit to be representatives of the Irish democracy, and cannot be removed too soon. The objection in itself implies a suspicion of the genuine nature of the patriotism so loudly vaunted by our party politicians. Unity is a good thing, no doubt, but honesty is better, and if unity can only be obtained by the suppression of truth and the toleration of falsehood, then it is not worth the price we are asked to pay for it. I would, in conclusion, earnestly recommend my readers to study the suggestions contained in this paper, and to act accordingly. Should

> this meet with a favourable reception, I may give in a future issue my ideas on the programme of political and social reform on which such a party might fight in Parliament and the country, while the public opinion of Ireland was ripening behind them, and pending the arrival of the propitious moment for action.'[16]

Connolly did not consider then the possibility that people might vote in an election such as that of 1918 to support an ideal such as republicanism but subsequently wish to settle for something less than that ideal, as the Irish were to do in 1921–2 when weary of war and facing the prospect of perhaps even greater British violence than that experienced between 1916 and 1921. The voters of Ireland were willing by then to accept an Irish Free State that was less than a republic and far less than Connolly's ideal socialist republic, and this fact became quite clear at the general election of June 1922. What the public settled for was dominion status, a form of dual monarchy more imaginative than Home Rule but less radical than the revolutionary state advocated by Connolly. If there was a popular Irish revolution in the first two decades of the twentieth century, that was its extent and achievement. No amount of wishful thinking or myth-making should obscure that fact.

The Anglo-Irish treaty was the democratic limit of 'the Irish revolution'. Had the vote accepting it in Dáil Éireann in January 1922 been respected by all of the elected representatives and by the IRA, a great deal of physical and psychological damage could have been avoided, and the considerable achievement of an independent state might from the start have been celebrated and built upon instead of condemned or lamented as less than ideal. If civil war had been avoided, the later counter-revolution of which Regan has written might have found it harder to make headway.[17]

The Irish Civil War was an interruption to the revolution, or even a counter-revolution in its own right, its object being the destruction of the treaty and of the provisional government, albeit in the name of the notional or unrealised republic declared in 1916. This is not to say that what happened was simply a struggle between constitutionalists with all moral right on their side and violent republicans who were entirely in the wrong. British insistence on limitations to Irish independence—backed up by the threat of overwhelming force—greatly thwarted the operation of democracy in Ireland. Both sides in the Civil War, and most voters in Ireland, would have chosen a united and independent Ireland had they been given that simple choice.

When de Valera's life was spared and he was freed soon after the Civil War and went back into Dáil Éireann to forge his new political career, it became clear just how much had been made possible by the Irish plenipotentiaries in London. But if de Valera's life was spared, Arthur Griffith's reputation would not be. As explained elsewhere in this book, a myth was to be fashioned from a lie that made Griffith the scapegoat for a national tragedy. This ultimately suited the main political parties, which were happy to put some distance between Griffith and themselves, but it left future generations a distorted political perspective that clouds our understanding of how Ireland developed to its present state of being.

A few years after James Connolly's execution in 1916, and after the Russian revolution of 1917 and the Irish War of Independence, the James Connolly Publishing Company in Dublin issued what it described as a reprint of *Erin's Hope: The End and the Means*. But this pamphlet of Connolly's articles now had a new and more glorious title: *The Irish Revolution: The End and the Means*.

However, it now came with a significant omission, for the editor purported to have included Connolly's 1896 article from *Shan*

Van Vocht that was considered earlier but the article was in fact absent. At least one Scottish reprint of *Erin's Hope* had likewise dropped the first of the four articles included in the first printing, that same one from *Shan Van Vocht*.[18] The pamphlet as published in the 1920s included a 'preliminary notice' by the 'director' of the James Connolly Publishing Company, R.J. Connolly, who was James Connolly's only son and who had been a teenager when in 1916 he joined his father in the Easter Rising. He cited 'technical reasons' in respect of the omission of 'certain valuable commentaries on the text' but did not claim such an excuse for the absence of the *Shan Van Vocht* article. Might this absence have been in fact a form of conscious or unconscious political censorship, marking an unwillingness to face the fact that 'the Irish revolution' for which Connolly aimed failed to muster the degree of 'moral sanction' or democratic support necessary for it to succeed?

As may be seen from his *Shan Van Vocht* article of November 1896, Connolly was at that time asserting, in the face of what he regarded as the overwhelming Irish revolutionary tradition, his own belief that 'those who see in an Irish Republic the only *political* idea worth striving for' should not eschew political action by seeking, in secret conspiracy alone, to prepare for revolution: 'Up to the present, every genuine Irish revolutionist has acted on this belief, that political action was impossible for republicans'. However, he continued,

> 'Now I assert the contrary. A revolution can only succeed in any country when it has the moral sanction of the people. It is so, even in an independent country; it is doubly so in a country subject, like Ireland, to the rule of another. Within this century, no Irish revolutionist had obtained this sanction before he took the field … In 1848 the majority of the Irish people pinned their faith to the Repeal Association, which had disavowed even the right to resist oppres-

> sion, and the Young Irelanders themselves had made no reasonable effort to prepare the popular mind for revolution, but had rather been precipitated into it against their will. Under such conditions, failure was inevitable. Those who were willing to "rise" had no means of knowing how far their aspirations were shared by their fellow-countrymen elsewhere, and lacking confidence in themselves, with the recognized leaders of public opinion against them, the effort ended in disaster. The history of the Fenian movement was somewhat similar. The number of actually enrolled members formed but an insignificant minority of the population, the vast majority of our countrymen, though perhaps sympathizing with the Fenian ideal, put their trust in politicians who preached tame submission under the name of "prudence" and "caution", and in the critical period of the movement flung the weight of their influence on the side of "law and order". In both cases the recognized leaders of national thought were on the side of constituted authority, and against every revolutionary effort. The facts are as undeniable as they are lamentable, and they speak in trumpet tones in favour of such a re-modelling of Irish revolutionary tactics as shall prevent a recurrence of similar disasters in the future. This, I hold, can be best accomplished by a political party seeking to give public expression to the republican ideal. One point needs to be emphasized in this connection, viz., it is not republicanism, but the counsel of insurrectionary effort to realize republicanism, which gave to previous Irish movements their odour of illegality.'

Both Connolly and Griffith, through their writing and political work, tried hard thereafter to win the moral sanction of the people for their republican ideals. While Griffith was more conservative if not less caustic in his opinions than Connolly, his policy during the first decade of the twentieth century—as reflected in his publication of *The Resurrection of Hungary* and his foundation of Sinn Féin, together with his advocacy of the withdrawal of Irish members of parliament from Westminster—was more radical than Home Rule. Griffith's vision was closer to what was achieved in practice within twenty years than was the revolutionary socialist dream of James Connolly.

The Easter Rising surely had no moral sanction from most Irish people. Had it not been for the manner in which the British responded, and in particular their execution of the injured James Connolly, that insurrection might be remembered today as foolhardy and destructive rather than daring and brave.

By the time that Roderic Connolly published the shorter 'reprint' of his father's *Erin's Hope*—notably and gloriously now entitled *The Irish Revolution*—Roderic himself had become a founding member of the Communist Party of Ireland. He may have come to regard his father's views in 1897 as too facilitating in the light of more recent revolutionary events in Russia and his own declared communist ideology. Nevertheless, the long and thankless task of building up the Sinn Féin movement and otherwise stimulating radical political opinion from the end of the nineteenth century had been a vital part of the struggle for Irish national liberation in the early twentieth century. It facilitated after 1916 the harnessing of popular support for political independence when the electoral franchise was greatly expanded in 1918.

To gloss over what went on before the years 1913–23 is to distort the story of 'the Irish revolution' of the twentieth century. To do so is to reduce a complex struggle for national liberation to a series of late violent episodes that in themselves could not have achieved the democratic result that fulfilled some of the ideals and sacrifices of generations. It does not do justice to the cultural ideals of the

Gaelic League, the business aspirations of the Irish-Ireland movement and the ideas of earlier intellectuals, such as those whom Connolly and Griffith admired.

Distortions of history arise for many reasons. Articles in the May/June and July/August 2025 editions of *History Ireland*, illustrate this fact. There, Conor McCabe challenges the confident assertion by C. Desmond Greaves in his *Life and Times of James Connolly* (London, 1961) that Connolly served in the British Army. McCabe writes 'Decades of repetition… have managed to turn legend into fact.' Anthony Coughlan rejects the challenge, relying on Greaves's journals that are in the process of being archived. While journal records of interviews are hearsay, they are at least ostensibly a contemporary record of what has been said to an author. No such notes have been found to support Pakenham's version of what Chamberlain told him about some aspects of the Treaty talks when the latter refused to share his papers with Pakenham.

The erasure from the later editions of *Erin's Hope* of an article that rationalised the sort of pragmatic co-operation in which Connolly engaged with the man whom he came to call an 'old friend', namely Griffith, seems to this author's mind an omen of Griffith's erasure from and debasement within later accounts of 'the Irish revolution'. While some writers who identify with one or other side in the Civil War support Fine Gael or Fianna Fáil or Sinn Féin and have found Griffith perhaps a bad fit for their narratives of Ireland's political development, others who are leftist or liberal have seen in Griffith a repository for their contempt of the less than purely republican or socialist idealist. We need scapegoats, as de Valera is said to have told Griffith when the latter left for London as captain of the team of treaty negotiators.

Once civil war erupted in Ireland in 1922, it was not long before Collins and Griffith were warned that some on the anti-treaty side were out to kill them. The offices being used by the new government in Upper Merrion Street were heavily fortified and ministers sometimes had to sleep there for their own safety. Griffith was horrified at having to be defended physically against some of his own people. In the National Library of Ireland, among the papers of Seán Ó Lúing, who as late as 1953 wrote the first substantive biography of Griffith, I found this anonymous note on a small scrap of paper:

> 'Arthur Griffith died of a broken heart. Shortly after the start of the civil war workmen were delayed in getting into his office as he was seated at his desk with his hands to his face. On arranging his desk for removal, one of the workmen discovered the blotting pad was quite wet with his tears.'[19]

When founding Sinn Féin in 1905, Griffith regarded it very much as a 'movement' more than a mere political party, one that would allow a range of proud Irish people to work together. He believed that Ireland's hope for the future lay in co-operation, as Connolly had argued. In his papers, which he worked long hours for little remuneration to sustain, Griffith railed against social injustice and against the kind of nationalist sectarianism that had brought down Parnell and that was to result in civil war in 1922–3. That he was blamed by some for being a cause of that civil war, including by Frank Pakenham in his own tortured way, is egregious.

30

'*THE* IRISH REVOLUTION'?

If there was an 'Irish revolution' in the early twentieth century, it was incomplete for women and for working-class activists, for those who aspired to social and economic equality, for those who wanted a parliament for the whole island of Ireland and/or a full Gaelic revival, and even for those who might have been satisfied with just part of Ireland becoming a new state if only it were a republic entirely free of the symbolism of the British Crown. The 'revolution' was certainly judged wanting by those who embarked on a civil war. And when some define 'the Irish revolution' as somehow including that civil war they serve to sweep under their glorious carpet a national embarrassment, to appropriate a secondary insurrection that tried to subvert the first and set at naught the independent Irish Free State as it emerged.

While there may have been a 'spirit of revolution' in Ireland in the years before 1923, the actual contents of a book of that name, which was edited by John Cunningham and Terry Dunne and published in 2024 with the subtitle *Ireland from below 1917–23*, illustrate its limitations. The essays in that volume range across various labour and other social upheavals and radical interventions then, including the establishment of 'soviets' or quasi-soviets when workers briefly seized control of workplaces, but a common theme of the book is that such radicalism did not result in notable change or long-term gains. In fact, the volume might have been better named *Labour, Gender and Class in the Struggle for Irish Independence*, which was the title of the conference at which it originated and which implicitly recognises that the decade before 1923 was more 'struggle for Irish independence' than 'revolution'.

During his presidential address at the Irish Trade Union Congress in Waterford in August 1918, the labour leader William O'Brien declared that 'The only real and genuine remedy is to be found in the control of industry in the interest of the community by the working class'. He added that he meant all industries, agricultural and manufacturing, and admitted: 'This proposal is revolutionary, but it is the only proposal that can ultimately satisfy the conditions of the new social order we all desire …'. Such workers' control was certainly not a lasting fruit of 'the Irish revolution'. After O'Brien's subsequent release from Wormwood Scrubs prison in England, one newspaper commented that 'The special interest of the case of William O'Brien is that he is not primarily a Sinn Féiner but is a Labour leader. Hitherto, owing to the influence of the clergy, the Sinn Féiners have fought shy of Labour. If O'Brien became a sure connecting link, their power would be much extended.' No doubt it had not gone unnoticed by the clergy and others that O'Brien's election literature included a quotation from the *Communist Manifesto* by Marx and Engels. Given that O'Brien had been present at the secret meeting that, as seen earlier, Seán T. Ó Ceallaigh convened for the IRB in 1914 to plot Irish revolutionary strategy for the duration of the great war begun in Europe—a meeting attended by most of the future signatories of the 1916 proclamation and by Griffith and a few others—it is striking that the newspaper described him and his comrades as being kept at arm's length by Sinn Féin in 1920.[1]

WHAT YEARS?

The term 'the Irish revolution' has come to be applied most commonly to events in a period roughly commensurate with the eleven years celebrated or commemorated by the Irish government a century later during the official 'decade' of commemorations between 2012 and 2023. Yet as long ago as 1912 William Blackwood & Sons of Edinburgh and London had already published a challenging history by Michael McCarthy boldly entitled *The Irish Revolution*.[2] For McCarthy, a rural Irish unionist, 'the Irish revolution' was over by the time he wrote. Four more years were to elapse before the Easter Rising of 1916. In an author's note at the beginning of his account, McCarthy describes himself as 'a child and product of the Revolution of which he attempts to give a complete short history'. James Joyce in Trieste had a copy of this work among his books.[3]

McCarthy's concept of the Irish revolution is explained by his book's subtitle, *The Murdering Time, from the Land League* [founded 1879] *to the First Home Rule Bill* [1886], and by his intended second volume's subtitle, *The Decline and Fall of Parnell, from the First Home Rule Bill to the Second* [1893]. He was not alone in believing that a revolution had already occurred in Ireland, a revolution of lasting and major significance. It was a socio-economic revolution in respect of land ownership, and McCarthy described 'the solid effects of the revolution in Ireland' as follows:

> 'The power of rent-fixing had been taken from the landlords, the divinity which had hedged them was no more, the process of converting the tenants into proprietors had begun. The farm-labourers

> had won the right to a good house and plot of land which the community could give them without the leave of the lords of the soil. Five-sixths of the parliamentary representation of Ireland had been "nationalised" and transformed into a machine for the confusion of the British parliament. The spirit of revolution was abroad in the land, and it seemed as if even the ecclesiastics would soon have to fight openly for their power over the awakened people. Many other fortresses too remained to be captured in the course of the revolution, but the story of how they were assailed and the result must be told in another volume.'[4]

Some may not agree with McCarthy's belief that between 1879 and 1893 '*the* Irish revolution' had already happened. Nevertheless, in his *Davitt and the Irish Revolution, 1846–82*, the prominent historian T.W. Moody had little doubt about the significance of changes already achieved. Moody wrote of Davitt's career 'in the context of two Irish revolutionary movements, the Irish republican or Fenian movement and the Land League movement, which during 1879–82 interacted on each other with momentous results'.[5]

To judge, however, from the titles of a spate of books in recent years, the very earliest date to which many authors of more recent works would assign the start of 'the Irish revolution' is 1912, the actual year of publication of McCarthy's retrospective volume. This is no quibble. The meaning of words and of concepts matters. To define events in the decade leading up to and including the Civil War of 1922–3 as 'the Irish revolution' suggests a coherence and finality that is too neatly rounded. It may be reassuring for citizens of the Irish state founded in 1922, but it is also potentially misleading.

It is useful for marketing purposes to keep 'the Irish revolution' simple. It flatters the main political parties that grew out of events then, as well as being beneficial for book publishers and historians, for whom the recent long decade of commemorations was a welcome promotional platform. When the term is applied to the period between 1912 and 1923 it lends weight to claims by various configurations of nationalists or republicans in the early twentieth century (and by assumption to the present Fine Gael, Fianna Fáil and Sinn Féin parties)—claims to the fruits of a much longer struggle for Irish liberty from English control.

There should be heroes or action men and women involved in the story of any 'revolution'. It makes neat accounts of 'revolutions' enticing for publishers, historians and readers alike. The authors of a recent study of 'the Irish revolution' highlighted a tendency in writing history that is relevant in this context:

> 'The focus on IRA violence in popular and scholarly accounts, a perspective reinforced by the release of valuable archival material from the Military Service Pensions collection and Bureau of Military History, has reinforced public understanding of the struggle for independence as a primarily military conflict. By foregrounding the impact of small-scale events—ambushes and the burning of empty barracks—over popular mobilization, elections, strikes, and other protests, this approach marginalizes the importance of nonviolent forms of resistance. Political and state commemoration in Ireland during the current Decade of Centenaries has also tended to focus on the 'raids and rallies' that preoccupied nationalist accounts in the years after independence.'[6]

To define '*the* Irish revolution' as a distinctive armed phenomenon of the second decade of the twentieth century is to downplay the great significance not only of earlier uprisings but also of land wars, cultural struggles and even political movements in the nineteenth century or earlier, and to sideline major constitutional and social changes that were in any event coming within the United Kingdom of which Ireland was a part. Not the least of the latter was the UK franchise act of 1918 that greatly extended the right to vote among men and women in Britain and Ireland. In his remarkable critique 'An Irish revolution without a revolution', published in 2016 and available free online, Aidan Beatty points out, for example, that Conor Kostick's Marxist text entitled *Revolution in Ireland: Popular Militancy, 1917 to 1923* (2nd edn, Cork University Press, 2009) begins by tracing Ireland's socio-economics back to the Act of Union of 1800, 'thus more than tacitly recognizing the slow pace of class-based histories'.[7]

Historians who use the definitive term 'the Irish revolution' to describe the period immediately before and around the emergence of an Irish Free State do not seem to agree on its span. This fact is indicative of its fuzziness as a concept. Each gives a range of dates that seems to express his or her view on the first and last significant moments of the revolutionary process. Thus the revolution is usually said to have begun in one of the five years leading up to and including 1916 and to have ended in one of the three years from 1921 to 1923. Some rebels sang of being 'on the one road swingin' along', but the 1916 Rising, the 1917 general election, the War of Independence and the Civil War never constituted a single, clearly marked highway.

In his *The Making of Modern Ireland 1603–1923*, published by Faber, J.C. Beckett defined the period 1914–23 as that of 'the Revolution in Ireland'. However, the editors of another major general history of Ireland that also appeared around the time of the fiftieth anniversary of the 1916 Rising were more circumspect. In *The Course of Irish History*, produced by RTÉ and edited by T.W. Moody and F.X. Martin, the chapter devoted to the period

1891–1921 is entitled simply 'From Parnell to Pearse'. It weighs in the balance peaceful movements such as the Gaelic League and the Anglo-Irish literary revival and in passing uses a title for the period that was once quite common among citizens and quite apposite, namely 'the Troubles'. When that title was increasingly appropriated to designate more recent events in Northern Ireland its use seemed to fade away for the earlier period.

In 2017 Cork University Press launched its omnibus *Atlas of the Irish Revolution*, edited by John Crowley, Donal Ó Drisceoil and Mike Murphy. Heavyweight in bulk and academic status, it boasts that its one hundred contributors 'offer multiple perspectives on the pivotal years from the 1912 Home Rule Crisis to the end of the Irish Civil War in 1923'. These were also the years chosen by Four Courts Press for its recent series of county histories of 'the Irish Revolution'. The thick *Atlas* has much to commend it, yet its first 140 pages are devoted to events *before* 1912, and its editors struggle unconvincingly to justify its title, admitting that the term remains contested by 'some' historians. They write:

> 'It [the title] has been chosen here simply because it provides the most convenient, and now generally accepted, umbrella term under which to gather the multifarious subjects and themes thrown up by these years of political change, social upheaval, cultural ferment and military conflict. Its use does not signify a specific, ideological approach to the history of the 1912–23 period, or suggest a particular understanding of the nature of what occurred.'[8]

If the title 'Irish revolution' does not indicate 'a particular understanding of the nature of what occurred', might 'non-revolution' have served as well or even better? Some might also argue that the idea of a successful revolution serves a fine ideological purpose for the state in the face of republican or socialist criticism.

The revolution of Cork University Press and Four Courts Press was a year longer than that of Diarmaid Ferriter's *A Nation and Not a Rabble: The Irish Revolution 1913–1923* (Profile Books, 2015), two years longer than Beckett's 'The Revolution in Ireland, 1914–23'—as the relevant chapter of his general history was entitled—and four years longer than Marie Coleman's *The Irish Revolution, 1916–1923* (Routledge, 2013), but it was shorter than Robert Lynch's *Revolutionary Ireland, 1912–25* (Bloomsbury, 2015). Cal McCarthy's *Cumann na mBan and the Irish Revolution, 1914–1923* (Collins Press, 2014) followed Beckett's precedent.

Pádraig Óg Ó Ruairc's photographic history was headed *Revolution*, but its subtitle referred adjectivally and somewhat less conclusively to *Revolutionary Ireland 1913–1923* (Mercier, 2014). Michael Barry's *Illustrated History of the Irish Revolution, 1916–1923* (Andalus, 2020) presumably required fewer images for fewer years, with Fergal Tobin's *The Irish Revolution: An Illustrated History 1912–25* (Gill & Macmillan, 2013) needing more for more.

The editors of a recent collection of essays on the 'global history' of 'the Irish Revolution' confidently refer to 'the revolution that took place in Ireland between 1916 and 1923', when Ireland came to be counted not only among the nations of the world but also among the fields of revolution of the early twentieth century, apparently. These editors plead for greater attention to be paid in the context of Ireland to factors such as the collapse of Europe's empires after World War I, the redrawing of national boundaries to accommodate new republics, the strengthening of ethnic nationalism by mass suffrage, the Russian Revolution, and a wider British crisis spanning from Egypt to India. Their pleas have merit, no matter how one defines the Troubles between 1916 and 1923, for the changes in Ireland at that time were part of an international trend in the assertion and winning of national and democratic rights.[9]

An author who breaks with the consensus by starting her account in the first decade of the twentieth century is Marnie Hay, in *Na Fianna Éireann and the Irish Revolution, 1906 to 1923* (Manchester, 2019). Richard Killeen's study lengthens the period at the other end in a *Short History of the Irish Revolution: 1912 to 1927* (Gill, 2007).

One might argue that supplying a range of dates in a title is merely an indication of the necessary limitations of any volume, and simply announces the period covered by the author in respect of what might indeed have been a longer process. But these titles seem more declamatory or definitive than that, and the dates ought to have been placed within brackets if that was not intended to be signified. When the French journalist Simone Tery's contemporary reports of events were collectively republished as a book in the 1920s, the word 'revolution' was not in its title, but brackets were: *En Irlande de la guerre d'indépendance à la guerre civile (1914–1923).*[10] The presence of just one capital letter, that being in the name of Ireland, is also relevant, for the use of initial capital or upper-case letters in nouns in the title of books in English ('title case') lends emphasis to the word 'revolution' after the word 'Irish' in the particular context under consideration here and suggests that any dates following it define the period of revolution and not just the period of the study.

One should not judge a book by its cover but covers may tell their own stories. In 2020 an impressive tombstone volume edited for Yale University Press by Eunan O'Halpin and Daithí Ó Corráin was published. Its simple title, *The Dead of the Irish Revolution*, includes no dates, but the volume itself gives details of deaths during 'the Irish revolution' for only the years between 1916 and 1921. By default, the Civil War is excised from the revolutionary process. One might define the Civil War in fact as some kind of counter-revolution or separate revolution of its own.[11]

Two books edited by Desmond Williams in 1966, on the fiftieth anniversary of the Easter Rising, avoided in their titles reference to any revolution, these being *The Irish Struggle, 1916–26* and *The Years of the Great Transition 1916–1926.* Their titles may be more accurate descriptions of what happened then than is the word 'revolution'.

RECURRENT REVOLUTION

Revolution was a constant or recurrent feature of Irish history in the face of invasion, colonisation and imperialism and the concept cannot be confined exclusively to years immediately before and after the foundation of the Irish Free State.

The Irish revolution that led to the creation of an independent state in 1922 had its immediate roots in the soil of land wars and in the aftermath of the Fenian rising of 1867 (the one in Dublin in which one of my great-grandfathers participated). The work of the Gaelic League of Douglas Hyde and of the Irish-Ireland industrial movement were also crucial for it. Given the interplay between theory and practice which is part of a revolutionary process, the theorists and associations that gave rise to what has been called an 'Irish Renaissance' then readied the public mind for its shift from the support of relatively modest Home Rule objectives to more radical political options after 1916. Hence the appropriate full title of Dominic Daly's 1974 book, *The Young Douglas Hyde: The Dawn of the Irish Revolution and Renaissance, 1874–1893* (Irish University Press), with its appreciative foreword by Erskine Childers, who was the namesake and son of one of the secretaries to the Irish treaty team in London in 1921 and was president of Ireland in 1974.

By including some years before the turn of the century in any consideration of events leading to the creation of an independent Irish state one can acknowledge more comprehensively too the role of the Irish Republican Brotherhood, as well as the foundational work of a range of activists and small political organisations. These activists include perhaps most notably Arthur Griffith, both as a journalist producing his influential weekly papers and as the founder of Sinn Féin and author of *The Resurrection of Hungary*. James Joyce, according to his brother, described Griffith's *United Irishman* as 'the only paper in Dublin worth reading'[12] and it was sent to him when he lived abroad. As witness statements of the Bureau of Military History indicate, people who became active in the War of Independence had been eager readers of Griffith's papers. His papers had an impact beyond Ireland, partly owing to the socialist Fred Ryan, who had sometimes written for Griffith and also sometimes disagreed with him:

> 'Ryan ... reprinted Griffith's Sinn Féin writings in the short-lived *Egyptian Standard*, which Ryan co-edited with W.J. Maloney at Cairo between 1908 and 1909. Indian nationalists who preached passive resistance against British rule in their own country, through the Swadeshi Movement, also took a keen interest in Griffith's teachings. One Indian-nationalist newspaper described Griffith's Sinn Féin policy as identical with that of Swadeshi, and argued that Griffith had provided that movement with a practical scheme for implementing its program.'[13]

If Griffith's foundation of Sinn Féin is elided from the Irish revolution of this period, or if his publication of the best-selling pamphlet *The Resurrection of Hungary* is forgotten, or his attendance at a crucial IRB meeting in 1914 is ignored, he becomes less visible as the influential force that he was, and this makes it easier for writers to repeat unchallenged what Griffith called the 'damnable lie' about his handling of the treaty negotiations in London in 1921 that has been examined at some length above.

By allowing the period of 'the Irish revolution' to run on until 1927, the present author brings the curtain down at the entry of Éamon de Valera's new Fianna Fáil party into Dáil Éireann that year. De Valera's decision then to abandon his policy of abstention from the parliament in Dublin, to overcome the obstacle of the oath mentioning the king that the deputies of Dáil Éireann were expected to take, may not have been as momentous as that of Sinn Féin to abstain from Westminster in 1918, but it was surely revolutionary in its own way.

Others, too, have found the concept of 'the Irish revolution' difficult to understand within a narrow range of years. In an original critique through the lens of 'masculinity', for example, Aidan Beatty has written that

> 'The period from 1912 to 1923 is the most heavily privileged period in modern Irish historiography and it has become commonplace to describe this period as "The Irish Revolution". Moreover, a number of Irish historians have built on this to see the post-1922 period as the "Irish Counter-Revolution", when more radical political impulses were suppressed in favour of the Free State's vision of conservative law and order. This paper challenges these paradigms by arguing that the themes commonly associated with the "Revolution"—meritocracy, violence, the excitement about acquiring national power—had currency within Irish nationalism long before 1912. Similarly, the defining features of the "Counter-Revolution"—coercion, fear of socialism and feminism, a desire to force Irish citizens to live up to certain prescribed social

> roles—were already implicit in the politics and culture of the "Revolution".'[14]

The difficulties involved in using the word 'revolution' as a reductive or overarching term to describe what happened in Ireland during the years 1914–23 are well illustrated by an early case of the word's defence not just as a concept but as a strategy. This was in a paper on 'ethics of the Irish revolution', published in March 1924 by the remaining hard-line republican rump of Sinn Féin, in which the author chose explicitly to begin with the Easter Rising of 1916 (whose leaders had proclaimed 'the Irish Republic as a Sovereign, Independent State') and in the course of which the author demonstrated the subjective and arbitrary nature of the description. One does not have to agree with the definitions to appreciate this effort at intellectual clarity:

> 'Easter week may be defined as a revolt, viz., against the *de facto* Government; it may also be described as war waged against England's forces by the forces of the Provisional Government of the proclaimed Irish Republic. The conflict of 1920 was war in the full sense, being an encounter between the forces of the elected Independent Government of the Irish people and British forces. The armed conflict of 1922 may be described as war on the Irish Republic, no longer waged by England's own army, but by the forces of the Free State Provisional Government, established by England; or a revolt of citizens against the lawful Republican Government; or the continuation of the revolt and war against English rule and domination in Ireland. It was clearly civil war. It partook also of the nature of international war, because it was begun by forces paying allegiance, through the "Provisional Government", to England's King, and because it was initiated under England's threat and carried on with England's help.'[15]

So the Easter Rising was 'revolution', the War of Independence was purely 'war in the full sense', the Civil War begun in 1922 was a war of suppression or a revolution ('revolt of citizens') or a revolution *and* war of independence—but in any case 'clearly civil war'. Yet it was an 'international war' too.

How much simpler and more serviceable are terms such as 'the War of Independence' or 'the Troubles' for the period between Easter 1916 and the end of the Civil War, and how much more accommodating of nuance and perspective within the complex framework of those times when set against the arc of a far longer revolutionary struggle for Irish freedom from England.

Crown forces (Blank and Tans and Auxiliaries) happy to have escaped injury in an IRA attack of 11 April 1921 on the London and North Western Hotel, North Wall, Dublin, where they were billeted. Petrol bombs were thrown through the windows (courtesy National Library of Dublin, HOGW117)

31

OTHER MYTHS?

Sometime after conceiving of the present volume I came across a pamphlet by Rayner O'Connor Lysaght (1941–2022) entitled *The Great Irish Revolution: Myths and Realities, a Handbook* (Dublin?, *c.* 2006). I waited to read it until I had formed my own views and completed my first draft of this book. Lysaght's thoughtful pamphlet addresses a broad range of topics, in a small space and generally without referencing. His 'myths' by no means all coincide with those considered above.

Revisionism—or 'myth-busting', if one wishes—has many forms. It can be just as tedious as predictable orthodoxy if taken to iconoclastic extremes. Lysaght does not do so, and I do not think it necessary to seek out the various points on which I disagree with him and contest or confound them here. His is a short work worth reading, as is any serious and spirited consideration of the contentious developments that have made Ireland and other countries what they are today.

More recently, and more explosively, a provocative historian at the University of Dundee has also fuelled continuing controversy about the reassessment of the past within the context of contemporary events and perspectives—or 'revisionism', as this trend is known.[1] In his *Myth and the Irish State* (Irish Academic Press, 2013), Dr John M. Regan discusses the role of the historian in interpreting matters such as the part played by Michael Collins in the creation of the Irish Free State.

Regan asks to what extent in 1922 was Collins prepared to ignore the parameters of the very treaty with the British that he himself had helped to negotiate, and later to assume to himself dictatorial powers that might have in time—had he lived—threatened the fledgling democracy that was the Irish Free State? Or was the new Irish government simply exercising the sort of special powers to which any democratically elected state might resort when faced with an existential threat? These are uncomfortable questions to which there is not an entirely unambiguous answer. In a review of the book on his *Irish Story* website, John Dorney observes that

> 'Regan's thesis is that Collins, driving force within the IRA from 1919–21, bolstered by his personal network within the Irish Republican Brotherhood, in both the Dáil and the Army, was in fact a dictator in waiting. He cites, among other things, Collins' assuming, without consultation with his cabinet colleagues, simultaneous supreme command of the National Army and head of government on the outbreak of the Irish Civil War. Moreover, Regan notes that Collins would not let the Third Dáil, elected in June 1922, meet in session, nor did he consult it about the declaration of war on the anti-Treaty IRA. It was not until after his death in ambush in Cork in late August 1922 that the Dáil was finally recalled.'[2]

Regan argues that the notion of 'elision', simply ignoring unhelpful evidence, threatens Irish history. He believes that some historians have ignored unhelpful facts that perhaps do not further their points or that perhaps contradict them altogether. One may note, of course, that this is not an exclusively Irish sin.

More generally, in his *Myth and the Irish State*, Regan asks questions such as 'Why do some historians deny or marginalise the British threat of war and re-conquest in 1922?', 'Why do so many Irish historians describe Michael Collins as a "constitutionalist" or a "democrat" when the evidence argues otherwise?' and 'Was the Irish Civil War really fought between "democrats" defending the state and "dictators" attempting its overthrow?'. He believes that some of what historians have written about militant republicanism in the early twentieth century has gone too far in designating sectarianism as the motivation for certain acts of violence, and that this is at least partly because historians did not want to be thought to provide a moral alibi for paramilitary violence during 'the Troubles' in Northern Ireland in the late twentieth century.

By no means all historians have agreed with or taken kindly to Regan's critique. In a strong review of *Myth and the Irish State*, Diarmaid Ferriter, professor of modern history at UCD, has accused Regan of excessive invective and personalisation, of 'extreme repetition' and of insulting the intelligence not just of historians but also of the public more generally.[3]

It was a previous professor of modern history at UCD, Robert (also known as Robin) Dudley Edwards, along with his counterpart at Trinity College Dublin Theodore Moody, who in 1938 founded the journal *Irish Historical Studies*. The two were, as Aidan Clarke has put it,

> 'involved in a series of organisational initiatives aimed at promoting systematic improvements in the standards of Irish historical scholarship. Their motives transcended the disciplinary: both were convinced of the ameliorative power of an informed and objective understanding of the past.'[4]

Yet, notwithstanding their undoubtedly high ambitions, their own careers and opinions illustrate the benefits of eternal vigilance when it comes to history and to the proud boast of 'scientific' methods in any field, if by 'scientific' is meant a mode of research that can entirely exclude subjective motivation and evaluation. For, ironically, given their outstanding reputations for promoting an objective approach to history, the pair found themselves differing as paid experts on Irish history concerning a great fisheries dispute in Ulster that included in 1947–8 what is said to have been at that time the longest court case in the history of the Irish state. Moody was in the witness box for twelve days. Other historians were also involved in the case, with one barrister later observing that 'The experts hardly agreed on anything'.[5] Other historian witnesses in that case included Daniel Binchy of UCD, 'professor of Roman law, jurisprudence, and legal history' (in his case mainly ancient Irish law), who was subjected to a bruising cross-examination that exposed inconsistencies in his position that might also be called 'revisions'. Binchy in turn accused Eoin MacNeill, Edwards's mentor, of letting political considerations colour his views of Gaelic Ireland. Among the papers of Robert Dudley Edwards in the UCD Archives are files relating to his work as an expert witness for the Erne, Laune, Moy, Foyle and Bann and Ballycroy fisheries cases, dated 1928–63.[6]

Not every 'professional historian'—if by that term one means someone who has graduated with an advanced degree in history and who is employed by an educational establishment—is always objective or free from conscious or unconscious bias. As against that, any citizen who takes an interest in interrogating received historical wisdom may aspire to fairness and objectivity.

For his part, O'Connor Lysaght was born in Wales and moved to Ireland, where he studied history and espoused revolutionary Marxist theory and causes. He participated in many street protests and was respected by people who did not share his Trotskyist views. The 'theses' that Lysaght challenges are not simply dismissed by him. He begins responses with phrases such as 'Subjectively, this is true …' and 'This can be accepted only by accepting …' and 'This is more challenging…' that express a critical capacity when it comes to the sort of 'positive facts' or 'absolute certainties' that Napoleon remarked 'ought to be incontrovertible' but that remain contested even by the most candid of observers. And what, indeed, will be the case 'if the narrators be not sincere, or if they should be actuated by interest or passion', as Napoleon then asked?[7]

Unfortunately, Lysaght's challenge does not go far enough when it comes to a principal concern of the present volume, namely the 'damnable lie' that Griffith somehow bound the plenipotentiaries by doing a dirty deal with Lloyd George. Like too many other writers, Lysaght appears to assume some sort of 'common knowledge' rooted in Pakenham's *Peace by Ordeal* when in his Section 24 he writes that 'Griffith is to be criticised for giving his word to Lloyd George not to leave the talks on the partition issue' and refers to Griffith's 'surrender on partition'. This is not only misleading and untrue, as I hope the present volume demonstrates clearly, but is a narrative that has had a malign impact on our idea of the origin of the Irish state. At least Lysaght does not simply stay 'on side' by condemning the treaty outright, for he concedes that it may be true that it gave Ireland the best possible deal then, 'given the margin available for error on the part of the Irish plenipotentiaries'. The Irish were also convinced, rightly or wrongly on the basis of discussions with the British, that the boundary commission to be set up under the treaty would result in significant changes to the border.

Perhaps it is the neat Oxbridge style of Pakenham's English, if not a certain veneer of even-handedness, that has seen him escape the kind of critical reading in recent times to which other early accounts of the new state's creation written by authors such as P.S. O'Hegarty and Dorothy Macardle are subjected. On first looking into Pakenham's *Peace by Ordeal* the present writer joined the number of those who have praised it, but since then familiarity with the text has bred a revision of my views on a book that was in practice a project calculated to a political end.

Myth-busting should be even-handed. One finds a recent volume on revisionist scholarship and Irish politics, published in Britain, promoted on the basis that 'Almost nowhere are politics and history so intimately bound up as in Ireland. Over the course of several hundred years rival political and religious camps have shaped their identities according to particular interpretations of their shared history.' More bound up than in the Netherlands or Russia or the United States of America or England? Are national and imperial politics and history not bound up in powerful myth in Britain, as Brexit has surely shown?[8]

I have illustrated elsewhere how a biased and misleading account of the development of Kenmare, Co. Kerry, was framed by the famous Thomas Babington Macaulay in his *History of England* to further British interests in Ireland. Macaulay's seat in parliament had been arranged by the most influential landlord in Kerry, Lord Lansdowne, who was a brother-in-law of Sir Charles Trevelyan–the powerful British civil servant who oversaw the cataclysmic years of the Great Famine. Oscar Wilde mocked the prominent English historian of Ireland J.A. Froude who followed Macaulay when writing on Kenmare.[9] History published in Ireland is not somehow unique. It is not only smaller nations that continue to cherish myths in need of busting.

32

A UNITED IRELAND?

In April 1922, as the anti-treaty IRA occupied the Four Courts at gunpoint, a frustrated Éamon de Valera told the *Manchester Guardian* that 'If the Irish people were allowed a free choice I am certain they would choose by an overwhelming majority exactly what these armed forces desire'.[1] What was it 'exactly' that he thought the anti-treaty forces 'desired'? Renewed negotiations with the British? A renewed war of independence for a 32-county Irish republic? At what price?

In early 1922 Michael Collins was despairing of the Northern Ireland government. Catholics north of the border were being killed by sectarian murderers, while unionist politicians showed little or no intention of working with Dublin on any all-Ireland basis. Collins urged de Valera to 'consider where his language, if translated into action, was hurrying the nation', and 'could he not cease his incitements—for incitements they were, whatever his personal intentions'.[2]

In late April Winston Churchill, 'knocked out for the time being by a bad fall at polo', wired Collins to encourage him to continue talking with Northern Ireland's premier James Craig, claiming that 'a great deal of good has resulted from the agreement and we must at all costs preserve it as the foundation on which the future peace and unity of Ireland is to be erected'. Given Britain's partition of

Ireland two years earlier, the fact that Churchill—one of the British team that negotiated the treaty and now as secretary of state for the colonies responsible for its implementation—held out the prospect of the 'unity of Ireland' cannot have greatly impressed Collins. He replied impatiently, outlining outrages against Catholics in Northern Ireland that included seven further deaths over the previous weekend and 'raids and searches of a provocative character'.[3]

At a fundamental level, there is little doubt that most Irish people did not wish *any* part of Ireland to be governed from London. The British remained in Ireland down the years owing to their use of overwhelming force. Britain had repeatedly crushed political and military efforts to remove their armed forces from the island and to achieve Irish independence. There was a long and bloody history of repression, slaughter and dispossession through which a colonial or imperial superiority was asserted and maintained. If the republican Easter Rising of 1916 did not have widespread popular support, the United Kingdom franchise itself before the reforms of 1918 was scarcely very democratic. Many people had no vote, and the British occupation of Ireland was certainly not chosen by the majority of Irish people.

Had the British respected the opinions of the majority of the people on the island of Ireland, a form of 'Home Rule' would have been in place long before 'the Irish revolution' and Ireland might have already declared itself to be an independent state. When it came to violence and force, the United Kingdom government had no moral high ground from which to lecture the Irish. The Irish did not have a free choice. Sinn Féin had fought but not beaten the British during the War of Independence. The truce of 1921 was a stalemate in chess terms. The British were determined to keep the whole island of Ireland within the empire—or 'the commonwealth', as that imperial network could now be less provocatively called—and to keep the king in Ireland as head of state. Lloyd George, quite flexible in some ways and no ardent supporter of unionism, had made it clear to de Valera from the outset where his government's red lines lay. He would not yield on the 'Crown' for, as he told his own cabinet 'It will give the impression that we have lost our grip, that the Empire has no further force and will have an effect in India and throughout Europe'. He thought that 'without acceptance of Throne and Empire you march into the bog'.[4]

The British were also unwilling to see all unionists in Ulster included in a united Ireland against their wishes, and any attempt to force them in would have led to the replacement of Lloyd George's government by a more conservative or reactionary one and to a civil war in Ireland far more deadly than that which ensued. The fact that many unionists were armed and prepared to fight to stay out of a united Ireland meant that a full military confrontation between Ulster unionists and the IRA might have been a disaster for Sinn Féin's objectives and for its armed Volunteers and, indeed, for all Ireland.

But was a united and independent Ireland in fact what de Valera intended to signify by the words 'what these armed forces [in the Four Courts] desire'? He had already conceded, as shown above, that counties with a unionist majority might vote themselves out of an Irish republic.

Did those who seized the Four Courts really believe that they could have fought on with whatever limited resources remained in IRA hands and driven a refreshed British Army entirely out of Ireland and forced all of unionist Ulster into a 32-county Irish republic? Some may have thought so but these were probably deluded. In fact, as noted earlier, the immediate demands of anti-treaty activists tended to focus on a more limited objective: to turn the clock back a few months by tearing up the treaty, abolishing the Provisional Government of the Irish Free State and restoring a united Dáil that would be almost exclusively composed of Sinn Féin members (under the presidency again of de Valera, one assumes). But then what? Going back to war was not an attractive prospect for most people, who feared further instability and suffering and saw no immediate possibility of a settlement superior to the one already achieved.

The pro-treaty argument, that the plenipotentiaries had come away from London with enough to allow future development and progress towards greater independence and prosperity, was broadly shared within every class of the community. In early May 1922 some anti-treaty IRA officers angered colleagues when they joined with Michael Collins and Richard Mulcahy to recognise this fact publicly. Among them was Dan Breen, one of the most remarkable figures of the War of Independence and a future Fianna Fáil TD. The group urged 'the acceptance and utilization of our present national position in the best interests of Ireland'. The officers described the situation as grave and declared that 'if the present drift is maintained a conflict of comrades is inevitable'. They added that 'this would be the greatest calamity in Irish history, and would leave Ireland broken for generations'. To avert such a catastrophe, they called for a closing of ranks and 'the acceptance of the fact—admitted by all sides—that the majority of the people of Ireland are willing to accept the treaty'. They foresaw the result of the election in June 1922 in which a clear majority of deputies in favour of the treaty was returned to Dáil Éireann.[5]

Meanwhile, de Valera had been mocking Michael Collins in terms that now seem ironic, given what we know of de Valera's own later use of the treaty freedoms to strip away residual British powers in Ireland once he returned to Dáil Éireann with his new Fianna Fáil party. During an interview with him for the Hearst newspapers of America, a journalist pointed out that Collins and many on the pro-treaty side 'accepted the treaty as a means to securing an Irish republic in time' and asked de Valera why he did not accept that point of view. De Valera replied waspishly,

> 'Mr Collins may accept the "Treaty" with that view, or pretend to accept it with that view. A Missouri man would say to him, I think, "You will have to show me." Mr Collins has never yet shown anybody how he may, by his "Treaty", secure the Republic "in time" or eternity. If Mr Collins has discovered this new primrose path to the Republic, he might map it out for us in advance a little. That would be far more convincing than ever so many bald assertions which no one who really tries to gauge the future without being interested in deceiving himself will accept for a moment.'[6]

De Valera himself later trod the 'primrose path to the Republic' when Collins lay dead and buried. Bit by bit, stepping-stone by stepping-stone, de Valera and others were to dismantle the residual symbols of empire that he so detested By the end of the 1930s, as Ruane observes, 'de Valera had substantially emasculated the Treaty and had a republic in all but name'.[7] It was a coalition government of his opponents under Taoiseach John A. Costello that in 1949 finally and formally declared the Irish Free State a republic. Ireland had not been divided by an international land border before 1920 and, if a simple headcount were applied, the democratic choice of a majority of its people would have been for the island to become an independent state of thirty-two counties—albeit with a large minority in the north-east resistant to leaving the United Kingdom. Democracy, however, must be tempered by other considerations if it is not to be a tyranny of the majority. Most Irish people recognised in 1922 the difficulties and undesirability of trying to force a large Protestant minority of largely British origin into a new Irish state that was largely Catholic. These were difficulties not only of military practicality, given that the War of Independence had already been fought to a standstill, but of principle, such as de Valera identified in Dáil Éireann on 22 August 1921. That day, as we have seen above, two months before the plenipotentiaries left for London, de Valera told his fellow deputies that, for his part, 'if the Republic were recognised, he would be in favour of giving each county power to vote itself out of the Republic if it so wished. Otherwise they would be compelled to use force.' Today the Belfast/Good Friday Agreement of 1998, as endorsed by the public in referendums on each side of the Irish border, affirms that

> 'It is for the people of the island of Ireland alone, by agreement between the two parts respectively and without external impediment, to exercise their right of self-determination on the basis of consent, freely and concurrently given, North and South, to bring about a united Ireland, if that is their wish, accepting that this right must be achieved and exercised with and subject to the agreement and consent of a majority of the people of Northern Ireland'.

The Belfast Agreement also acknowledges that 'a substantial section of the people in Northern Ireland share the legitimate wish of a majority of the people of the island of Ireland for a united Ireland'. An overwhelming majority of voters in the Republic of Ireland voted in favour of the Belfast Agreement, notwithstanding the fact that for many years the 'majority' in Northern Ireland had discriminated against the 'substantial section' there that has been principally Catholic and nationalist. Once again, as in the case of Irish voters who in the general election of June 1922 endorsed the proposed Anglo-Irish treaty by electing a clear majority in favour of it, the preference of most Irish people is for peaceful democratic change, where force or violence is ever a last resort.

It would be just another 'damnable lie' to pretend that most people in Northern Ireland currently want a united Ireland. However, many people, north and south, hope that such an objective can be achieved peacefully, in the best interest of all who live on the island. If Ireland is to be united again and if the border is to be dissolved, the voters' preference is still for a settlement based on winning the argument for unity rather than one predicated on fighting a war against other Irish people.

If there was an Irish revolution during the twentieth century, it was essentially a democratic one.

APPENDIX

IRISH DELEGATION OF PLENIPOTENTIARIES

SECRET.

CONFERENCE ON IRELAND.

MR. GRIFFITH'S NOTES OF TWO SUB - CONFERENCES HELD ON December 5th/December 6th. 1921 at 10, DOWNING STREET.
No.1 - at 3 p.m.
No.11 - at 11.30 p.m. to 2.30 a.m.

Present:

BRITISH REPRESENTATIVES	IRISH REPRESENTATIVES
Mr.Lloyd George	Mr.A.Griffith
Mr.Chamberlain	Mr.M.Collins
Lord Birkenhead	Mr.R.C.Barton
Mr.Churchill	

The following is the barest outline of what happened on Monday- 5th.December. We were there all day and probably half the night - with a couple of breaks.

Mr.Barton is making, at my request, a long Memo. of events, which we shall bring with us for you to-morrow night.

Things were so strenuous and exhausting that the sequence of conversation is not in many cases clear.in my mind to-day.

Mr.Barton, Mr.Collins and myself were on our side. Mr.Lloyd George, Birkenhead, Churchill and Chamberlain on theirs.

The Conference opened with the British Delegates in a bad mood. They had had a full Cabinet meeting previously and apparently had had a rough time.

Lloyd George began by suggesting we had let him down over the Ulster proposals.

We denied this and argued we must have a reply from Craig refusing or accepting these proposals before we proceeded.

The others pointed out that as they were prepared to go ahead with their proposals irrespective of Craig there was no ground for our contention.

We went on this line of argument for a while when Lloyd George declared we were trying to bring about a break on Ulster. The question was,would we or would we not come within the community of nations known as the British Empire. The question must be answered because it was the question of peace or war.

(1)

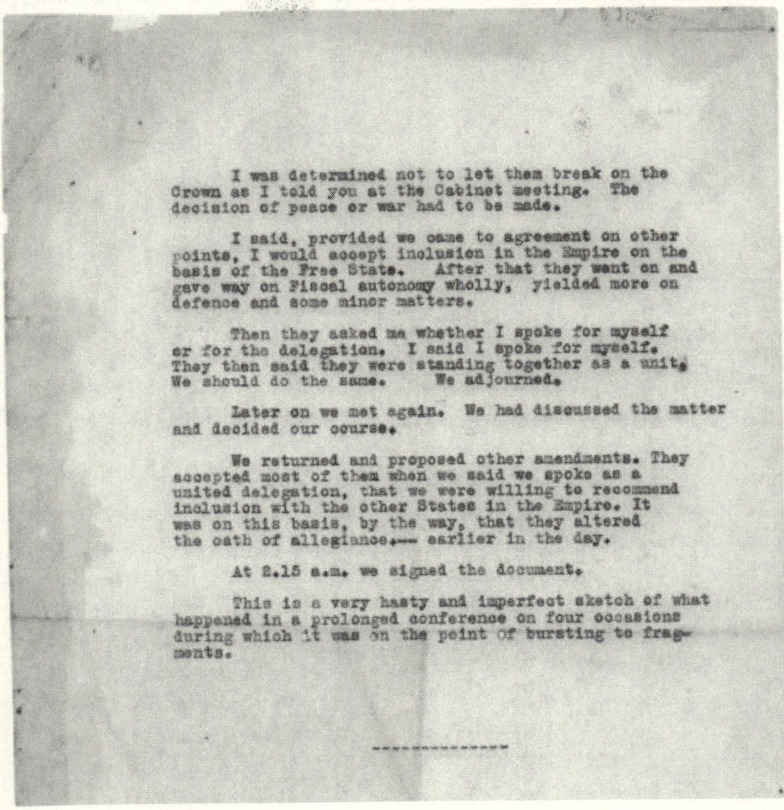

I was determined not to let them break on the Crown as I told you at the Cabinet meeting. The decision of peace or war had to be made.

I said, provided we came to agreement on other points, I would accept inclusion in the Empire on the basis of the Free State. After that they went on and gave way on Fiscal autonomy wholly, yielded more on defence and some minor matters.

Then they asked me whether I spoke for myself or for the delegation. I said I spoke for myself. They then said they were standing together as a unit. We should do the same. We adjourned.

Later on we met again. We had discussed the matter and decided our course.

We returned and proposed other amendments. They accepted most of them when we said we spoke as a united delegation, that we were willing to recommend inclusion with the other States in the Empire. It was on this basis, by the way, that they altered the oath of allegiance.— earlier in the day.

At 2.15 a.m. we signed the document.

This is a very hasty and imperfect sketch of what happened in a prolonged conference on four occasions during which it was on the point of bursting to fragments.

Chairman Griffith's prompt report for de Valera, on the crucial final session of the Treaty conference in London on 5/6 December 1921 (NAI DE 2/304/5/6), has been inexplicably omitted from the series *Documents on Irish Foreign Policy*. The session lasted over eight hours (not including a long break). Yet Griffith's outline is just 450 words, and the 'long memo' he asked Barton to write is fewer than 2,600 words (NAI DE 2/304/1/DIFP 213). There were no formal minutes. Their original hand-written notes have not been found. In Dáil Éireann (15 December 1921) Barton described his notes as an 'impression', after 'the strain' of a 'pretty severe' struggle.

ENDNOTES

Preface

1. '"An extraordinarily clever journalist": Arthur Griffith's editorships, 1899–1919' in *Periodicals and Journalism in Twentieth-Century Ireland*, ed. Mark O'Brien and Felix Larkin (Dublin, 2014), pp 16–30.
2. Nicholas Mansergh, *The Unresolved Question: The Anglo-Irish Settlement and its Undoing 1912–72* (New Haven and London, 1991), p. 2.
3. National Archives of Ireland DE 2/304/5/6.
4. Dwayne H. Mulder, 'Objectivity', *Internet Encyclopedia of Philosophy: A Peer-Review Academic Resource* (https://iep.utm.edu/objectiv/). See also https://plato.stanford.edu/entries/scientific-objectivity/. Both accessed 14 July 2025.
5. C. Kenny, *Irish Patriot, Publisher and Advertising Agent: Kevin J. Kenny (1881–1954)* (Bray, 2011), pp 2–3; C. Kenny, *Kenmare: History and Survival—Fr John O'Sullivan and the Famine Poor* (Dublin, 2021), pp 7, 8, 11, 32, 39, 152–3, 238.

1. 'Call it what you like'?

1. *Evening Echo*, 15 April 1922.
2. *Belfast Newsletter*, 15 April 1922.
3. *Irish Times* and *Irish Independent*, 15 April 1922; *Cork Examiner*, 23 March 1922.
4. Dan Edelstein, *The Revolution to Come: A History of an Idea from Thucydides to Lenin* (New Haven, CT, 2025), p. 3; 'Book Talk' with Dan Edelstein, the Hoover Institution, 29 April 2025 (at 5.25–7.15 minutes) (https://www.hoover.org/events/revolution-come-history-idea-thucydides-lenin; accessed 17 May 2025).
5. Ernie O'Malley, *On Another Man's Wound* (London, 1936), pp 59, 144.
6. Nicholas Allen, 'Ernie O'Malley (1899–1957)', in John Crowley, Donal Ó Drisceoil and Mike Murphy (eds), *Atlas of the Irish Revolution* (Cork, 2017), pp 874–5.

2. 'Pure Spanish blood'?

1. Terry de Valera, *A Memoir* (Dublin, 2004), pp 141–9.
2. M.J. MacManus, *Éamon de Valera: A Biography* (Dublin, 1944), p. 9. For the street ballad see also chapter 13.
3. C. Kenny, *Dangerous Ambition: The Making of Éamon de Valera* (Dublin, 2024), pp 28–61.

4. Owen Dudley Edwards, *Éamon de Valera* (Cardiff, 1987), p. 150, cites 'private information' as his source for Blythe's description.
5. Patrick Murray, 'Obsessive historian: Éamon de Valera and the policing of his reputation', *Proceedings of the Royal Irish Academy*, vol. 101C (2001), pp 37–65.
6. Terry de Valera, *Memoir*, pp 141–9.
7. NLI MS LO P116, item 68.
8. Sinéad de Valera to Frank Hughes, 11 July [1916] (Blackrock College Archives); De Valera Papers, UCD P150/3375; Robert Schmuhl, *Ireland's Exiled Children: America and the Easter Rising* (New York, 2016), pp 119–48 ('Éamon de Valera: The Myth of Exile'); Gallagher Papers, NLI MS 18,375 (19), Memorandum of Michael Rynne (civil servant and lawyer) regarding the Taoiseach's American citizenship, 25 April 1946.
9. C. Kenny, 'Spanish blood in Ireland: Éamon De Valera and Dáil Éireann—from revolutionary assembly to parliamentary institution 1918–1926', in *Proceedings of the 76th Conference of the International Commission for the History of Representative and Parliamentary Institutions, Toledo, 2024* (forthcoming); C. Kenny, 'Éamon de Valera's long but fruitless search for his mysterious Spanish father', *Sunday Independent*, 8 September 2024.
10. The Nursery and Child's Hospital registers are now kept at the New York–Presbyterian/Weill Cornell Medicine's Medical Center Archives, which kindly furnished me with a photo of the entry in the hospital register.
11. New York City Municipal Archives, B–M–1882–0352241 (https://a860-historicalvitalrecords.nyc.gov/view/68888; accessed 1 May 2025); Correspondence with the church of St Agnes, East 43rd Street, which kindly sent the author a photograph of the baptismal record as 'amended' (March 2023).
12. Seán P. Murray, 'The case for Éamon de Valera's birth and baptismal records being forgeries', *Iarmhí: Journal of the Westmeath Historical Society* vol. 1, no. 2 (2025), pp 1–7.
13. Daphne Maginess, *Tales from the Emerald Isle: Jottings from Bray, Co. Wicklow* (Brighton, 2010), p. 82.
14. Reminiscences by de Valera, noted in the hand of Dorothy Macardle, apparently at Government Buildings in Dublin on 30 July 1934 (UCD Archives P150/3662), include Crusoe references.
15. UCD Archives P150/25; Minutes of debates (Blackrock College Archives).
16. UCD Archives P150/379; John S.C. Abbot, *Napoleon at St. Helena; or, Interesting Anecdotes and Remarkable Conversations of the Empire* (New York, 1855), p. 497; Kenny, *Dangerous Ambition*, pp 7–11. The Count de la Case recorded the observation on Saint Helena.
17. Murray, 'Obsessive historian', *passim.*
18. Interview with Jean Tulard, *Le Figaro*, 20 March 2025 (Littéraire, p. 8).
19. *Cork Examiner* and *Freeman's Journal*, 27 October 1917. The *Irish Times* omitted the adjective 'brave' before 'dead'. See also Róisín Kennedy, 'The death of Cúchulainn in the GPO', in John

Crowley *et al.* (eds), *Atlas of the Irish Revolution* (Cork, 2017), pp 917–20.

3. Griffith was a monarchist?

1. *United Irishman*, 5 December 1903.
2. *Ibid.*, 20 July 1901, by 'Cuguan' (a common pen-name of Griffith).
3. Brian Maye, *Arthur Griffith* (Dublin, 1997), pp 94, 111.
4. *Freeman's Journal*, 29 Nov. 1905; *United Irishman*, 9 Dec. 1905; *The Sinn Féin Policy* [speech by Griffith at the Convention of the National Council, 1905] (Dublin, [1906]), 32pp; Arthur Griffith, *The Resurrection of Hungary: A Parallel for Ireland* (Dublin, 3rd ed. 1918, with appendices), pp. 139–63.
5. Maye, *Griffith*, pp 228–34; O'Malley, *The Singing Flame* (Dublin, 1978), p. 193.

4. De Valera never accepted partition?

1. NLI MS L P116, item 61, 'Vote for de Valera!'.
2. D.H. Akenson, 'Was de Valera a republican?', *The Review of Politics*, vol. 33, no. 2 (1971), 233–53.
3. John Bowman, *De Valera and the Ulster Question 1917–73* (Oxford, 1972), p. 55.
4. Thomas Jones, *Whitehall Diary, Vol. 3: Ireland 1918–1925* (ed. Keith Middlemas) (London, 1971), *passim* re 1921; *Documents on Irish Foreign Policy, Vol. 1: 1919–1922*, ed. Fanning, Kennedy *et al.*, in a series published by the Royal Irish Academy (hereafter *DIFP*), no. 188, NAI DE 2/304/1 (Griffith to de Valera, 3 November 1921); *DIFP* no. 187, UCD Archives P150/1914 (Griffith to Lloyd George, 2 November 1921); *DIFP* no. 185, NAI DE 2/304/1 (Memorandum by the Irish Delegation, 29 October 1921). In publishing no. 187, the editors of *DIFP* wrote in a footnote that 'George Gavan Duffy and Robert Barton were very much opposed to the sending of this letter and there were numerous alterations to the text before it was despatched' but gave no source for this statement. As Griffith points out to de Valera in no. 188, he had already in *DIFP* no. 187 (to Lloyd George) 'adhered to the basis' of the memo agreed by delegates (no. 185).
5. Houses of the Oireachtas, 'Organising and publishing the Treaty Debates', (https://www.oireachtas.ie/en/visit-and-learn/centenaries/treaty-debates/organising-and-publishing-the-treaty-debates/; accessed 1 May 2025).
6. Mansergh, *The Unresolved Question.* (New Haven and London, 1991), p. 177.
7. *DIFP* no. 209, NAI DE 2/304/1.
8. *DIFP* no. 214, DE 2/304/1, 'Final text of the Articles of Agreement for a Treaty between Great Britain and Ireland as Signed', London, 6 December 1921.
9. *Dáil Éireann Debates*, 10 January 1922, Appendix 17, 'Proposed Treaty of Association between Ireland and the British Commonwealth presented by President De Valera to the secret session of An Dáil, Articles 17–21'; *Dáil Éireann Debates*, 10 January 1922: 'Appendix 18: The President's Alternative Proposals' (https://www.oireachtas.ie/en/debates/debate/dail/1922-01-10/23/ and /24).

5. '*Ulster* will fight and *Ulster* will be right'?

1. Jones, *Diary*, p. 134.
2. *Ibid.*, pp 135–7.
3. Boundary Commission Papers 1922 (NAI TSCH/3/S1801A).
4. C. Kenny, 'Lord Birkenhead, ambiguity and the Irish border: lawyers and the Anglo-Irish treaty', in D. Capper, C. McCormick and N. Dawson (eds), *Law and Constitutional Change* (Cambridge, 2025), pp 198–215; C. Kenny, '"It is notorious that a lawyer cannot draft his own will clearly": framing the Boundary Commission in the Anglo-Irish treaty 1921', *Irish Jurist*, vol. 68 (2022), pp 1–24; Kevin Matthews, *Fatal Influence: The Impact of Ireland on British Politics, 1920–1925* (Dublin, 2004), pp 75ff, 169–70, 288–90.
5. Boundary Commission Papers (NAI S1801A), typescript, pp 2, 7; *Irish Independent* and *Freeman's Journal*, 4 February 1922.
6. Boundary Commission Papers 1922 (NAI TSCH/3/S1801A), typescript, p. 8; *Irish Independent* and *Freeman's Journal*, 4 February 1922.
7. Griffith to Collins, 15 February 1922, typed copy said to have been extracted from 'the Griffith papers' (Boundary Commission Papers 1922, NAI TSCH/3/S1801A).

6. Collins led the Treaty team, founded FG?

1. Gerard Shannon, 'Griffith and Collins: a deteriorating relationship, January to August 1922', *Cut & Paste* ['Remembering Arthur Griffith'], vol. 8 (2025), 19–25.
2. Allen, 'Ernie O'Malley (1899–1957)', p. 874.

7. They disobeyed the cabinet?

1. NAI DE 2/304/1, 7 October 1921; *Dáil Éireann Debates*, 14 Sept. 1921
2. De Valera to the plenipotentiaries, *DIFP* no. 160, UCD Archives P150/1925.
3. *DIFP* no. 195, NAI DE 2/304/1.
4. Catalogue of the National Library of Ireland, Markievicz (Ke 82); Ronan McGreevy, 'How the most famous painting of the Irish war of Independence was staged', *Irish Times*, 25 May 1921.
5. *DIFP* includes quite a few but by no means all such relevant letters and documents.
6. Colum Kenny, 'A fateful weekend in 1921: at the crux of negotiations for an Anglo-Irish treaty and an independent Irish parliament', *Parliaments, Estates and Representation*, vol. 39, no. 1 (2019), pp 1–15.
7. *DIFP* no. 206, UCD Archives P150/1914.
8. UCD Archives P150/1560, De Valera to Joseph McGarrity, 27 December 1921.
9. *Dáil Éireann Debates*, 19 December 1921.

9. Duress and *immediate* war?

1. Thomas Jones, *Whitehall Diary, Vol. 3: Ireland 1918–1925* (ed. Keith Middlemas) (London, 1971), pp 152, 154, 171.
2. M. O'Malley, 'Military aviation in Ireland 1921–1945' (Ph.D thesis, NUI Maynooth, 2007), pp 25–32.
3. *Irish Times*, 1 November 1924.

4. Jones, *Diary*, pp 132, 134, 139, 149, 167.
5. Michael Collins, *The Path to Freedom* (Dublin and London, 1922), pp 34–5; for the terms offered in July see *DIFP* no. 141, reprinted from *Official Correspondence Relating to the Peace Negotiations June–September 1921* (Dublin, 1921).

11. An 'oath of allegiance' to the king?

1. Lloyd George's draft at *DIFP* 207, NAI DE 2/304/1; Copy of secretary's notes of meeting of the cabinet and delegation held 3 Dec. 1921 at *DIFP* 209, NAI DE 2/304/1.
2. *Dáil Éireann Debates*, 20 August 1919.
3. Tom Garvin, *1922: The Birth of Irish Democracy* (Dublin, 2005 ed.), p. 55.
4. H. Duncan Hall, 'The British Commonwealth of Nations', *American Political Science Review*, vol. 47, no. 4 (1953), 997–1,015, at p. 1,004, n.10.
5. Thomas Mohr, 'Dismantling the Anglo-Irish Treaty: removing the oath and the repugnancy clause from the constitution of the Irish Free State' in *Confluences of Law and History*, ed. Niamh Howlin and F.M. Larkin (Dublin, 2025), pp. 288–9.
6. *DIFP* no. 207, NAI DE 2/304/1 (Lloyd George to Arthur Griffith, with draft of treaty, 30 November 1921); *DIFP* no. 206, UCD Archives P150/1914 (Griffith to de Valera, 29 November 1921).
7. Above, chapter 7.

12. Griffith was a 'pacifist'?

1. Colum Kenny, 'Arthur Griffith's rifle', *The Irish Sword: Journal of the Military History Society of Ireland*, vol. 32, no. 130 (2020), pp 361–72; *ibid.*, pp 373–6, for a reprint of Arthur Griffith, 'Bringing in the guns', *The Southern Cross* (Buenos Aires), 28 August 1914.
2. BMH Witness Statement 205 (Maud Griffith, 3 March 1949).
3. BMH Witness Statement 1,765 (Seán T. Ó Ceallaigh (O'Kelly), vol. 2, pp 144–280 (year 1952), at pp 154–9).

13. De Valera 'knew nothing' about politics?

1. Thomas Jones, *Whitehall Diary, Vol. 3: Ireland 1918–1925* (ed. Keith Middlemas) (London, 1971), p. 110 (7 September 1921).
2. *Dáil Éireann Debates*, 9 January 1922.
3. Padraic Colum, *Arthur Griffith* (Dublin, 1959), p. 33.
4. *Freeman's Journal*, 27 October 1917; *Dáil Éireann Debates*, 14 September 1921.
5. *TIME*, 16 January 1933; *Irish Independent*, 12 November 1932; 'The voice of the multitude', *Irish Press*, 20 February 1932; *Southern Star*, 15 October 1921; *Connaught Telegraph*, 17 April 1920; 'Kiltimagh news' in *Mayo News*, 5 July 1919, for its being sung at a concert in Kiltimagh Town Hall; Seán Ó Faoláin, *The Life Story of Éamon de Valera* (Dublin, 1933), p. 10; Kevin Boland, *The Rise and Decline of Fianna Fáil* (Cork, 1982), p. 69.

14. The plenipotentiaries bound Ireland?

1. Jones, *Diary*,, p. 138.
2. Frank Pakenham, *Peace by Ordeal* (London, 1935), pp 205, 221.

15. Not all five signed or voted for the treaty?

1. *Dáil Éireann Debates*, 20 August 1919.
2. *Dáil Éireann Debates*, 10 Jan. 1922, appendix 18.
3. Diary of Erskine Childers, Trinity College Dublin MS, f. 88v, f. 102; BMH WS 979, pp 41–2; C. Kenny, *A Bitter Winter: The Irish Civil War 1922–23* (Dublin, 2022), p. 90.

16. Partition was the crunch issue?

1. At https://www.oireachtas.ie/en/visit-and-learn/centenaries/treaty-debates/explore-the-treaty-debates/ (accessed 1 May 2025).
2. Cormac Moore, *Birth of the Border* (Newbridge, 2019), pp 63–4; D.R. O'Connor Lysaght, *The Great Irish Revolution: Myths and Realities, a Handbook* (2006), p. 20.
3. Seamus Woods to C-in-C, 29 September 1922 (Boundary Commission Papers 1922, NAI TSCH/3/S1801A, 5pp).
4. BMH WS 979, p. 41.
5. *Ibid.*, pp 44–5.
6. Memorandum of an interview between Michael Collins and David Lloyd George, 5 December 1921 (*DIFP* no. 212, NAI DE 2/304/1).
7. Griffith to Collins, 15 February 1922 (NAI TSCH/3/S1801A).
8. *The Times* (London), 14 December 1921.
9. *Ibid.*
10. C. Kenny, 'Lord Birkenhead, ambiguity and the Irish border', pp 198–215; C. Kenny, '"It is notorious that a lawyer cannot draft his own will clearly"', pp 1–24; Thomas Mohr, *Guardian of the Treaty: The Privy Council Appeal and Irish Sovereignty* (Dublin, 2016), *passim*; Matthews, *Fatal Influence*, pp 169–70, 290; Padraic Colum, *Arthur Griffith* (Dublin, 1959), pp 295–6.
11. Jones, *Diary*, pp 164–5.
12. *Ibid.*, p. 178.

18. The oath was 'almost meaningless'?

1. *DIFP* no. 209, NAI DE 2/304/1 (Notes, 3 December 1921).
2. Thomas Jones, *Whitehall Diary, Vol. 3: Ireland 1918–1925* (ed. Keith Middlemas) (London, 1971), p. 183 (interposition by Middlemas).
3. NAI DE 2/304/5/6, not published in *Documents on Irish Foreign Policy*.
4. BMH WS 1,280 (Eamon Broy, 31 October 1955), p. 141.
5. Jim Maher, *The Oath is Dead and Gone* (Dublin, 2011), pp 213–29.
6. Mohr, 'Dismantling the Anglo-Irish Treaty', pp 272–302 for a recent overview.

19. Dangers of Bolshevism?

1. Patrick Mannion and Fearghal McGarry (eds), *The Irish Revolution: A Global History* (New York, 2022), p. 16.
2. *Berner Tagwacht*, 9 May 1916, cited at http://www.columbia.edu/~lnp3/mydocs/race/lenin_ireland.htm (accessed 1 May 2025).
3. 'Larkin, James' by Emmet Larkin, in the RIA's *Dictionary of Irish Biography* (*DIB*).
4. Geoffrey Bell, *Hesitant Comrades: The Irish Revolution and the British Labour Movement* (London, 2016), *passim.*
5. Olivier Coquelin, 'Utopian impulse in revolutionary Ireland: a case study

of the 1918–1923 Irish soviets', *Études Irlandaises*, vol. 49, no. 2 (2024), pp 109–24.

6. 'Peace and Prosperity or Red Ruin', de Valera handbill, 1917 (NLI LO P116, item 63).
7. *Belfast Newsletter*, 23 November 1921.
8. *Irish Citizen*, November 1917, p. 387.
9. *Voice of Labour*, 10 November 1923, p. 8. The allegation is not corroborated.
10. *Freeman's Journal*, 19 October 1921.

20. Dev 'heartily disagreed with [Rory] O'Connor'?

1. NLI MS 31,284/3, O'Donaghue to Mary C. Bromage, 30 December 1950, p. 3.
2. 'O'Donoghue, Florence ("Florrie")', by Marie Coleman, in the RIA's *Dictionary of Irish Biography* (*DIB*).
3. Earl of Longford [Frank Pakenham] and Thomas P. O'Neill, *Eamon de Valera* (London, 1970), p. 187; *Evening Echo*, 23 March 1922.
4. Mary C. Bromage, *De Valera and the March of a Nation* (London, 1956), pp 163–4.
5. *Evening Herald*, 14 October 1922; *Cork Examiner*, 16 October 1922; Kenny, *Dangerous Ambition,* (Dublin, 2024), p. 263.
6. Longford and O'Neill, *Eamon de Valera*, p. 185
7. *Ibid.*, p. 185.
8. Charles Lysaght, 'Review of *Atlas of the Irish Civil War: New Perspectives*', *History Ireland*, vol. 33, no. 2 (2025), p. 60.
9. Bromage, *De Valera*, p. 166.
10. Kenny, *Dangerous Ambition*, pp 255–60.
11. As reported in the *Irish Independent*, 11 April 1922, and other Irish papers; Bromage, *De Valera*, p. 168.
12. Michael Gallagher, 'The Pact General Election of 1922', *Irish Historical Studies*, vol. 22, no. 84 (1979), pp 404–21, at pp 412–13; Dorothy Macardle, *The Irish Republic* (London, 1937), p. 715.
13. Longford and O'Neill, *Eamon de Valera*, p. 197.
14. *Ibid.*, p. 196.
15. *Ibid.*

21. 'The Civil War started on 22 June 1922'?

1. See https://www.ria.ie/2022/06/28/28-june-1922-the-assault-on-the-four-courts/.
2. D.R. O'Connor Lysaght, *The Great Irish Revolution: Myths and Realities, a Handbook* (Dublin, 2006), p. 21.
3. *Cork Examiner*, 4 March 1922; BMH WS 822 (William James Stapleton).
4. *Evening Herald*, 22 March 1922.
5. *Irish Independent* and *Irish Times*, 23 March 1922. The *Cork Examiner* that day has his reply as 'You can call it what you like'.
6. *Northern Standard*, 14 April 1922; *Skibbereen Eagle*, 15 April 1922.
7. *Irish Times* and *Irish Independent*, 15 April 1922.
8. *Evening Echo*, 15 April 1922.
9. *Irish Independent*, 18 April 1922.
10. Bromage, *De Valera*, p. 169; *Southern Star* and *Fermanagh Herald*, 15 April 1922 etc., for the English newspaper's questions and de Valera's answers.
11. *Irish Independent*, 18 April 1922.
12. *Belfast Newsletter*, 27 April 1922.

13. *Irish Independent*, 5 May 1922 and other newspapers.
14. Eoin Swithin Walsh, at kilkennylibrary.ie/eng/our_services/decade-of-centenaries-resources/battle-of-kilkenny-1/ (17 May 2025).
15. *Evening Echo*, 15 and 21 April 1922.
16. *Irish Times*, 26 August 1922.
17. See https://www.ucc.ie/en/theirishrevolution/irish-civil-war-fatalities-project/research-findings/republican-fatalities-1922-23/ (accessed 23 April 2025).

22. Michael Davitt was a philo-Semite?

1. *The Correspondence of Daniel O'Connell*, ed. Maurice R. O'Connell (8 vols) (Dublin, 1972–80), vol. 4, pp 95, 277–8.
2. William Fagan, *The Life and Times of Daniel O'Connell* (2 vols) (Cork, 1847–8), pp 388–98.
3. *Irish Times*, 5 December 1892.
4. R.M. Douglas, 'Irish and continental European antisemitism', in Aidan Beatty and Dan O'Brien (eds), *Irish Questions and Jewish Questions: Crossovers in Culture* (Syracuse NY, 2018), p. 32.
5. C. Kenny, 'Sinn Féin, socialists and McSheeneys: representations of Jews in early twentieth-century Ireland', *Journal of Modern Jewish Studies*, vol. 16, no. 2 (2017), pp 198–218.
6. 'Griffith, Arthur Joseph', by Michael Laffan, in the RIA's *Dictionary of Irish Biography* (*DIB*).
7. Colum Kenny, 'Two Irish Zionists and their antisemitism: Michael Davitt (1846–1906) and Arthur Griffith (1871–1922)', in Zuleika Rodgers and Natalie Wynn (eds), *Reimagining the Jews of Ireland: Historiography, Identity and Representation* (Oxford, 2024), pp 63–92.
8. C. Kenny, '"Manufactured news" and Michael Davitt's journalism for William Randolph Hearst in South Africa and Russia', in D. van Tuyll, M. O'Brien and M. Broersma (eds), *Politics, Culture and the Irish-American Press 1784–1963* (Syracuse NY, 2021), pp 203–24.
9. C. Kenny, 'Political ambiguities: John Redmond, Michael Davitt and Arthur Griffith on the Limerick Boycott', in Seán W. Gannon and Natalie Wynn (eds), *The Limerick Boycott in Context* (Oxford, 2025), pp 97–128, at pp 101–2.
10. C. Kenny, 'James Larkin and the Jew's shilling: Irish workers, activists and anti-Semitism before independence', *Irish Economic and Social History*, vol. 44, no. 1 (2017), pp 66–84.
11. C. Kenny, *The Enigma of Arthur Griffith: 'Father of Us All'* (Newbridge, 2020), p. 52; 'Briscoe, Robert Emmet', by L.W. White, in *DIB*.

23. Griffith kept Dev in the dark?

1. Jones, *Diary*, pp 174, 176, 179 for 24–29 November and 2–4 December 1921; Kenny, *The Enigma of Arthur Griffith*, chapter 14.
2. Lloyd George to de Valera, 20 July 1921, in *Official correspondence Relating to the Peace Negotiations June-September 1921* (Dublin, 1921); *Dáil Éireann Debates*, 14 Sept. 1921.
3. *Dáil Éireann Debates*, 27 April 1922.
4. Diarmaid Ferriter, *A Nation and Not a Rabble: The Irish Revolution 1912–1923* (London, 2015), p. 251, citing Thomas Jones, *Whitehall Diary, Vol.*

1, 1916/1925 (ed. Keith Middlemas), (London, 1969) p. 174.
5. *DIFP no. 182, NAI DE 2/304/1 (AG to Dev, 27 October 1921).*
6. Jones, *Diary*, p. 165; *DIFP* no. 196, NAI DE 2/304/1.
7. Cormac Moore, *The Root of All Evil: The Irish Boundary Commission* (Dublin, 2025), p. 1
8. Jones, *Diary*, p. 147.
9. Seán Cronin, *The McGarrity Papers: Revelations of the Irish Revolutionary Movement in Ireland and America 1900–1940* (Tralee, 1972), pp 107–11.
10. Jones, *Diary*, pp 148–50; *DIFP* no. 185, NAI DE 2/304/1.
11. Jones, *Diary*, p. 171.
12. *Ibid.*, pp 154–5.
13. *Dáil Éireann Debates*, 27 April 1922.
14. C. Kenny, 'The "Inverness Formula": Lloyd George, Ireland and the first UK cabinet meeting outside London', *Journal of Scottish Historical Studies*, vol. 43, no. 2 (2023), pp 136–60.
15. BMH, WS 979 (Robert Barton, 27 July 1954).

24. Frank Pakenham: author of quality?

1. Anonymous reviewer at https://www.askaboutireland.ie/reading-room/digital-book-collection/digital-books-by-subject/history-of-ireland/pakenham-peace-by-ordeal/ (accessed 16 June 2025).
2. Pakenham, *Avowed Intent* (London, 1994), p. 3. Ferriter, *A Nation and Not a Rabble*, p. 250.
3. Robert Barton, BMH WS 979, p. 28 (1954); Frank Pakenham, *Peace by Ordeal* (London, 1935), pp ix–x; Peter Stanford, *Lord Longford: An Authorised Life* (London, 1994), pp 96–9.
4. Brian Maye, Letter to the Editor, *Irish Times*, 31 May 2021.
5. *Ibid.*
6. Stanford, *Lord Longford*, pp 98–9, 134–6.
7. Mansergh, *The Unresolved Question*, p. 177.
8. Longford, *Avowed Intent*, p. 41.
9. Adam Sisman, *Hugh Trevor-Roper: The Biography* (London, 2010), p. 108.
10. Longford, *Avowed Intent*, pp 26, 37–41, 49, 60–1.
11. Pakenham, *Born to Believe: An Autobiography (*London, 1953), *passim*; Stanford, *Lord Longford*, pp 60–2.
12. Robert Blake, 'Smith, Frederick Winston Furneaux, second earl of Birkenhead', in *DNB*.
13. Pakenham, *Avowed Intent*, pp 49–58; Stanford, *Lord Longford*, pp 89–90.
14. Mary Craig, *Longford: A Biographical Portrait* (London, 1978), p. 46.
15. Birkenhead to Churchill and Chamberlain, 21 August 1924 (Churchill Archives Centre, Churchill College, Cambridge, CHAR 2/750).
16. Craig, *Longford*, p. 42.
17. Longford, *Avowed Intent*, p. 61; Elizabeth Longford, *The Pebbled Shore* (London, 1986), p. 146.
18. Longford, *Avowed Intent*, p. 61.
19. De Valera Papers, UCD Archives P150, nos 382 (especially correspondence with Nicholas Nolan, secretary to the government), 1474 and 1579; *ibid.*, 383 (correspondence with Robert Lusty and Hutchinson publishers).
20. Murray, 'Obsessive historian: Éamon de Valera and the policing of his reputation', pp 37–65.
21. *Irish Times*, 15 August 1968.

22. Longford, *Avowed Intent*, p. 61; Longford, *The Pebbled Shore*, p. 145.
23. Childers diary, TCD MS, f. 88v, f. 102; BMH WS 979, pp 41–2 (italics added here).
24. Brian P. Murphy, *John Chartres: Mystery Man of the Treaty* (Dublin, 1995); 'Childers, (Robert) Erskine', by M.A. Hopkinson, in *DIB*; Dr Nancy Power, 'Chartres meets Collins', *Irish Independent*, 4 November 1935. *Nationality* first appeared in June 1915. Its publication ceased immediately after the Easter Rising 1916 but resumed in February 1917.
25. Charles Bewley, *Memoirs of a Wild Goose* (Dublin, 1989—but written at least twenty years earlier), pp 77–8; Student Admission Papers and Call Book, 1884 (Society of King's Inns MS), but no terms are listed as having been kept by Chartres at King's Inns; *Register of Admissions to the Honourable Society of the Middle Temple*, vol. 2 (London, 1949), p. 648 (7 January 1885); J.S. Chartres, *The Public Authorities Protection Act 1893* (London, 1912); J.S. Chartres, *Judicial Interpretation of the Law Relating to Workmen's Compensation* (London, 1915); John Chartres, *Judicial Interpretations of the Munitions of War Acts 1915 and 1916* (London, 1917).
26. *Tipperary Star*, 8 April 1944.
27. Stanford, *Longford*, pp 149–50.
28. Sisman, *Hugh Trevor-Roper*, pp 108–11; Eunan O'Halpin, *Spying on Ireland: British Intelligence and Irish Neutrality During the Second World War* (Oxford, 2008), p. 138.
29. Stanford, *Longford*, pp 94, 392.
30. Moya Llewelyn Davies to P.S. O'Hegarty, 28 August 1941 (NLI MSS 41,780/1–10); Longford, *The Pebbled Shore*, p. 146. There are lively biographies of Pakenham and his clever wife Elizabeth in the Oxford *Dictionary of National Biography* (by Paul Johnson) and one of Frank in the *DIB* (by Patrick Maume).

25. Secret assent?—'Damnable lie!'

1. Pakenham, *Peace by Ordeal*, p. 205.
2. De Valera Papers, UCD Archives P150/25; Minutes of debates (Blackrock College Archives); *Sunday Independent*, 19 March 1922; *Cork Examiner*, 20 March 1922.
3. Childers diary, 7 December 1921 (Trinity College Dublin MS 7813, f. 103).
4. C. Kenny, *Midnight in London: The Anglo-Irish Treaty Crisis 1921* (Dublin, 2021), pp 110–18, where the document is also reproduced.
5. Pakenham, *Peace by Ordeal*, pp 199, 205, 218.
6. Kenny, 'Redeeming Dev, damning Griffith', *passim*.
7. Jones, *Diary, 5* (ed. Keith Middlemas) (London, 1971), p. 120; Austen Chamberlain, *Down the Years* (London, 1935), p. 143.
8. Jones, *Diary*, pp 155–6, 171; J.O. Hannay ('George A. Birmingham'), *Pleasant Places* (London, 1934), pp 187–8, for a characteristic example of references by acquaintances to Griffith's tendency towards silence.
9. Tentative 'suggestions' for a treaty presented by Thomas Jones to Arthur Griffith, 16 November 1921 (NAI DE 2/304/1), where Article 11 states that 'a Commission shall be appointed

to determine in accordance with the wishes of the inhabitants the boundaries between Northern Ireland and the rest of Ireland'; Griffith to de Valera, 18 November 1921 (NAI DE 2/304/1).

10. Childers diary, f. 55, f. 59 (15 and 16 November 1921).
11. Copy letter from John Chartres to General Richard Mulcahy, 5 Feb. 1924, etc. (NAI TSCH/3/S.1801E)..
12. See, for example, Mícheál Ó Fathartaigh and Liam Weeks (eds), *Birth of a State: The Anglo-Irish Treaty* (Newbridge, 2021), pp 119–21, 186–91; Paul Murray, *The Irish Boundary Commission and its Origins 1886–1925* (Dublin, 2011), pp 78–9.
13. N.C. Fleming, 'The conservative right, Ulster unionism and the partition of Ireland', in N.C. Fleming and J.H. Murphy (eds), *Ireland and Partition: Contexts and Consequences* (Clemson SC, 2021), pp 283–303.
14. Jones, *Diary*, pp 132, 134, 139, 149, 167.
15. 'Lloyd George, David', by K.O. Morgan in *DNB*.
16. Frances Stevenson, *Lloyd George: A Diary* (ed. A.J.P. Taylor) (London, 1971), cited by John Bowman in the *Irish Times*, 10 July 2021.
17. Jones, *Diary*, pp 159–60.
18. Ruane, 'The "so-called Treaty": the implications of legal form for achieving settlement of the Irish War of Independence', in *Confluence of Law and History*, ed. Niamh Howlin and F.M. Larkin (Dublin, 2025), p. 270.
19. Austen to Ivy Chamberlain, dated 13 November 1921, but postmarked 12.45 a.m. on 14 November (University of Birmingham, Chamberlain Papers, AC 6/1/463).
20. *Ibid.*
21. Michael Laffan, *The Partition of Ireland 1911–1925* (Dundalk, 1983), p. 123.
22. The words quoted were first articulated by Lloyd George in a letter from Inverness to de Valera, 7 September 1921 (*Dáil Éireann Debates*, 14 September 1921), but with the word 'can' instead of 'may' then being used; Lloyd George to de Valera, 29 September 1921, and de Valera to Lloyd George, 30 September 1921 (in *DIFP*), for de Valera's acceptance of the formula; *Irish Independent* and *Irish Times*, 5 October 1921.
23. Kenny, 'The "Inverness Formula", pp 136–60.
24. A.R.H., 'Boundary delimitations in the Treaty of Versailles', *Geographical Journal*, vol. 54, no. 2 (1919), pp 103–13.
25. Charles Townshend, *The Partition: Ireland Divided, 1885–1925* (London, 1921), pp 202–4.
26. Notes by Robert Barton of two sub-conferences held on 5–6 December 1921 at 10 Downing Street (NAI DE 2/304/1, also in *DIFP*). Childers also then referred to it as a 'memo' (Childers diary, f. 103 (7 December 1921). See also https://www.difp.ie/viewdoc.asp?DocID=213 (accessed 1 May 2025).
27. Kenny, *Midnight in London*, p. 113.
28. Jones, *Diary*, p. 164.
29. Lionel Curtis, UK Secretary to Peace Conference, to Prime Minister Lloyd George, 'Proposals to Ulster', memorandum dated 8 November 1921, p. 14, at Parliamentary Archives, Houses of Parliament, London, LG/F/181/4/1.

30. *Dáil Éireann Debates*, 22 August 1921. See above, chapter 4.
31. Jones, *Diary*, p. 110 (7 September 1921).
32. *Ibid.*, p. 163 (12 November 1921).
33. Parliamentary Archives, Lloyd George Papers P/181/4/1. For Curtis see John McColgan, 'Implementing the 1921 Treaty: Lionel Curtis and constitutional procedure', *Irish Historical Studies*, vol. 20, no. 79 (1977), pp 312–33.
34. Reproduced in Kenny, *Midnight in London*, p. 113.
35. Jones, *Diary*, pp 127–32.
36. Griffith to de Valera, 8, 9 and 12 November 1921 (de Valera Papers, UCD Archives P150/1914) and 15 November 1921 (NAI DE 2/304/1). These four letters are reproduced in *DIFP*.
37. Jones, *Diary*, pp 154–62.
38. Frank Gallagher, *The Anglo-Irish Treaty* (ed. T.P. O'Neill) (London, 1965), p. 118.
39. Jones, *Diary*, pp 156–7.
40. *DIFP* no. 192, UCD Archives P150/1914, Griffith to de Valera, 9 November 1921.
41. Griffith to de Valera, 3 and 15 November 1921 (NAI DE 2/304/1), 8, 9 and 12 November 1921 (de Valera Papers, UCD Archive P150/1914), and de Valera to Griffith, 9 November 1921 (NAI DE 2/304/1), all also in *DIFP*; Jones, *Diary*, pp 154–64.
42. Jones, *Diary*, p. 157.
43. Griffith to de Valera, 12 November 1921 (UCD Archives P150/1914), and de Valera to Griffith, 9 November 1921 (NAI DE 2/304/1), also in *DIFP*.
44. Pakenham, *Peace by Ordeal*, p. 205.
45. Jones, *Diary*, p. 158.
46. Townshend, *The Partition*, p. 202, appears to assume that he did.
47. Lloyd George to James Craig, 10 November 1921. Arthur Griffith's copy of this letter, headed and stamped 'secret'—and also carrying the stamp of the Irish Delegation of Plenipotentiaries—is at NAI DE/2/304/8/2. Also see *Correspondence Between His Majesty's Government and the Prime Minister of Northern Ireland Relating to the Proposal for an Irish Settlement* (HMSO, 1921) for this and what follows.
48. Griffith to de Valera, 11 November 1921 (NAI DE/2/304/8/2). This letter is not published in *DIFP*.
49. Craig to Lloyd George. Copy at NAI DE/2/304/8/2.
50. Jones, *Diary*, pp 162–3.
51. The reference in this context is to 'the area' within the special jurisdiction of Northern Ireland should it participate in an all-Ireland parliament, as raised by Lloyd George in his letter of 10 November 1921 to Craig.
52. In fact, Lloyd George had not yet made this explicit in writing to Craig, his letter of 10 November to Craig only hinting at the possibility when referring to problems caused by the 'jagged line' of the existing border.
53. Griffith to de Valera (12 November 1921). Copies at NAI DE/2/304/8/2 and de Valera Papers, UCD Archives P150. The Irish 'inner cabinet' then consisted of de Valera, Griffith, Collins, Barton, W.T. Cosgrave, Cathal Brugha and Austin Stack.

Sassoon's house, at what was then No. 25 Park Lane, has been demolished.

54. Stevenson, *Lloyd George*, p. 237 (14 November 1921). Stevenson earlier noted on 14 July (p. 227) that 'I have never seen D. so excited as he was before De Valera arrived, at 4.30'. That was just days after the truce in Ireland was declared, when de Valera came for talks alone with Lloyd George in London about a possible peace conference. 'Trent' (Trent Park in Enfield, north of London) was the location of one of Philip Sassoon's lavishly decorated properties, where he liked to play host to members of the British royal family and others. He was an art collector and a second cousin of the poet Siegfried Sassoon.
55. Austen to Ivy Chamberlain, 13 November 1921 (University of Birmingham, Chamberlain Papers, AC 6/1/463).
56. Austen to Ivy Chamberlain, 23 November 1921 (University of Birmingham, Chamberlain Papers, AC 6/1/470).
57. Austen Chamberlain, *Down the Years* (London, 1935), p. 148.
58. Lloyd George to Craig, drafts (National Archives, CAB/2/4, ff 147–9). A very few words were changed when incorporating the text into the Craig drafts.
59. Griffith to de Valera, 15 November 1921 (NAI DE 2/304/1).
60. Gallagher, *Anglo-Irish Treaty*, p. 119.
61. Jones, *Diary*, pp 170–1.
62. NAI DE 2/304/1 and NAI DE/2/304/8/2.
63. Jones, *Diary*, p. 171.
64. Griffith to de Valera, 23 November 1921, NAI DE 2/304/1 (as published in *DIFP*). There is also an extract from this at DE/2/304/8/2. For lawyers involved as delegates or advisers on both sides during the treaty negotiations see C. Kenny, '"It is notorious that a lawyer cannot draft his own will clearly": framing the Boundary Commission in the Anglo-Irish treaty 1921', *Irish Jurist*, vol. 68 (2022), pp 1–24, *passim.*
65. Griffith to Lloyd George, 2 November 1921 (UCD Archives P150/1914; also in *DIFP*).
66. Jones, *Diary*, pp 151–4.
67. *Ibid.*, pp 170–3.
68. Notes by Robert Barton of two sub-conferences held on 5–6 December 1921.
69. BMH, WS 979 (Robert Barton, 1954), pp 41–2.
70. Childers diary, TCD MS, f. 88v, f. 102; BMH, WS 979 (Robert Barton) pp 41–2. Barton's assertion (WS, p. 42) that 'Childers was active all the time, but he took no part in the final dispute' is difficult to square with Childers's diary entry, unless referring to exchanges between plenipotentiaries in the very final hours.
71. Childers diary, f. 103 (7 December 1921).
72. Kenny, 'Lord Birkenhead, ambiguity and the Irish border', pp 198-215.
73. Mohr, *Guardian of the Treaty*, pp 51–4.
74. Reader's report, in Seán Ó Lúing Papers, NLI MS 12,038, box 1.
75. Pakenham, *Peace by Ordeal*, pp 294–5; Griffith to de Valera, 12 November 1921 (NAI DE/2/304/8/2 and UCD Archives P150).

76. Pakenham, *Peace by Ordeal*, p. 294.
77. Gallagher, *Anglo-Irish Treaty*, p. 162.
78. Chamberlain, *Down the Years*, p. 149.
79. C.P. Scott, *The Political Diaries 1911–1928* (ed. Trevor Wilson) (London, 1970), p. 412.
80. Jones, *Diary*, pp 151–2; 'Premier's triumph. Sweeping Majority for Peace. Conference Policy Vindicated', *Irish Times*, 1 November 1921. *Hansard* online does not have the full day's debates.
81. Scott, *The Political Diaries*, p. 411, n. 21.
82. Colin Murphy, *The Treaty* (2021). See above, chapter 27.
83. Pakenham, *Peace by Ordeal*, p. 213.
84. *Ibid.*, pp 214–19.
85. *Ibid.*, p. 218.
86. *Ibid.*, p. 222.
87. *Ibid.*, pp 218–20.
88. *Dáil Éireann Debates*, 10 January 1922.
89. Pakenham, *Peace by Ordeal*, p. 219.
90. *Ibid.*, p. 221n.
91. *Ibid.*, p. 222.
92. *Dáil Éireann Debates*, S2, no. 5 (27 April 1922) (https://www.oireachtas.ie/en/debates/debate/dail/1922-04-27/3/).
93. Pakenham, *Peace by Ordeal*, p. 223.
94. *Ibid.*, p. xii.
95. *Hansard* 5 (Commons), cxlix, cc 351–60 (16 December 1921).
96. I have not found any corresponding contemporary notes of the 1921 negotiations among Chamberlain's papers in the University of Birmingham.
97. UK National Archives, CAB 43/2/4/102/.
98. Memorandum of an interview between Michael Collins and David Lloyd George, 5 December 1921 (copy) (NAI DE 2/304/1); also in *DIFP*.

26. Michael Portillo's poisoned gas?

1. Winston Churchill, *The World Crisis: The Aftermath* (London, 1929), p. 348.
2. Paul Addison, *Churchill: The Unexpected Hero* (Oxford, 2005), p. 74.
3. Jones, *Diary*, pp 211–12.
4. 'Lynch, William Fanaghan (Liam)', by William Murphy in *DIB.ie*.
5. *Sunday Independent*, 14 May 2023; Letters, *Irish Times*, 16 May 2023.
6. A.M. Prentiss, *Chemicals in War: A Treatise on Chemical Warfare* (New York and London, 1937), pp 114, 138.

27. Only play-acting?

1. Frank Pakenham, *Peace by Ordeal* (London, 1935), p. 218.
2. Above, chapter 25, *passim*.
3. Colin Murphy, 'First night nerves as I play Treaty for laughs', *Sunday Independent*, 21 November 2021.
4. Interview by Nick Zidarescu at https://www.buffedfilmbuffs.com/post/an-interview-with-daniel-kehlmann-the-author-of-g-w-pabst-novel-the-director (accessed 7 July 2025).
5. C.G. Duffy, 'George Gavan Duffy', *Dublin Historical Record*, vol. 36 (1983), pp 90–106, at pp 90–2; Kenny, 'Lord Birkenhead, ambiguity and the Irish border', pp 201–2.
6. *De Valera san Fhásach* ('De Valera in the Desert'), broadcast in January 2025.

28. Griffith was poisoned?

1. Oliver St John Gogarty, *As I Was Going Down Sackville Street* (London, 1937), pp 185–9.

29. A majority favoured revolution?

1. *Shan Van Vocht*, vol. 1, no. 11 (6 November 1896).
2. Thomas E. Mayne, 'The development of Ireland', October 1896.
3. James Connolly, *Erin's Hope: The End and the Means* [ISRP, March 1897]. There is a copy in the National Library of Ireland (NLI A17963).
4. Kenny, *Enigma of Arthur Griffith: 'Father of Us All'*, pp 114–16; 'The origin of the Abbey Theatre', *Sinn Féin*, 14 February 1914.
5. Published in 1909 as part of the Harp Library by J.E.C. Donnelly (https://www.marxists.org/archive/connolly/1909/hope/erinhope.htm). Unfortunately, this website appears to reproduce what is not, as stated there, the 'first published' version of *Erin's Hope* of 1897 (note 302 above) but a later and shorter version.
6. See, for example, *Shan Van Vocht*, vol. 3, no. 8 (August 1898, by 'Griffiths' [*sic*] while still in South Africa), no. 9 (September 1898) and vol. 4, no. 1 (January 1899).
7. *United Irishman*, 22 April 1899; *Shan Van Vocht*, vol. 3, no. 8, pp 146–9, and no. 9, pp 163–4; Maud Gonne MacBride, *A Servant of the Queen* (ed. A. Norman Jeffares) (London, 1993), p. 176; Pádraic Colum, *Arthur Griffith* (Dublin, 1959), p. 45. The James Connolly who occasionally wrote for the *United Irishman* and who was later 'best man' at Griffith's wedding was not the socialist James Connolly (C. Kenny, Letter, *History Ireland*, vol. 25, no. 6 (2017)).
8. *Irish Nation*, 23 January 1909.
9. Kenny, *Enigma of Arthur Griffith*, pp 106–9; *Workers' Republic*, 30 December 1899; *United Irishman*, 23 December 1899.
10. T.W. Moody, *Davitt and the Irish Revolution, 1846–82* (Oxford, 1984), pp xv–xvi.
11. James Connolly, *Shan Van Vocht*, November 1896; Connolly, *Erin's Hope* [1897], pp 4–5.
12. 'Griffith, Arthur Joseph', by Michael Laffan, in *DIB*; Gerard Shannon at *The Irish Story* (https://www.theirishstory.com/2015/10/11/travelling-the-same-road-arthur-griffith-the-irb-pre-1916/#.Wfe8ZmKoPR0; accessed 22 April 2025).
13. James Connolly, *Shan Van Vocht*, November 1896; Connolly, *Erin's Hope* [1897], pp 4–5.
14. BMH WS 1,765, part 2, p. 163 (1952). Griffith edited two short-lived weekly titles between *Sinn Féin* and *Nationality*, namely *Éire–Ireland* (26 October–4 December 1914) and *Cut & Paste* (12 December 1914–27 February 1915).
15. Éamonn Ceannt, 'The consistency of Arthur Griffith', *Irish Nation*, 5 February 1910, p. 7.
16. For James Connolly on the relationship between Sinn Féin and socialism see *Irish Nation*, 23 January 1909.
17. John M. Regan, *The Irish Counter-Revolution, 1921–1936: Treatyite Politics and Settlement in Independent Ireland* (Dublin, 1999), *passim*.

18. Undated; published at Rutherglen, Glasgow; price twopence (NLI BB3037).
19. Ó Lúing Papers, NLI MS 12,038, box 3.

30. *The* Irish revolution?

1. Above, chapter 12 for the IRB meeting; 'What O'Brien Stands For' (1918) and election leaflet (1920), NLI MS LO P116, items 129 and 135; *Sunday Chronicle*, 16 May 1920.
2. There is a full text of McCarthy's volume online at Hathi Trust Digital Library (https://catalog.hathitrust.org/Record/005944915; accessed 16 June 2025).
3. Richard Ellmann, *The Consciousness of Joyce* (Oxford, 1977), at 'Appendix: Joyce's Library in 1920'.
4. Michael McCarthy, *The Irish Revolution* (Edinburgh and London, 1912), p. 494.
5. Moody, *Davitt and the Irish Revolution, 1846–82*, p. xv.
6. Patrick Mannion and Fearghal McGarry (eds), *The Irish Revolution: A Global History* (New York, 2022), p. 2.
7. Aidan Beatty, 'An Irish revolution without a revolution', *Journal of World-Systems Research*, vol. 22, no. 1 (2016), pp 54–76, at p. 56 n.1 (https://jwsr.pitt.edu/ojs/jwsr/article/view/602/725; accessed 17 May 2025).
8. John Crowley, Donal Ó Drisceoil and Mike Murphy (eds), *Atlas of the Irish Revolution* (Cork, 2017), p. xvii.
9. Mannion and McGarry, *The Irish Revolution*, p. 2.
10. Published by Ernest Flammarion, Paris [1923]. The title may be translated as *In Ireland from the war of independence to the civil war (1914–1923)*.
11. For a chronological list of Irish Civil War fatalities, by Andy Bielenberg and John Dorney, see Hélène O'Keeffe, John Crowley, Donal Ó Drisceoil, John Borgonovo and Mike Murphy (eds), *Atlas of the Irish Civil War* (Cork, 2024), pp 443–80.
12. Stanislaus Joyce, *My Brother's Keeper* (New York, 1958), pp 173–4; Frank Callinan, 'James Joyce and the *United Irishman*, Paris 1902–3', *Dublin James Joyce Journal*, vol. 3 (2010), pp 51–103.
13. Virginia E. Glandon, *Arthur Griffith and the Advanced-Nationalist Press Ireland, 1900–1922* (New York, 1985), pp 63–4.
14. Aidan Beatty, 'Counter-revolutionary masculinities: gender, social control and revising the chronologies of Irish nationalist politics', *Irish Studies Review*, vol. 29, no. 2 (2021), pp 229–42.
15. Columban na Banban, *Lecture on Ethics of the Irish Revolution* (Dublin, 1924), pp 10–11. M.P. McCabe, 'Vatican involvement in the Irish Civil War: Monsignor Salvatore Luzio's Apostolic Delegation, March–May 1923', *Journal of Ecclesiastical History*, vol. 62, no. 1 (2011), p. 100, n.43, identifies this pen-name as that of Fr Patrick Browne (Pádraig de Brún)—for whom see the *DIB*.

31. Other myths?

1. See, for example, Nicholas Canny, 'Review: Revising the revisionist', *Irish Historical Studies*, vol. 30, no. 118 (1996), pp 242–54; Ciaran Brady, *Interpreting Irish History: The Debate*

on Historical Revisionism, 1938–94 (Dublin, 1995); Brendan Bradshaw, 'Nationalism and historical scholarship in modern Ireland', *Irish Historical Studies*, vol. 26, no. 104 (1989), pp 329–51; Roy Foster, 'We are all revisionists now', *The Irish Review*, vol. 1 (1986), pp 1–5.
2. See https://www.theirishstory.com/2014/02/08/book-review-myth-and-the-irish-state/ (accessed 17 May 2025).
3. *Irish Times*, 5 April 2014.
4. 'Edwards, Robert ("Robin") Dudley', by Aidan Clarke, in *DIB*. See also Neasa MacErlean, *Telling the Truth is Dangerous; How Robert Dudley Edwards Changed Irish History Forever* (Browndogbooks, UK, 2005).
5. T.P. O'Neill [B.L.], 'Fish, historians and the law: the Foyle Fisheries case', *History Ireland*, vol. 17, no. 6 (2009), pp 62–5, at p. 64; *Irish Independent*, 17 January 1948.
6. Papers of R. Dudley Edwards, 1926–74 (UCD Archives LA22, files 653–94); Thomas Mohr, 'Salmon of Knowledge: Brehon Law before twentieth century courts', *Peritia*, vol. 16 (2002), pp 352–88.
7. Abbot, *Napoleon at St. Helena*, p. 497.
8. Robert Perry, *Revisionist Scholarship and Modern Irish Politics* (Farnham, 2013). See https://www.routledge.com/Revisionist-Scholarship-and-Modern-Irish-Politics/Perry/p/book/9781409451273?srsltid=AfmBOo-qceKNU3V4ErOtQ36ytjv2m2a6Gb-cvRNPDWwzeDNL2Eoq9xqz_1.
9. Kenny, *Kenmare*, pp 15–25, 239–40.

32. A united Ireland?

1. *Fermanagh Herald*, 15 April 1922.
2. *Westmeath Independent*, 15 April 1922.
3. Boundary Commission Files, [Collins] to Churchill, 25 April 1922, and Churchill (wire no. 82) via Alfred Cope to Collins, received 24 April 1922 (NAI TSCH S1801A).
4. Jones, *Diary*, vol. 3, p. 110 (7 September 1921).
5. *Nationalist and Leinster Times*, 6 May 1922.
6. *Irish Independent*, 15 April 1922.
7. Ruane, 'The "so-called Treaty"', p. 271.